D0371968

Rain Forest Into Desert

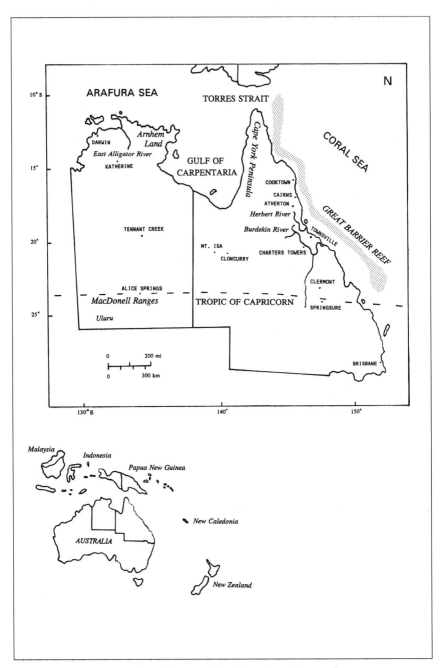

Location map of northern Australia.

Rain Forest Into Desert
Adventures in Australia's Tropical North

Ellen E. Wohl

UNIVERSITY PRESS OF COLORADO

© 1994 by the University Press of Colorado
P.O. Box 849
Niwot, Colorado 80544

The University Press of Colorado is a cooperative publishing enterprise supported, in part, by
Adams State College, Colorado State University, Fort Lewis College, Mesa State College,
Metropolitan State College of Denver, University of Colorado, University of Northern Colorado,
University of Southern Colorado, and Western State College of Colorado.

Library of Congress Cataloging-in-Publication Data

Wohl, Ellen E., 1962–
Rain forest into desert: adventures in Australia's tropical North / Ellen E. Wohl
p. cm.
Includes bibliographical references and index.
ISBN 0-87081-334-x
1. Rivers — Australia — Northern Territory. 2. Rivers — Australia — Queensland.
3. Geomorphology — Australia — Northern Territory.
4. Geomorphology — Australia — Queensland. I. Title.
GB568.89.W64 1994
508.9429 — dc20
94-11605 CIP

In memory of Keith Katzer,
good friend,
who would have written a better book

~

Contents

Preface

This book is the result of a year spent in Australia doing field research for my doctoral dissertation in geology, and of a second visit three years later to complete that research. In the tradition of geologist and river explorer John Wesley Powell, I have combined various trips into a single narrative for the purpose of brevity and accordingly have taken some liberties. I focused on my initial, most challenging experiences, when I worked alone. On subsequent visits to the sites, I had excellent field assistants, who made both the work and the whole experience much more enjoyable.

My specialty within geology is fluvial geomorphology; *fluvial* means river, *geo-* means earth, *morph* is form, and *-ology* is the study of. I study the processes and landforms associated with rivers, which Thoreau has likened to the veins of a leaf crossing the earth's flesh. I am fortunate in my profession. Rivers occur in every environment on earth, and with the globe as my laboratory I follow my work across its surface. My choice of Australia grew from my fascination with tropical rivers, which have received relatively little attention from geomorphologists. Australia provides an accessible tropical region with no language difficulties, no political unrest or guerilla activities, no real danger of tropical diseases like malaria, and a fairly good support system of roads and equipment access: in short, the physical and climatic setting of the tropics, without all the usual social and logistical difficulties. I also chose Australia because of its geographic location with respect to global climatic circulation patterns.

My research in Australia involved using sedimentary deposits emplaced by floods to reconstruct flood characteristics and then relating those floods to past climate and to channel morphology. During the summer wet season in northern Australia, the monsoonal rains keep the rivers high. Superimposed on this widespread precipitation are the intense rains associated with tropical cyclones moving inland from the sea. The great clockwise gyres of the cyclones whirl inland, bending the resilient palm trees and flattening the houses as they pass, dumping twenty-five centimeters of rain in a few hours. Behind them come the floods, massive pulses of water sweeping everything before them. The floods inundate the flat river basins, sending the animals into the treetops or floating on rafts of vegetation. I wanted to use the distribution through time of these large floods as a record of cyclone fluctuations.

I examined flood deposits along three Australian rivers: the Burdekin and Herbert Rivers in northeastern Queensland and the East Alligator River in the Northern Territory. Although I describe my work, this book is primarily a chronicle of my reactions to the unique and unfamiliar Australian landscape and culture and is organized along the progression of my travels in northern Australia. Each of the two principal sections begins with a "work" chapter describing the rivers I studied. This is followed by a chapter about the more general coastal region through which the rivers flow and, finally, by a chapter describing an inland progression from the coast to the central deserts.

The relative abundance of water has exerted a major control on all aspects of life in Australia, from the distribution of eucalypts and kangaroos to the customs of Anglo-Australians and Aborigines. Water is thus one of the dominant themes of this book, as are my ambivalence toward many of the situations in which I found myself, and my gropings toward a philosophy of balance between humans and their environment.

The relationship of people to their land has always been one of my primary interests, and in an effort to understand this relationship in Australia, I read widely in both human and natural history, for understanding is impossible without a knowledge of the crucial context of time. As a geologist realizes that a landscape records physical events long past, so a student of culture and national characteristics understands that these qualities have been forming over generations. The attitudes recorded in a nation's literary heritage provide an index to this development.

Raised in the context of North American environmental philosophy and activism, with a tradition reaching back through John Muir and Henry David Thoreau to English writers like Gilbert White, I found myself in a culture with a different attitude toward its natural surroundings. Like the rest of the world, the Australian environment is currently under siege from a variety of destructive influences: uranium mining, hydroelectric power, woodchipping, and resort development all threaten the few remaining areas of wilderness. As they make land-use decisions relative to these issues, the Australian people are redefining their view of their land.

During the course of my research, I was able to travel widely throughout the continent and to see a variety of environments. I was, of course, unable to attain the detailed knowledge and understanding of place that comes only with continued observation, and my comments reflect initial impressions of each environment during one season. Despite these limitations, I returned from Australia with new insight into both that land and myself. Thoreau wrote that one should not travel blindly and that inner travel is more important than outer. I found that outer travel served as a stimulus to inner, and during my Australian sojourn I covered more than physical distance. It was difficult to write of these distances. Many times I wished for a magic pen, that I might bring forth on the page the play of light and shadows on the curving fronds of a rainforest palm. I wanted to dip my pen into history and send sprawling across the clean white paper the excited, milling chaos of a gold rush, or the deep faith in progress and the golden opportunity that impelled men and women into the harsh openness of an unknown land. Most of all I wanted to open for you a window on the Australia that I perceived, so I included in this book much of what most interested me: landscape, biota, human history and culture, geology. Perhaps among all of these I have approached an understanding.

~ ~ ~

I extend my sincere thanks to all the organizations and individuals who made my visit to Australia possible. Funding from a Fulbright-Hayes Research Grant, The National Geographic Society, Sigma Xi, The Scientific Research Society, The Geological Society of America, and The University of Arizona allowed me to travel to Australia. Once there, I was greatly assisted by the faculty and staff of the Department of Geomorphology and Biogeography at The Research School of Pacific Studies, Australian National University; the Australian Institute of Marine Science; and the Office of the Supervising Scientist, Alligator Rivers Region Research Institute. I would particularly like to acknowledge Drs. John Chappell, Peter Isdale, and Jon East of these institutions. Without exception, the Australians are the most open, friendly, and generous people I have met. From people I met on the road to officials in various government institutions, the Aussies were eager to share themselves and their wonderful land with me, and they made my visit to Australia immeasurably richer.

Once I returned to the United States and began to write this book, I received assistance and encouragement from several individuals. Keith Katzer, Lisa Ely, and Sara Rathburn all read early versions of the manuscript and provided helpful suggestions. Keith had the first draft of the manuscript with him when he was killed in an automobile accident in the summer of 1988. I thought of him often when revising that first draft, and his tremendous enthusiasm for life will always be a source of inspiration for those fortunate enough to have known him.

Daniel Moses, Paul Martin, and an anonymous reviewer provided crucial encouragement and critical reviews when the manuscript was submitted for publication, and Deborah Korte provided careful editing; I am grateful to each of these individuals and to the staff of the University Press of Colorado for their assistance.

Finally, my parents have provided a lifetime of encouragement, support, and love. If they had not raised me to be confident and independent, I would never have journeyed to Australia or embarked on the adventures of this book, which I expect to be only the beginning of a long and delightful career. For this, and for so much more, I thank them.

Part I

Queensland: Reef and Rain Forest ~

No two voyageurs enter their doors in the same way or have identical adventures, but all have in common the final impact which is in the evolution of vision and perspective, and when there are no longer any beckoning mirages ahead, a man dies. With an open horizon constantly before him, life can be an eternal challenge.

Sigurd Olson, *Open Horizons*

The water there was all brightness and color, blue swirling into green like veins of azurite and malachite dancing with one another. The sunlight fragmented on the tiny waves, and I closed my eyes to stop the glare. So much beauty was painful and could only be absorbed in small doses. The clean white sand was coarse and warm, and on the wind were the thick, fecund scents of the rain forest. Behind me the forest swelled swiftly upward into a huge wave. The wave broke on the crest of the mountains, and the farther side was dry. There, the sun dominated. The land stood bared to the sun, spare and self-contained, and the sun glared down day after day, sucking up the heavy wet mantle of moisture sheltering the forest and the sea. The broken wave ran quietly out into the flat sand and rocks, lapping away to the horizon.

Such is the disparity between the lushly vegetated coastline and the arid interior of Queensland. Sugarcane, rice, and bananas flourish along the flat coastal plain, where the dry season is heavy with humidity, and tropical cyclones drench the land in the wet season. Less than 400 kilometers to the west, across the Great Dividing Range, cattle cluster around the scant watering ponds produced by bores, and a thousand small shafts pock the hills where the gold miners labored. To the south, winter snows dust the hills where the town of Stanthorpe straddles the range.

The state of Queensland sprawls across 1,735,000 square kilometers of northeastern Australia, an area roughly equivalent to the U.S. states of California, Montana, Wyoming, and Texas combined. Like Montana and Wyoming, Queensland is sparsely populated by politically and socially conservative rural folk. Their ancestors sought their fortunes extracting the resources of a rugged land as miners and lumber cutters, pastoralists and fishers. The land was rich in these resources, with an abundance of gold, copper, silver, pasture for cattle and sheep, sugarcane, bananas, rice, fish, pearls, sea slugs, and timber all waiting to be harvested. Today many of these extractive industries are faltering for one reason or another — exhaustion of the resource, increasing extractive costs, declining world demand — but Queensland has found a new resource in its scenery, luring visitors from all over the world. The Great Barrier Reef and the magnificent rain forests support a booming international tourist industry, and the portions of reef and rain forest that survived earlier eras are now subject to new threats of degradation and destruction.

Stretching along 2,300 kilometers of coastline from the southern edge of Papua New Guinea to just beyond the Tropic of Capricorn, the Great Barrier Reef is the world's largest coral province. It is actually an amalgamation of more than 2,000 individual reefs strewn along Australia's east coast and extends out to 200 kilometers offshore. Everything here is on a vast scale: paralleling the reef along the east coast of Queensland, the peaks of the Great Dividing Range and a series of lesser ranges run 5,000 kilometers from Cape York south to Wilson's Promontory, a distance greater than that from New York to San Francisco. Though low in comparison to many of the world's mountains, the Great Dividing Range is impressive when seen from sea level. At Cairns it reaches heights of 1,600 meters, comparable to the Adirondack Mountains of New York. The range acts as a major orographic barrier to the rainbearing southeasterly trade winds and is responsible for the diversity of environments in Queensland. When the trades sweep in from the Coral Sea, they drop most of their moisture on the seaward side of the range, where the rain forests grow thick and dark. This narrow strip between the innermost peaks and the outermost reefs, 400 kilometers at its widest, is the world of reef and rain forest where I came to study floods.

1

The Restless Earth ~

Water is always arriving or departing. It is the restlessness of the Earth.

Peter Steinhart, "Trusting Water"

It all began with poring over topographic maps and aerial photographs of Queensland, searching for rivers with promising shapes where flood deposits could be hidden. I went to the rivers to study the great floods that roar down their channels during the wet season, gouging and scouring holes in the solid bedrock of their gorges and rushing rampant across the flat sandy plains, uprooting trees and changing the face of the landscape in a few days. Sands and silts carried by the floodwaters are left high in crevices and hidden margins of the gorges when the floods begin to wane. I wanted to use these sediments to reconstruct a history of the floods that had occurred before anyone kept systematic records of river flow.

Unravelling the history of flooding was difficult enough, but the greatest challenges I faced were my own fears and uncertainties about my first solo field research, done in a place of heat and isolation where the murky river water held the threat of danger. Saltwater crocodiles inhabit the fresh- and saltwater rivers of tropical Australia, and saltwater crocodiles attack people. Although my study areas were well inland, my awareness of these crocodiles formed an underlying current of fear throughout my work.

The Burdekin River

I came there alone and as a stranger, slightly mistrusting, yet also trembling with a dream coming true. The land was dusty with red and orange, and the old mountains on the horizons were low and scattered. Clumps of pale, faded grass straggled out across the plains, and when the gum trees came together in a clump, I looked carefully beneath them for rusty-scuffed wallabies with skeleton-jutting hips. Hunched kookaburras sat smirking on the tree branches.

That was the dry season. Only a few months later, when the Northern Hemisphere curled itself against the snows of January, the rivers of the Burdekin basin would be raging over their banks, coating the land in fresh green growth. From December to April the cyclones and monsoonal troughs sweep inland from the Coral Sea, bringing the heavy rains that drive the life cycles of the plants and animals in the seasonal tropics, just as the winter storms set the tempo for life in the North American deserts. The Burdekin River and its tributaries drain a vast expanse of 130,000 square kilometers, encompassing extremes. Rain falling in narrow basalt canyons shadowed by rain forest at the northern end of the basin loses itself in the open sand channels of the semiarid savanna at the southern end.

It was a long time before whites visited this land of extremes and began to keep written records of its floods and other characteristics. Such records begin in the mid-1840s, courtesy of an eccentric German explorer named Friedrich Wilhelm Ludwig Leichhardt.

Leichhardt named the Burdekin River on his epic 1844–1845 overland journey from Moreton Bay (Brisbane) north through Queensland and then west to Port Essington, near present-day Darwin. He is one of the more romantic figures in the pantheon of Australian explorers, an enigmatic man portrayed in Patrick White's novel *Voss*. Apparently a self-styled "Dr.," Leichhardt studied botany at the universities of Göttingen and Berlin. He was a strange mix of Victorian idealism and vanity: he dreamt equally of extending the knowledge of mankind and of ensuring his own place among the heroes of geographic discovery. Leichhardt came to Australia in 1842 knowing nothing of what Australians call "the bush." Somehow he convinced colonial society that he had the skill and determination to successfully undertake what no white Australian had yet done, an exploration of the northern and northeastern interior.

With the financial backing of the merchants of Sydney, who were anxious to establish a new port on the northern coast, Leichhardt and nine others set off into the unknown north on October 1, 1844. Fourteen months later, Leichhardt and six followers staggered out of the tropical bush and into the settlement of Port Essington on the north-central coast of Australia, having long since been given up for dead. Often lost in the flat, featureless monotony of scrub plains, they starved for lack of skill at finding bush tucker and all but died of thirst through ignorance of water holes. The sun burned them, sent mirages, dried their tongues and throats, and cracked their skin. Bad water racked their insides, and anxiety tortured their minds — with good reason, for they knew the Aborigines were shadowing them. John Gilbert, a member of the party, was killed in an attack by blacks in the Cape York Peninsula, and it has since been asserted that Gilbert, a native Australian well skilled in bushcraft, actually kept the expedition going. But Leichhardt's journal of the trip gives no indication of the importance of Gilbert's role, and Leichhardt managed to continue to his destination after Gilbert's death.

Part of Leichhardt's fascination lies in the contradictions of his character. He was shortsighted, could not use a gun, and had little sense of direction, but in his determination he taught himself to sight on the sun and stars during the sea voyage to Australia. An overbearing leader, his men were soon at odds with him; two abandoned the expedition and returned to the settlements, and the journals of those who remained show that they soon lost their trust in him. Tactless in dealing with the Aborigines, he also refused to post a camp guard at night, resulting in Gilbert's death. He spent much of his time lost but reached his destination in the end. In his journal, written with one eye toward the hero-craving public, he wrote of his ideals of uncovering the unknown and bridging the vast distances for the greater good, yet in the bush he begrudged his companions their dwindling rations.

Leichhardt returned to the colonies a hero, to be feted and admired. He had no trouble finding the funds and new volunteers for his next expedition, which left the Darling Downs of southeast Queensland in December 1846 with the intent of traveling at least 5,000 kilometers across the continent to the west coast before turning south along the coast to Perth. Looking at the proposed route on a map, and knowing something of its wild aridity, one can only marvel at Leichhardt's overweening ambition. The journey he contemplated, having barely survived its predecessor, was on a truly epic scale. It is difficult to fathom both the relentless personal drive and the depth of self-confidence that must have lain behind such an undertaking.

Leichhardt had overstepped himself this time, however. The eight-man expedition returned to the Downs seven months later, having encountered the floods of an exceptional wet season. This was not the last time that the rains of arid Australia played havoc with human plans. Australia's coefficient of variability of precipitation is exceptionally high by world standards, meaning that the same terrain that remains bone dry four years straight may be awash in water the next year. Leichhardt was a victim of rainfall variability; I am its student.

Returning to the Darling Downs, Leichhardt felt that his luck had failed and his men were incompetent, but his subordinates were more outspoken about his failings as a leader than those of the first expedition had been. They accused him of selfishness and callous indifference to the suffering of others, inability, and, most damaging, periodic insanity.

Leichhardt's spirits improved when he returned to Sydney and learned that the Geographical Societies of both London and Paris had awarded him gold medals. With his self-esteem restored by public acclaim, his relentless ambition drove him into the unknown bush yet again, and in April 1848 he led the six members of his third expedition west from the Darling Downs, Perth again in his sights. Although many have looked for them, their remains seem to have vanished without a trace.

It has been suggested that Leichhardt and his companions may have drowned in one of the inland's notorious floods. When incoming cyclones suck great masses of moisture from the warm tropical seas, the whole countryside can flood, drowning people in what was, hours before, a parching desert. In Xavier Herbert's epic novel of the outback, *Poor Fellow My Country,* he describes the struggles of a boy caught in such a flood:

> Often he stopped and stood for respite behind trees, only to be fouled up by gobs of rank froth spat down from sodden trunks and branches. Time itself was a grey thing, getting greyer. The ground became a grey thing, a sheet of dirty water lashed into steam by rain. Water everywhere. No creeks now. Only one grey seething pulling mass. He floundered into holes, fell over submerged objects. It was swampland, grown with spindly tea-tree stuff that grew thicker, thicker, and allowed no way out. He came to moaning and whimpering with the effort it cost to go on, as he must go, or lie down and drown.

Leichhardt's explorations make an interesting comparison to the adventures of Álvar Núñez Cabeza de Vaca, the first European to explore on foot the interior of arid North America. In 1527 Cabeza de Vaca was shipwrecked on the Florida coast, and during the next eight years he traveled 9,700 kilometers, around the Gulf of Mexico, west to Arizona, and south to Mexico City. During his travels, Cabeza de Vaca was everything from slave to king among the American Indian tribes he encountered, but always he was open to the Native Americans, carefully observing and recording their customs. Had Leichhardt been more open to the Aborigines and used their skills and knowledge, he might have succeeded in crossing the vast arid interior of Australia.

Later, out in the Center, I began to understand what Leichhardt had felt. The land itself. It was flat mostly, the occasional low hills only enhancing the flatness. The longest straight run of railroad track in the world lies here. Driving in that country, I clung to the roads like lifelines. Few landmarks there for the uninitiated, and fewer second chances. I watched the sun set early on a winter evening stretching out into the hours ahead and thought how easy it would be to lose the habits of self-control. I imagined his thoughts. Hunger. Boredom with the monotony. Fear of his own lacking. Why not eat the extra food? Why bother with the conventions that lace up our sagging will in public? He had to succeed: he had no children, no personal relations, nothing to outlast the anonymity of death. But he could make his name ring out so that it would overcome the sting of death. Here, in this anonymous land, he could achieve greatness.

~ ~ ~

Leichhardt crossed the Burdekin basin during his first expedition and named the river after Mrs. Burdekin, a wealthy Sydney society woman and one of his financial supporters. His published journal is all facts and figures for this portion of the journey, but he must have had misgivings when he realized that now he must actually accomplish his ambitious goals. Perhaps some of his fierce pronouncements were a reaction to unacknowledged misgivings: "The interior, the heart of the dark continent, is my goal, and I will never relinquish the quest for it until I get there." His own dark heart proved more formidable an obstacle.

I certainly had misgivings of my own while on the Burdekin. In this world of mechanized transport, transitions often occur too suddenly, and one afternoon I found myself, seemingly abruptly, in the Burdekin Gorge. The gorge is a long drive and a moderate hike from any place where people live, but it was not until I arrived that I realized my isolation. Standing on the bank of the river, I found myself surrounded by phantoms largely of my own making.

It was close there, trees behind and the river before me, and I was nervous. What I could face with a companion strengthening my flank was almost too much alone, but I was ashamed of hesitation. Across the river

Camp along a quiet stretch of the Burdekin River.

the gum trees on the crest of the hill stood out sharp and stiff. Below them the hill softened into shadows, coming out clear again where the dark river flecked with white ran swiftly down the stones, raising a confused, jumbled sound. Just below the rocky stretch, the water collected itself quietly in a bottomless green-black pool, and I stood cautiously on the bank, wondering about the crocodiles. The flies buzzing about my head settled on my cheeks, crawling inquisitively toward my eyes. The sun was hot on my head, and there were things to do in camp, but I stood by the pool, wondering.

Then I put a brave face on it. Brave faces are necessary to beginnings, as prescribed by heroic tradition. Leichhardt acknowledged this in his journal, describing the first expedition as it set out: "Many a man's heart would have thrilled like our own, had he seen us winding our way round the first rise beyond the station with a full chorus of 'God Save the Queen' which has inspired many a British soldier — aye, and many a Prussian too — with courage in the time of danger." Later, when he realized that the friendly onlookers were no help in the face of starvation and death, he may have felt differently.

I struggled with ambivalence throughout my stay on the river, and my journal for those days records my mood swings from happiness at the quiet beauty all around me to tense fear of the dangers and uncertainties I faced. There should be a primer given to new graduate students embarking on solo field research for the first time, explaining that uncertainty and fears of inadequacy are to be expected. I am not inherently timid, and I had little patience for the prolonged struggle with fear and anxiety that I faced on the Burdekin partly because of the physical environment and partly because of my own inexperience. I knew that there were crocodiles in that murky water, and this knowledge made it difficult to come to terms with the river and get on with the flood research. All I wanted to do was get done and get out as quickly as possible, although I never acknowledged this until long after.

As large carnivores, crocodiles pose a threat to humans and have thus come under the same opprobrium as tigers, bears, or wolves. Crocodiles are not accorded the saving graces of dignity or intelligence that humans often perceive in the other major predators. Reptiles have never been particularly attractive to most people, and the grim, hard, sharply efficient appearance of crocs argues against affection.

Freshwater crocodiles, or "freshies," *Crocodylus johnstoni,* get their specific name from Sub-Inspector Johnstone, who collected the original specimen in the Herbert River in the early 1870s. These crocodiles feed on fish, frogs, and other small animals and are described as "relatively harmless to humans." The "relative" presumably refers to *Crocodylus porosus,* the big "salties." These can attain lengths of more than six meters and are responsible for the crocodile-caused human fatalities that have given the rivers of northern Australia a certain notoriety, as described in grim detail in Hugh Edwards's book *Crocodile Attack.*

The saltwater crocs build meter-high nests of soil and vegetation in which they lay up to fifty eggs that incubate for ten to twelve weeks while the mother crocodile remains near the nest, on guard and aggressive. Before hatching, the young call from inside the eggs, and the mother excavates the nest for them. She even carries some of the young, gripped gently among her razored teeth, to the water, remaining nearby to guard them during their early, vulnerable stages. Fortunately for fluvial geomorphologists, many eggs and young are destroyed by the large lizards called goannas, by pigs, and by fluctuating water levels.

One of the more fascinating, and to humans sinister, aspects of crocodile behavior is their ability to reduce their breathing and heart rate so as to remain hidden, submerged in murky water, patiently awaiting their prey. Suddenly the seemingly torpid crocodile bursts from the water to catch a bird on the wing. Perhaps that is why, in the Book of Job, the crocodile is described as "the chief of the beasts." The early civilizations centered in the Tigris and Euphrates valleys must have been well aware of the power, menace, and unpredictability of crocodiles.

Today we can destroy whole crocodile populations, as the Australians nearly did before crocodiles were given protected status in the late 1960s and early 1970s. That was a controversial decision in a land where crocodiles have killed humans, and it was tangled up in notions of the rights of other creatures to exist, the value of crocodiles in attracting tourists to northern Australia, and the rights of local residents to have free and unfearing access to fishing and swimming.

Perhaps it is good for humans to sometimes have the fear and thus know the anxiety of wild creatures. Without that element of truth, if you will, we only play at being in a pristine world or a wilderness. Humanity has a free reign, and free run, over the vast majority of the land surface, and if our words about stewardship and responsibility are to have any meaning, then we must try to preserve ecosystems outside the range of human ethical values of predator versus prey or animal versus human. We can afford such a little generosity, both for the predators and ourselves.

~ ~ ~

Despite my initial misgivings, the days soon fell into a rhythm as I sorted out the work before me. My first task was to identify sites of flood sedimentation. When the energetic waters of a flood come down a river channel, they usually carry fine-grained sediments like silt and sand with them. The turbulence of the flowing water keeps these sediments in suspension, much as powdered chocolate rises through a glass of milk when stirred with a spoon. When the floodwaters spread into sheltered nooks and crannies, like the mouths of tributary channels or the quiet edges of the main channel, their velocity and turbulence decrease and the fine sediments settle out of suspension and down to the bottom, just as the powdered chocolate will settle to the bottom of the glass once the stirring stops. As the floodwaters recede, the accumulations of sediment are left behind along the channel, and the highest sediments are not disturbed by subsequent smaller flows. Over hundreds of years, numerous layers of flood sedimentation accumulate at a given site, creating a complex three-dimensional mosaic.

In order to decipher the record of floods contained in these mosaics, I had to use the stratigraphy, or layering, of each site to develop a mental image of how the individual sedimentary deposits related to each other. This involved designating layers within the deposit, describing the color, grain-size characteristics, thickness, and other notable features of each layer and then correlating physically separate but similar layers that appear at different sites but could have been produced by a single flood.

The greatest challenge of geology is to extrapolate to the third and fourth dimensions from a two-dimensional stratigraphic exposure. It is difficult enough to unravel the individual "footprints" left at a site by numerous floods, but it becomes even more aggravating to try to reconstruct a history of events from these footprints when there is no standard against which to judge the accuracy of interpretation.

Unravelling site stratigraphy often involves digging trenches or soil pits to expose the contacts between depositional units. If you are lucky, tools like seismic arrays or backhoes provide access to the subsurface. If you are more limited, as I was, then you rely on natural exposures in gullies and spend endless sweaty, dusty hours with a small shovel and blistered hands. Once I thought I understood the geometry of the deposits, I set out to determine the ages of the floods that had deposited them. For this I relied on radiocarbon dating.

Radiocarbon dating is based on the decay of the radioactive carbon-14 (^{14}C) isotope. Bombardment of nitrogen-14 (^{14}N) in the upper atmosphere by neutrons from cosmic rays causes atoms of ^{14}N to break down into a proton and a ^{14}C atom. This ^{14}C is oxidized to $^{14}CO_2$ and distributed evenly through the global atmosphere in minute concentrations relative to the more common $^{12}CO_2$. The radioactive carbon is assimilated by living organisms until their death, when it begins to decay at a constant rate of 1 percent every eighty years. The production of ^{14}C has not been constant in the past, and tree rings of known age have been used to refine the calibration curve of the $^{14}C/^{12}C$ ratio through time. From the resulting calibration curve, a sample of dead organic matter such as wood or charcoal can be used for dating. Through radiocarbon dating of organics associated with the flood deposits, I was able to determine the ages and frequencies of floods that had occurred over the past 2,000 years.

Radiocarbon dating sounds relatively straightforward, but in practice it is difficult to interpret the results of radiocarbon analyses in terms of the history of a site. Much of the material that I submitted for analysis from the Burdekin River consisted of pea-sized charcoal fragments. In a classic scientific paper published in 1976, the Australian scientists Russell Blong

Flood sediments accumulated as a large mound at the
mouth of a tributary to the Burdekin River. Features
resembling steps going up the mound are stratigraphic
exposures. The shovel in the foreground is approximately
one meter in length.

and Richard Gillespie demonstrated that charcoal being transported down
the bed of a modern channel was up to 10,000 years old, with the smaller,
rounded fragments, which are most likely to have been reworked from
older deposits, having the greatest ages. This is not good news when you
are trying to unravel the history of flooding using a chronology based on
small, rounded charcoal fragments because no other organic materials are
available in the flood sediments. In this situation, I treated the radiocarbon

dates as maximum limiting ages for the flood sediments and was generally encouraged when the oldest radiocarbon ages came from the most deeply buried flood sediments, and the youngest ages from the uppermost sediments.

The final step in my field research was to survey the river channel. In a stable channel like the bedrock gorge of the Burdekin, the height of flood sediments above the channel bottom approximates the high-water level of the associated flood. With a computer model developed by the U.S. Army Corps of Engineers, a series of high-water marks along a channel can be used to estimate the discharge, or volume of water per unit of time, necessary to produce such marks, if channel geometry is known. My field surveys involved measuring both the cross-sectional and longitudinal dimensions of the length of channel containing the flood sediments, and the height of those sediments above the channel bottom.

Working alone, I used a theodolite to triangulate the vertical and horizontal distances between a reference point and the points I was measuring along the channel, where I could see those points. In situations where I could not get a clear line of sight, as with the channel below the water level, I used a measuring staff to physically determine distances between points. This might normally have made for pleasant swimming on hot days, but I was worried about what the crocodiles would think of such a rude intrusion into their territory. My channel bottom surveys consequently were not extremely detailed.

Using these methods, I could reconstruct both the magnitude and frequency of past floods along the river. What I found was a record of at least seven large floods during the last 1,200 years, all of which ranged in discharge from 11,000 to 30,000 cubic meters per second — tremendous volumes of water. By comparison, the mean annual discharge of the Mississippi River is 18,000 cubic meters per second, while that of the Amazon River is 175,000 cubic meters per second.

The discharge estimates for floods on the Burdekin River developed from channel sediments compare well with the discharge values measured at a stream gauge located at the head of the Burdekin Gorge that has been recording floods since 1967. Stream gauges are instruments set up at a surveyed, stable cross section of the channel. The gauges are calibrated with a rating curve that relates water height to discharge. Some type of recording device, often a float inside a tube positioned in the channel, indicates water height during the flood, so that discharge may be estimated from the rating curve. These water-height measurements may record only the highest level attained during a flood, as in a crest-stage gauge, or they may be connected to something like a strip-chart recorder that indicates changes in water level at fifteen-minute or other time increments.

Gauge records are generally regarded as the most accurate indicator of flood discharge, as compared to geologic records like flood sediments or historical records like eyewitness accounts. However, gauge records may be inaccurate if the channel cross section changes as a result of erosion and deposition during the flood. These records may also be incomplete if the gauge is destroyed by a very large flood, as is too often the case. Finally, the gauged discharge record for any river is usually of short duration relative to the recurrence interval of the largest floods. Gauged records in northern Australia generally cover seventy years at most and are thus of limited utility in trying to determine the magnitude of the largest floods, which may recur only once every 50, 100, or 500 years. These are the situations where sedimentary flood records, which may cover more than 1,000 years, are useful in predicting flood frequency and magnitude.

The physical labor and the heat often left me exhausted. I was subsisting on a diet of dried instant foods: primarily muesli, the Australian version of granola; rice cakes (because they keep better than bread); and instant noodles. Once I hooked a catfish in a shaded pool guarded by paperbark trees bent with the force of past floods. I had the cooking of the fish all planned out, as only those who have been on sparse rations for some time can do: I would coat it in mud and bake it in the embers with some of the lemon verbena growing along the channel, a bit of onion, some soy sauce. . . . But the fish escaped from the line in a patch of reeds, taking with it the only hook and all my gastronomic hopes.

The main difficulty I faced during my work along the Burdekin was crossing the river. On the early trips I had no boat, which left me the options of wading across at a rapid or swimming across at a pool. How could anyone justify swimming across a crocodile-infested river? Many people have since asked that question, but I am unable to provide them, or myself, with a satisfactory answer. I was provoked into a desperate act by a blend of perceived necessity and obstinacy. I could justify it to myself at the time, but not now.

Each method of crossing had its disadvantages. There were rapids at the upstream and downstream ends of the reach on which I worked, and I vividly remember my first crossing of the lower rapids. Sitting in the shade of a gum tree, I studied them warily. The river was quietly menacing in a hundred slender green channels between black rocks. There was nothing grand or inspiring in its menace, only a quiet possibility of evil. Some of the rocks were big enough to support a scraggly bush, and on these I pinned my hopes. But make it to those islands, and I was safe. The green water lay between, still and opaque in the hot noon sun.

I struck off across the river, slipping and swimming my way through each of the little subchannels. Where the rocks dropped off suddenly into the murky water, I held my pack above my head and did a desperate sidestroke for the next spot of terra firma. I finally reached the opposite side, as wet with nervous sweat as with river water.

The alternative to crossing at one of the rapids was to swim across a quiet pool. I did that twice without incident, but the third time quenched my confidence in the method. I was returning to camp one afternoon, trudging reluctantly, the heat of the day on me. Even the flies were silent under the harsh exposure of the sun. The trees along the valley walls stood straight and flat in the absence of shadows, and on the green water not a ripple. Topping a sandbank, I had a clear view of the river. At its edge lay something large and dark, rigid in a hardened skin studded with knobs. I stared, mesmerized. It slid smoothly and soundlessly into the inscrutable green water, confirming all my fears, and my breath came out suddenly in a harsh word.

I scurried on, the river watching me now. Down to the river, up to the thickets, down to the river again, seeking a narrow crossing, my breathing harsh and fast until I plunged, swearing to the god of desperation I'd make it. Viscous water and turgid limbs holding me back. Then the frightful shock of the unseen rock swelling out beneath the water's edge at the bank, and I was on the hot, dry rock, gasping, almost crying, half laughing, out, away, safe.

I estimated the croc to be four meters long. I was particularly unnerved by its complete disappearance once it entered the water, without even surface ripples to indicate subsurface movement. There would be no way to see a croc approaching in this river, and if one decided to attack me, I stood no chance. I had hoped that any crocodiles found this far inland would be freshwater crocodiles, but a crocodile four meters long had to be a big salty. That was the last time I crossed at a pool.

The third crossing point I used on the river, the upstream rapids near my camp, proved to be a figurative and literal crossing. I used a heavy theodolite and tripod for the early surveying on the river and left them in the car when I first set out, intending to return when I finished the stratigraphy and sampling and exchange sets of gear. My last site was on the right bank, as was my car, while camp was on the left bank. When I finished at that last site, I hiked back along the river and camped on a giant sandbar opposite the tent, using my rucksack for a pillow and my poncho for a blanket. I intended to minimize river crossings by sleeping on the right bank and then hiking out along it the next day to the surveying equipment.

As the sun sank toward the horizon, the bases of the flat-bottomed cumulus clouds darkened beneath their pale gold crowns. I started a fire at dusk, as the clouds smoldered orange, and cooked my supper. It was a windy night, presentiment of a weather change. I put out the fire after supper and was immersed in night — blue-black night, and the wind rising. Pale green clouds flowed swiftly by beneath the heavy gold moon, seen as though at the bottom of a well when it appeared through holes in the clouds. I lay on my back, hands clasped behind my head, on a sand island high between rivers of water and air. The midnight black water snagged itself on the prow of the island, divided into smooth, swift, deep branches that snagged again on jumbled rocks and snarled into tangles of white foam and noise. Above the water rushed the wind, stooping to snatch and pluck before flinging itself boisterously on. I lay in the midst of all this motion perfectly still, concentrating on the color of the moon. I felt good and free, at ease with the sweeping wind and unmindful of the rush of dark waters. The high ridges on either side of the river smudged into the darkness, and I was left alone on a sandy island rushing through black space, only the moon to guide me.

I lay there all unmindful as the river flowed ceaselessly onward. One of the greatest unappreciated miracles, all the rivers of the world with their ceaselessly flowing waters. The river was both the background and the source for everything there: the flutings of the rock, the green of the grasses, the calls of the birds, the shapes of the hills. All these existed because the river bound them together, and I, too, was briefly a part of all this because of the river. I adjusted my life and my rhythms to those of the river world, and the river carried me into its world.

It took little effort to set my thoughts adrift and let the river carry them. Down they flowed, through the silent crocodile pools, among the green-black threaded channels, down into the wide canyons I had never walked. They spread out, flowing shallow and pale over sandy channels unshaded by trees, thinning as they went, diverted for agriculture, sinking into the deep, loose sands, finally reaching the restless ocean, dark metal under moonlight. And there I pulled them back with a rush, reeling in thought as a fisher a fish, for the ocean is too vast and dark to be comprehended at night. I let my thoughts float upward in the other direction instead. They paused at the moon, lead-dark in its earth shadow but for the mercury shining at its edges, and then floated beyond, wandering among the planets. On to the stars, strolling easily the broad, well-lighted path of the Milky Way, the galactic center a megalopolis of distant light. But I turned back before it was reached, down and inward into the impenetrable depths of sleep.

I awoke with a start from a dream of the moon and sat up abruptly, thinking of my car keys in the tent across the river and another river crossing to make. I finally decided that I might as well cross that night and sleep comfortably in my bag. Necessity lay on the opposite bank, and not even the rush of winds and waters could drown its call. Stripping down to tennis shoes, mind freed of all stored memories and fears, I went to the black water.

At the edge, the world condensed into a stretch of roaring black and white, so simple and direct. The water was thick and warm about me, viscously caressing my body, testing my lightness and fragility. I was a slender reed bending into the unstoppable current, working slowly and steadily across, borrowing strength from the stones like a crayfish. Nearly across, and tiring, I heard the rapids below roar louder. Slip once here, lose the steady security of those rocks, and I would be gone, on down through the twisting white and black in a pulping and splintering of flesh and bones. But then the bottom was rising beneath my feet, and the water growing stiller. Panting, half-stumbling, I grasped at the algae-slimed boulders on the grassy bank, limbs heavy in the thin air. Up the dark, quiet, uneven slope into the soft bed and quickly down, down, deep into safe dreams as the rain began to fall softly.

I came up slowly from the quiet depths into a tent of murky, indistinct green softly reverberating with raindrops. Outside the world was gray and green, everything sodden and hushed. The air was chill, and the raindrops surprised my sleep-warm flesh as I picked my way gingerly down to the river over rain-slick cobbles and thick, wet grass. At the edge of the water I stood again, seeking the demons of last night. They had gone, and the water lay quiet, smooth beneath the leaden sky. Even the rapids were subdued, and the raindrops hissed susurrously on the pool above. I entered the river quietly, no longer afraid. But an extended moment and I was across, warm with the river's warmth, striding on into the wide world.

~ ~ ~

It took me more than a week to come to terms with my fears, to move freely and observe carefully. Of necessity, my work, or thoughts of it, occupied most of my waking hours. Often, however, the other inhabitants of the river took me out of myself, revealing the hidden existences surrounding me. As I walked, I often flushed wallabies from the brush. Wallabies seem such improbable creatures at first. Their gentle faces and delicate forepaws contrast with their massive hindquarters, and when I startled them, they thumped away with their tails jerking up and down like pump handles. The many species of kangaroos, wallabies, and euros, herbivorous marsupials mostly of the genus *Macropus,* occur throughout the range of Australian environments. The first known description of a macropod (literally, big foot) was written in July 1629 by Francis Pelsart, a commodore of the Dutch East India Company sailing from Holland to the Dutch East Indies via the Cape of Good Hope. Blown off course to the east, his ship struck the Abrolhos reefs off Western Australia. As Hector Holthouse expressed it, the wreck was "a story of mutiny, bloodshed and mystery without equal in the annals of the sea." Suffering horribly, Pelsart and some of the others eventually made it to Batavia on a small skiff. Amazingly, Pelsart continued to write in his journal, and on one of the islands they passed, he described a creature that must have seemed to him to be drawn directly from a medieval bestiary, a small wallaby: "On these islands there are a large number of Cats, which are creatures of miraculous form, as big as a hare; the Head is similar to that of a Civet cat. . . . If they are going to eat they sit on their hind legs and take the food with their fore-paws and eat exactly the same as the Squirrels or apes do."

Mornings and evenings on the river were the most pleasant times. Often I woke to a thick fog, with unseen birds calling all around me. Some days the moon still shone brightly when I left camp, a frail symbol of purity that melted to a thin wafer at moonset.

Many mornings it was a contest of will to crawl out of my sleeping bag into the damp cold. But there are many beauties known only to early risers, beauties as small as a silken spider web loaded with dewdrops or rare as a double rainbow. One morning as I hiked along the channel's edge, I looked ahead to a bend in the river. From the actual river, invisible at the bend, rose columns and puffs of steam, backlighted to a pale gold by the rays of the sun, like clouds seen from an airplane. Continuing on to a rock overlooking the channel, I beheld the water river, still and smooth as though frozen, beneath the mist river. The mist river swirled and flowed with currents of its own, as silently as the vapor from dry ice, though no breeze disturbed the quiet morning. Every so often a fish dimpled the water river, or a bird skimmed low through the mist river. It was magic, and I simply sat down and watched.

The mornings rapidly grew hot after the fog burned off, and the flies woke up for the day and got down to their work. I have never encountered anything quite like Australian flies. They must always be referred to in the plural because, as with ants or termites, a single fly ceases to have any meaning; there arc simply too many of them in any one place. They begin their activity at first light, activity unending until after sunset, reaching crescendos at dawn and dusk. This is not to imply that they ever really cease at any time during the day; there are only relative lulls. The flies seek moisture, crawling restlessly across exposed skin and collecting at eyes and mouth. If they had been biters, I would have gone crazy.

As it was, I became efficient at swatting them with my hat, but by afternoon I usually had a cloud of twenty or thirty flies around me. At times there were so many of them crawling up and down my bare arms and legs that it felt like water running off. During my stay in Australia I met people who had spent all of their life outdoors and grown so used to the flies that they hardly bothered to brush them off their faces. I never reached that stage of nonchalance and constantly gave the Australian salute: two rapid passes of the hand before the face.

Often I returned to camp exhausted and sore, infuriated at the ceaseless taunting of the flies, irritated by the raucous cries of the cockatoos, cursing, filthy. Day after day it was hot and cloudless, and my journal grew more terse, with lines like "To bed early, very tired." I was too sensible of the heat-charged air at midday that tired my eyes and made my head ache. The vegetation seemed faded by the sun, bleached to the last shade of green and hanging weighted in the thick air. I was afraid of missing things or of misinterpreting the flood sediments. Filthy from digging, I found carrying the heavy gear wore me down until every muscle ached. Up cliff faces, down mud banks, across sandbars through wet grass. The river was malevolent, and I was tired of myself.

A not unusual example of the density of Australian flies.

Oh, well, yes. Even at times like that there were moments: trudging along once, sweating and straining under the burden of the equipment, I came upon a tiny water garden. A small pothole filled with water nestled in a massive knob of gray granite, a few small pebbles at its bottom. A tall, slender clump of bright green grasses and a small, delicately leafed aquatic plant grew in the pothole, creating a lovely, miniature world. Or other things that caught my attention from the margins of vision: small mud curls that crackled when I walked on them, superimposed on larger, deeper mud cracks at the water's edge. The bright, deep green of water lily pads in the coffee-colored billabongs, and the way the light on the sandbars faded from the white-hot of midday to late afternoon's gentle gold while the shadows slipped down the hillside to pool on the river's far edge. Late in the day the river picked up tones of silver and lead and seemed to be flowing randomly in different directions.

The river was bird-haunted. Cockatoos glided pure white, high against the blue sky, and cormorants spread their drying wings as they perched on the rocks. Little black-and-white willy wagtails continually tipped their long, slender tails up and down like metronomes, punctuating all their movements. In the cool mornings and evenings or the still heat of the day, the great wading birds stood in the shallows, unmoving until my blundering passage shocked them heavily up on their long wings. Along the river lived herons, egrets, and the big brolgas with their gray bodies and red heads. The brolgas, *Grus rubicundus,* probe the mud of wetlands in Australia and New Guinea searching for sedge tubers. Like other cranes, they are famous for their group courtship dances, and it amused me to imagine how such Ichabod-like cranes must dance.

Wherever I camped, I had a constant background of river music, and I remembered Robert Chazal's line, "Water speaks in long syllables, air in short." One of my favorite camps lay in an area of grassy swales interspersed with tall eucalypts and large, stream-polished boulders lapped by waves and ripples of sand. The surrounding forest was an open sclerophyll woodland with widely spaced eucalypts and an occasional bottle-trunked baobab. Beside the tent the land rose on one side into forested hills where the spiky trees girded the sky, on the other side falling to the river over a series of fluted and polished bedrock knobs.

A hundred bird voices echoed off the rocks. Each night at dusk the cockatoos, Xavier Herbert's "loud-voiced bosses of the river timber," came to roost in the nearby trees. Flocks of palely gleaming white in the thickening dusk, the cockatoos screeched and shrieked at each other until I was deafened to the sounds of the night beyond. At last they quieted, and across the river kookaburras chortled at each other. The bats came out in that special time of evening after the sun has set, before full dark, when it is good to have the clean, sharp smell of wood smoke in the air. There was something pleasantly mysterious about the bats as they stitched their way rapidly back and forth across the cooling evening sky.

Gentle evening breezes whispered over the softly rushing sound of the river, and occasionally the logs on the fire snapped. Across the river, the eucalyptus trees formed black silhouettes against the pale green western sky. As I lay before the fire, I felt at ease with my body. Tired with the fatigue of hours of exertion, I was beyond minding the worn and sore spots, the kinks and knots. I lay sprawled in the clean sandy grass, barefoot, in my loose, tattered field clothes that allowed me to forget I was wearing clothes. Some nights I saw the Southern Cross standing out clearly from a host of unfamiliar constellations and a faint Milky Way swirling sinuously across the meridian. Others, the moonlight subdued the landscape to a photograph in blacks and grays, and the sandbars beside the dark river glowed like snowbanks. Always, I grew quiet with the thought that this was what I had really come for: to sit before a camp fire on the banks of a river, beneath the southern stars. To come to know an unfamiliar land.

On such nights I lay back, trying to think like a river. It is easy to accept the age of the earth, and the changes of the earth's surface, in a book or in the classroom but hard to put such concepts into practice.

I watched the moon rise. So many countless nights the moon had risen over the Burdekin. I tried casting my mind back in time, imagining landscapes now long since gone. According to Australian geologists D. E. Clarke and A.G.L. Paine, the rocks that presently form the uplands of the Burdekin basin began (because all stories must begin somewhere) as sediments accumulating in a huge depositional basin called the Tasman Geosyncline stretching along what are now the eastern uplands. During the Paleozoic Era (570–245 million years ago) thick deposits of sediments accumulated and were subsequently folded and hardened into rocks, to be intruded by the hot magmas of volcanic and intrusive igneous rocks. Whole landscapes were created and worn away, leaving only subdued roots in the northwesterly structural trend of the upper Burdekin and its tributaries.

Much of the Burdekin catchment is flat, with only the remnants of long periods of erosion during the last 200 million years. These remnants take the form of flat-topped mesas with duricrusts, superficial hard crusts of weathered soils. Sometime in the last sixty to forty million years, the drainage of the gently westward-sloping surface changed as the present upland areas were lifted in relation to the coastal plain. With the uplift came eruptions of lava, damming some of the river channels and altering flow directions from the inland to the sea. The uplift increased the erosive power of the flowing waters, and the landscape was dissected and stripped, exposing old, deeply weathered soils. The eroded material was carried down to the edge of the sea, where floods and sea waves reworked it to form the present coastal plain.

A great deal of the landscape of the Burdekin basin has remained little changed for at least twenty million years. This is the case in much of Australia, in contrast to much of North America, where recent glaciations and continuing tectonic uplift have greatly altered the landscape over the past few million years. Australia, however, has been tectonically stable over this period and has not had appreciable glaciers for more than 200 million years. Thus the literary stereotypes of the Australian continent as ancient and subtle have many layers of meaning.

My images of these landscapes are constrained by my intellectual world. As Stephen Jay Gould has so persuasively demonstrated in his many essays, the attitudes of scientists toward their work to some extent reflect the larger society in which they live and are hardly the purely objective search for truth performed in an intellectual vacuum often imagined by non-scientists. The history of geomorphology thus provides an index to changes in the attitude of humans toward their physical environment. The earliest observations come from the Greeks, Romans, and Arabs: in 450 B.C. Herodotus noted the growth of the Nile delta, and sometime about A.D. 1000 Al-Biruni related the downstream decrease in the size of particles carried by the Ganges River to water-current strength. European scholars began taking interest in landforms during the Renaissance, and, predictably, Leonardo da Vinci was one of the earliest, with his 1519 note on the erosive ability of running water.

When British scholars turned to secular subjects in the second half of the seventeenth century, the prevalent belief, as summarized in Gordon Davies's history of geomorphology, *The Earth in Decay,* was that the earth was decaying due to human sin. This belief led students of landscape to accept easily the potency of the forces of denudation, relying on the Genesis account of earth history and the Mosaic chronology. They studied nature to learn of God, and when they needed analogies, they turned to the microcosm-macrocosm (man-universe) theory of the earth as an organism, in which mountains took on something of the role of offensive warts. Around 1700 interest peaked in the works of three major theorists: Thomas Burnet suggested that condensation from a cloud formed a fairly smooth, featureless earth that was then sculpted into mountains and valleys by the waters of the Noachian flood. John Woodward differed by claiming that sediment in the floodwaters had settled and immediately hardened into expansive, horizontal sheets of rock that were subsequently ruptured and disordered by unexplained mechanisms. William Whiston envisioned comets both shaping the earth and causing the flood. The basic explanations of topography were that the present relief had originally been molded by God, had resulted from the destructive Noachian flood, or was due to former catastrophic earthquakes. In any case, the rate of surficial erosion was drastically increased in order to squeeze earth history into the biblical allocation of 6,000 years, and mountains were viewed as senile remnants of a more glorious past.

For the next eighty years scientific interest turned to other fields, both because of the vogue for experimental science and as a reaction against the speculative work of Burnet, Woodward, and Whiston. A revival of interest in the natural landscape occurred in the 1780s, by which time Enlightenment Europe had accepted the account of Genesis as nonliteral. Geologists began to use the relative age of the rocks to determine the age of topographic features, and although catastrophes like huge floods and earthquakes were still regarded as important in the early history of the earth, a benevolent conception of God now viewed mountains as delightful scenery, and erosion as ineffective.

The 1780s also saw the recognition of the importance of field observations, and this at least put some checks on the bounds of speculative theorists. Men like the Scotsman James Hutton took a mechanistic view of the planet and eventually banned catastrophes altogether, opening up the view of an infinitely old earth that allowed Charles Darwin to theorize the infinitely slow evolution of life. It was the great age of the uniformitarians and the gradualists, and the theories of catastrophists were banished as a throwback to a more ignorant, superstitious time. However, the pendulum swung too far, and the natural sciences bore the bugbear of strict gradualism until the second half of this century, when the role of extreme events and episodic change again began to be acknowledged. But now we believe the extremes to be scattered more evenly throughout history, rather than being lumped at the beginning.

With the advent of a benevolent God and "good" mountains at the end of the eighteenth century, there was some difficulty in accepting that rivers could so alter the topography as to create the valleys in which they flowed. There were early pioneers like Hutton, but it was not until the 1860s that fluvialism, the idea that rivers sculpted their own valleys, was widely accepted. It was also in the 1860s that the great exploratory surveys of the western United States revealed to men like John Wesley

Powell that rivers, far from being impotent, were the major controls on landscape development in many regions.

After the exploratory fieldwork of the late nineteenth century, the first third of the twentieth was dominated by the qualitative theories of great systems builders like William Morris Davis of Harvard. Davis viewed the formation of landscapes in the context of the Cycle of Erosion. An evolutionary system in which landscapes progressed from young topography of steep mountains and high-gradient rivers to old rivers meandering across wide plains, the Cycle of Erosion was influenced by Darwin's ideas of biological evolution.

In another swing of the ideological pendulum following World War II, a quantitative rebellion set everyone to measuring and modeling on the smallest of scales, trying to see the world in a grain of sand, or at least a scaled-down flume model or simulation program on a computer screen. This emphasis on measurement of rates and processes was an attempt to put geomorphology on a solid, quantitative basis, akin to the envied "hard sciences" like physics and chemistry. In a world with the atom bomb and synthetic materials, precision and detail were seen as the keys to a deeper understanding than that embodied by Davis's comprehensive yet vague theories.

Now we are turning our sights outward again, and technological advances in remote sensing imagery are combining with global threats like greenhouse warming and desertification to tempt us to tackle problems on larger scales. This was part of the reason I had come to Australia: though it often got lost in the complexities of the immediate work, I kept reminding myself that I had a longer-term goal of relating the climatic controls on floods in Australia to those operating in other portions of the tropics, and thus clarifying a fragment of the huge puzzle that is global climate.

~　~　~

During my first field season on the Burdekin, a dam was being completed upstream. By the time I finished my work that season, they were testing the dam. The water level was noticeably lowered the day before I was to leave, and when I crossed the once-fearsome river on my way back to camp, the narrow flow hardly came to my knees. There was a bleached "bathtub ring" and a slight fishy smell all along the river. I was shocked at how much the river had dropped, but within a few hours it rose back to its former level. The rise was like seeing an old friend restored to health and made my going easier, although I knew that henceforward its health depended partly on the dam.

Each time we regulate a river, we lose a little of the wildness of a fresh world we can only age. The Burdekin dam is not a padlock, as are some dams. There will still be floods that rage freely down the gorge when the cyclones whirl in from the sea in the wet season. But inevitably the character of the river — its vegetation, sediment load, channel form, and ability to support life — will change. As dam builders, we often gain the illusion that we have mastered a river. But as often, we see through the illusion even within the short time span of our own lives. We may temporarily restrain rivers, but in so doing we alter them. Our alteration is trivial from the perspective of geological time, but it is often catastrophic from the time scale of the ecological community built on the present climatic and hydrologic conditions. As Rachel Carson wrote in *Silent Spring,* "The 'control of nature' is a phrase conceived in arrogance, born of the Neanderthal age of biology and philosophy, when it was supposed that nature exists for the convenience of man."

And so I left the Burdekin, troubled by the knowledge that I had seen the ending of a free-flowing, unregulated river. My home in the American West is no longer a land of free-flowing rivers either, though the rivers there were once the stuff of legend. We have neon lights in Las Vegas and green lawns in Denver, but we no longer have Glen Canyon or a Platte too thick to drink but too thin to plow. Somehow we must find a balance with the rivers before we alter all the river worlds we so little comprehend.

The Herbert River

> Oh, I have often been too anxious for rivers
> To leave it to them to get out of their valleys.
> The truth is the river flows into the canyon
> Of Ceasing-to-Question-What-Doesn't-Concern-Us,
> As sooner or later we have to cease somewhere,
> No place to get lost like too far in the distance.
>
> Robert Frost, "Too Anxious for Rivers"

The Herbert River drainage basin was named for Sir Robert George Wyndham Herbert (1831–1905), a native Englishman who served as Queensland's first premier in 1860–1866. The river heads in a particularly

Looking down into the Herbert Gorge. The tributary Blenheim Creek is in the foreground; the Herbert River runs right to left in the background.

steep, rugged portion of the Great Dividing Range and is one of a series of smaller rivers flowing from forested basaltic uplands down through narrow, rocky gorges to the sea. Almost four meters of rain fall each year in the perpetually wet coastal mountains of the upper Herbert basin. These waters collect for the steep plunge over the Herbert River Falls, the beginning of their seventy-kilometer journey through the Herbert Gorge. Here the river flows 400 meters below the surface of the surrounding plateau, its tributaries entering as white, spray-plumed falls.

Access to the mountains and plateaus of the upper basin is limited; logging roads approach the top of the gorge, but the river itself is accessible only on foot. The region has always presented a challenge for people eager to explore or exploit. The first white explorer through the area was the ill-fated Edmund Kennedy, a handsome, popular young surveyor who successfully explored the channel country of interior Queensland and New South Wales. In 1848 Kennedy and his expedition set out from Rockingham Bay, just north of the mouth of the Burdekin basin, intending to explore the northeastern coast from the landward side. A supply ship was to parallel him up the coast, but they became separated, and he and his party found themselves trapped among mangrove swamps, between the sea and mountains covered with dense rain forest. Six of his party starved, and one accidentally shot himself. For Kennedy, who was more than 600 kilometers on his way, the end came on the point of an Aboriginal spear only 30 kilometers from his goal of Port Albany.

Within thirty years the lower Herbert basin was settled enough for gentlemen scientists from Europe to venture into it on collecting expeditions. Beginning in 1880, the Norwegian Carl Lumholtz spent four years in the vicinity of the Herbert Vale station, collecting 700 individual birds, discovering four new species of mammals, and observing the local Aborigines. Lumholtz repeatedly described the Aborigines as "a race of people whose culture — if indeed they can be said to have any culture whatever — must be characterised as the lowest to be found among the whole genus *homo sapiens*," yet most of the 400 pages of his book *Among Cannibals* is devoted to Aboriginal culture.

Lumholtz began his adventures in high spirits, intent on discovery:

> Cheerful and happy, I started on my journey in beautiful, sunny spring weather, following the river upwards. All about me was fresh and green. . . . Before me I saw continually the scrub-clad hills, the foot of which I knew to be my destination. It was on these mountains that I based so many hopes. . . . [I] was prepared to submit to various kinds of privation if I could but get the opportunity of living amid this instructive Nature, where I anticipated such great results.

I went to the Herbert Gorge to reconstruct ancient floods from their sedimentary deposits, just as on the Burdekin. In the narrow Herbert Gorge the flood sediments were restricted to isolated pockets of sand forming terraces along the inner bends of the channel. Thus, the stratigraphy of the deposits was not as difficult to unravel as on the Burdekin, but in the Herbert Gorge reaching the deposits themselves presented a challenge. I made several trips into and through the gorge, and each one helped me to appreciate the endeavors of Kennedy, Lumholtz, and the other early explorers.

Heading inland from the small settlement of Kennedy, I followed an unpaved logging road up from the coastal highway over the rugged Cardwell Range and across the plateau to the edge of the Herbert Gorge. Steep, green mountains, and again I was entering them alone. Being alone was undoubtedly my greatest difficulty, for it is easier to be thorough and conscientious in my work when I have even an uncritical observer looking over my shoulder.

From the coast, there looked to be no room within the Cardwell Range for anything but trees, millions of trees and vines intergrown with one another. But somewhere up above lay the clear cut of a river, another river to follow back down to the sea. I followed a steep road cut into the burnt red, clay-rich soil of the tropics, crossed by numerous tiny rivulets where it had been carved out of the mountainside. Ill-defined dark masses of trees flickered by, casting patches of deep shade amid the sunlight. Occasionally a clearing provided a brief view of the slope falling swiftly away, crumpling into folds and ridges. As the road flattened and the trees thinned, I followed battered wooden signs to the road's end at a cliff edge.

I stepped gingerly out of the car after the long ride and walked quietly to the edge of the Blencoe Creek overlook, chosen from the map as one of the more accessible routes to the proposed study area, and peered down in to the Herbert Gorge. Standing at the top of the gorge, I had second thoughts. I looked down from nearly vertical walls, 400 meters deep, to a small stream curled around rocks, creating form without sound. Along the gorge walls the vegetation was thicker in the ravines, the green lines of plants mimicking the flow paths of water. Rainbow lorikeets, iridescent rainbows of purple-blue masks, fiery orange cravats, and emerald green coats, flashed among the branches above me. As though in delicate concession to the beauty of their plumage, they feed on flower nectar, lapped up with a specially formed tongue "brushed" at the tip.

Lumholtz was impressed by "the grand, wild, and romantic aspect" of the upper Herbert in the early 1880s:

> We descended from the table-land and suddenly got sight of Herbert river, flowing dark and restless far down in the depths below. . . . The natives had some strange superstitions in regard to this place. In the depths below dwelt a monster, Yamina, which ate men, and of which the natives stood in mortal fear. No one dared to sleep down there. Blacks who had attempted to do so had been eaten, and once, when a dance had been held there, some persons had been lost. . . . A gun would be of no use, they said, for the monster was invulnerable.

As I gazed down the walls of the gorge at the stubborn tree roots twined tenaciously into the rocks, I knew it might as well be here as elsewhere. I slid and stumbled down the steep, precarious route to the river, setting up camp where the eucalypts grew on the granitic sands and a quiet, clear little stream meandered between boulders and sandbars. That first night, I heard the bird calls that became so familiar I was no longer conscious of them: the descending hoot of the pheasant coucal, the percussive cry of the nightjar, and the eerie, high-pitched screams of the bush curlew, all so different than the night sounds of cockatoos and kookaburras along the Burdekin.

In many ways the Herbert was a more pleasant place to work than the Burdekin. The clear water and the numerous rapids and falls made me less apprehensive of crocodiles, and flies were miraculously absent. Coming from the Burdekin, I had developed work rhythms that were easily adapted to the Herbert, and many of the frustrations and pleasures were the same. When the sun shone brightly, the river was clear and cool, lying deep green and still between huge bedrock boulders or flowing noisily over rapids of smaller rocks. The river twisted and turned, twining the canyon with it, and my gaze always had to go up seeking space. So far from the stars down there. The details were as always — sun on pools, mosaics of boulders, breeze in leaves. Going barefoot to the river for a wash, I noticed the different textures of the rounded cobbles in the boulder bar on the tender skin of my arches: smooth away from the river, rough with dried algae near the river's edge, cool where the rock was in shadow, warm where it lay in the sun.

As on the Burdekin, the sun was sometimes a foe. On one trip, my small thermometer registered temperatures over 110°F each midday, and I couldn't drink enough water. A hot wind blew steadily throughout the day and early evening, making it difficult to dig in the fine sandy sediments and to cook supper. Each day I flopped down panting in the scant shade of early afternoon, dead to the world for the next two hours until the heat began to abate. The journal entry for such a day gives the idea: "Once more, three feeble cheers for exhaustion!"

During other trips, it rained frequently, generally when I had lightened my load by bringing only a tarp instead of a tent. Often I woke to mornings when the clouds hung low into the gorge, making ghostlike figures of the trees along the upper rim. The colors of the stream-worn boulders and the scents of the plants were enhanced by the dampness. Rows of droplets hung from the tree branches, and each grass blade was bent by fat globules of water. Climbing out of the gorge on such a morning, I looked back to the beautiful, insubstantial vision of a rainbow filling space. The tributary falls were at their loveliest, the white plumes of water wreathed by branches of cloud. Then I ascended into the clouds, hearing all around me the distant roar of unseen waters.

Too many rainy, tentless evenings were spent trying to make a shelter in imitation of the resourceful woodsmen heroes of my childhood. On more than one dripping dusk, I finally managed something I thought would last the night, barring a strong wind, but it was usually a pretty soggy affair. On such nights there was nothing to do but go to bed, no matter how early.

Perhaps it was the undercooked soup, chilled by the rain; it may have had the same effect on me as the 'fragment of an underdone potato' on Scrooge. Whatever the cause, it seemed that I was not alone on those nights as I lay beneath the tarp flapping in the dark, windy rain. Settling slowly and fitfully down into sleep I heard the voices of ghosts, and in my sleep-numbed mind I swapped stories with them of wet, windy nights and the terrible joys of life lived close and bare. There was Leatherstocking, stretching his lean, weathered frame closer to the fire's embers and smiling quietly as he spoke of the hard, fierce rains of early winter coming down swift and cold in the Mohican woods. Daniel Boone looked back across long years to the first spring rains, cutting as frozen steel on the dark and bloody ground of Kentucky. Darwin peered intently at the embers from his deep-set, cautious eyes and remembered rounding the Horn, into the teeth of the deadly gales of the Roaring Forties, men on deck gasping for breath as though drowning already. One of the voyageurs sung us a chanson, his cheeks rosy as his flaming scarlet cap, and joked of wet nights in the north woods when the rain sleeted through to snow by morning and pants froze to legs. The Major remembered nights on the Colorado, when the water that had pursued them all day caught them again at night, destroying the chance to dry spoiled food and notes. Burton screwed up his scarred face against memories of torrents of warm water dashing from the sky onto the steaming equatorial plains of Africa, and Leichhardt stroked his beard and sighed, the same tropical rains beating him down half a world away. I wanted to talk to Leichhardt particularly, ask him what the truth of it was, if it was a truth he could tell. But the whole insubstantial group faded back into the blackness of the rain, and I was left with silence, but for the wind and water voices of the night.

Pity I did not have the Aboriginal knowledge of how to make myself comfortable in that country. The rainforest areas of northeast Queensland were fully occupied by the Aborigines until very recently, but despite the observations of explorers like Lumholtz, we are more ignorant of many aspects of their culture than of the culture of the desert and seacoast people. The diet of the rain forest Aborigines consisted mainly of vegetables, as reflected in artifacts for cracking and grinding nuts and processing other plant foods. Protein came from insects, fish trapped in baskets of lawyer cane, or snared turkeys. Lumholtz vividly described an evening feast of beetle larvae in a cave along the Herbert:

> A big fire was kindled; outside it was pitch dark. . . . The large fire crackled lustily in the cave while we sat round it preparing the larvae. We simply placed them in the red-hot ashes, where they at once became brown and crisp, and the fat fairly bubbled in them while they were being thus prepared. After being turned once or twice they were thrown out from the ashes with a stick, and were ready to be eaten. Strange to say, these larvae were the best food the natives were able to offer me, and the only kind which I really enjoyed. If such a larva is broken in two, it will be found to consist of a yellow and tolerably compact mass rather like an omelette. In taste it resembles an egg, but it seemed to me that the best kind . . . tasted even better than a European omelette.

The Aborigines of the Herbert region defended themselves with their long wooden swords, clubs, spears, and kidney-shaped shields made from fig tree buttresses. They recorded their world in rock paintings and engravings depicting bird tracks, geometric shapes, humans, weapons, and various animals and fish. The oldest figures date back at least 13,000 years, and the youngest record domestic pigs and white explorers on horseback. Captain James Cook released pigs in Cape York in 1770 with the intention of providing a feral stock that could be hunted by shipwrecked sailors. The pigs prospered and were incorporated into Aboriginal legends as "little hairy men."

But the Aborigines had cold, wet nights, too. Lumholtz describes an unpleasant night in an Aboriginal hut of leaves and grass covering a framework of branches. These were temporary shelters, put up hastily each evening. "Later in the night a most violent shower of rain suddenly fell upon us; the water poured through the roofs of our huts and put out the fires. I awoke in inky darkness and heard the natives groaning in their disgust at this unexpected shower-bath on their naked bodies."

It was not always raining or swelteringly hot on the Herbert; there were also the calm evenings that are the only real reward for a hard day's work. As I bathed in the cool river at sunset, all the dirt and sweat of the day flowed away to leave me fresh and smooth. Watching the silver flashes of fish in the pools, I ate my suppers as the Southern Cross appeared just over the inner canyon wall in the darkening sky. There was the smell of wood smoke under the silent stars each night, even as I watched the small orange notebooks grow fat with data.

Evenings on the river — what a pleasant sound that has, such good memories and associations. Days for work and directed thought, evenings for relaxation and leisurely contemplation of the cosmos. I knew that when I finished my work on the Australian rivers, I would be sorry not so much for the days as for the evenings. It was so peaceful and simple in the evenings that I, too, was at peace. At home, surrounded by other people, even a quiet night is less relaxing, for I am never so quiet inside. There, it is never enough to simply be — I must always be doing. But on the river, after a few nights to relax into the new rhythm, I could sit and watch the clouds or listen to the water flowing by, and it was enough.

I wonder at the necessity of relearning the same lessons each time I venture beyond the formalized grid of civilization. But I worked with the river at last. Breathed and slept and walked with river, breeze, sunlight, stone rhythms. My blood flowed to the pulse of the rapids. It was a proper pulse for the place and time. My movements were unconscious, and fitting in so well, I couldn't go astray while my thoughts explored other existences, such as that of the sand grains at my feet. So clean and white and still. Could they be said to exist at all? Does existence imply consciousness?

The life history of a sand grain — subject matter for a hundred volumes. Single one out, any one would do — that small, slightly irregular one clinging to my toe. It had impressive antecedents. This particular grain traced its existence to a dim ancestral past when promiscuous atoms still dizzy from the Big Bang mated for eternity and communed with other atoms in a coalescing mass that grew and diversified, each to its own level. Our atoms, the heroes of our story, sank down together, lost in each other, deep into the proto-planet, trapped in a never-never existence of half liquid, half solid. And remained there some 4,600 million years — unimaginable length of time — churning and seething with the currents of their times, until an inevitable uprising bore them toward the surface, hardening them into rigidity with the drop of pressure and temperature.

And here the ancestry of the heroic sand grain becomes more certain; we can place dates, even if approximate, on the events of its history. For it had entered onto the pages of public history as a modest quartz crystal, one among billions in a granite pluton. There it sat, cheek by jowl with questionable neighbors — pink feldspars and black biotites — for 200 million years. Dark, silent, and motionless.

But things were happening above and around the quartz crystal. Memories of the mad motions of the cosmic dance were reawakened by the distant roar of waters as a tumultuous river ceaselessly carved its way down through the resisting rocks, carrying everything before it toward the sea. Dividing and conquering, the river used pieces of the rock itself to destroy the remaining rock, and our hero felt the surface approaching. Into the long dark night of the crystal's existence came a thin, twisting rootlet, twining down among the grains, forcing them apart, secreting acids to dissolve them. The rootlet swelled with absorbed moisture, and droplets of water followed in its path, knocking off crystals left and right. Our hero resisted, at first unyielding as the Rock of Gibraltar, but was finally overcome. Dislodged at last, thrust out into the bright, harsh air, the crystal took up a new life as a sand grain.

The grain was slow in reaching the river, now far below it. For a while our hero lingered near the place of release, forming a soil to nurture the invading plant. Then one morning the world collapsed in a roar of sound and tumbling motion as the grain was hurled down the canyon's side with billions of its fellows. It came to a stop not far above the river and worked its way slowly downward over the next few centuries, time and tide (or more accurately gravity and rain) carrying it relentlessly on.

At last the grain reached the embarkation of its next great stage and, late one afternoon, was suddenly swept in by the greedy water. Down and around, bounced and tossed and rolled, our hero traveled along the bed of the river, losing the rough edges of inexperience along the way, occasionally rising to the top in one of the great catastrophic upheavals of floods that are the lot of river sand grains.

There were quiet moments as well, periods of rest in the bright sunshine of the river beaches before being swept onward again in the impetuous green water. Our heroic sand grain was of the most admirable sort, able to accept the irresistible currents of the river with equanimity and yet control destiny if given the chance. Chance — so important in all these existences. Chance had left the hero stranded high and dry on yet another beach, where a great lumbering creature stepped on it and, by

A boulder bar (foreground) and bedrock beside the low-flow channel of the Herbert River.

chance, noticed it. And thus two existences met and mingled briefly, probably with fateful consequences for neither. The great creature lumbered off in another direction and was never seen again. And our heroic sand grain? Best inquire for it at a certain beach on the Herbert River. If it's not there, try the next one downstream, and the next after that, and so on to that eternal beach beside the endless sea where all sand grains eventually meet.

> To see a world in a grain of sand . . .
>
> William Blake, "Auguries of Innocence"

The sand grains of the Herbert share the river bars with giant boulders ranging from the size of a watermelon to that of a Volkswagen beetle. Where the wide-bottomed Burdekin Gorge has extensive, vegetated sandbars flanking the channel, the narrow bed of the Herbert Gorge is largely swept free of vegetation, the sand and boulder bars lying pristine and unhidden. The channel of the Herbert is steep through the gorge, and where the boulder bars cross the channel, they form rapids and falls. Clambering about like a pygmy among the jumbled piles of rock, I used the size of these boulders as another indicator of flood power, measuring diameters with a long tape.

Empirical relations between boulder size and hydraulic variables allow estimation of a flood's magnitude if the boulder sizes moved by the flood are known. Because I had no way of determining which among the jumble of boulders on each bar were moved by a given flood, I simply measured the largest boulders on each bar as an indicator of the largest floods. I found that flood characteristics estimated from the boulders along the Herbert River tended to differ from those estimated using sand and silt deposits, and I judged the latter to be more accurate.

If there is sufficient fine sediment available for transport by floodwaters, the relation between suspended sediment transport and hydraulic variables like velocity is fairly straightforward. The relation between coarse sediment transport and hydraulic variables is much harder to predict or understand because the movement of coarse sediment along the bed of the channel is highly stochastic. If I determined the diameter of a boulder along the Herbert River to be two meters, the best that I could do was to estimate a range of velocities for the floodwaters that moved the boulder. For example, if the boulder was surrounded by smaller cobbles, it would have begun to move at a lower flow velocity than if it was surrounded by larger boulders. Because there is no way of determining the influence of these initial conditions on boulder transport, I was left with rather vague estimates of flood hydraulics. But the results from the fine and coarse sediments made an interesting comparison, and measuring boulders gave me a change of pace from digging soil pits.

As I followed the river downstream, the character of the valley changed, and I knew the excitement of first explorers in rounding each bend. The deep, powerful river flowing over steep bedrock falls or between high ledges in still, green pools became a sparkling trout stream threading its way in hundreds of small rivulets over and between boulders. Ascending the river, Lumholtz also commented on the changes, noting how "the roar of the waters and the dark green vegetation clothing the hills on both sides of the valley from base to top . . . awakened in me hopes of interesting finds. . . . I was cheered by the sight of the luxuriant and beautiful surroundings." This contrasts strongly with his mood on another day along the upper Herbert: "It has been said that an Australian landscape breathes melancholy, and the truth of this statement is fully appreciated by a person who, on a day like this, wanders amid these sober, awe-inspiring gum-trees and acacias. One's mind cannot help being overcome by a sense of solitude and desertion."

As I continued downriver, I thought of things I might have missed, questions that might remain unanswered. But there will always be one more river, and I contented myself with the philosophy of Samuel Butler — "Life is the art of drawing sufficient conclusions from insufficient premises" — and of Mark Twain — "There is something fascinating about science. One gets such wholesale returns of conjecture out of such a trifling investment of fact."

Scientists aim to maximize their investment of fact and minimize their return of conjecture, but it is always tempting to speculate beyond firm ground. In Australia, my ultimate goal was to relate the history of flooding to regional climate. The paths of the cyclones each wet season are largely controlled by global atmospheric and oceanic circulation patterns. Cyclones are clockwise-rotating masses of air and moisture formed in association with the Intertropical Convergence Zone, or ITCZ. The ITCZ is a band of convective activity associated with warm sea-surface temperatures that moves seasonally north and south across the equator. During the Southern Hemisphere summer, a branch of the ITCZ swings down over northern Australia as sea-surface temperatures to the north and east of the continent rise and sea-level pressure drops. Cyclones originating in the Coral and Arafura Seas cross onto the Australian landmass, dumping their loads of moisture, and the rivers surge up into great floods.

While sea-level pressure is low over northern Australia and the western equatorial Pacific, it is high over Tahiti and regions to the east, reversing seasonally in a pattern known as the Southern Oscillation. Occasionally this pattern falters or breaks down, and sea-level pressure over northern Australia remains high during the summer, forcing cyclones north and east away from the continent and producing a drought even as the normally dry west coast regions of South America are being drenched by the rains of an El Niño.

The El Niño, named for its December appearance off the coast of Peru, is a pool of warm water associated with the Southern Oscillation. When the Southern Oscillation skips a beat, the warm El Niño waters grow much larger than usual, and the heightened evaporation produces disastrous flooding in Peru and Ecuador. The whole El Niño–Southern Oscillation system is like a stone chucked into a quiet pool, sending out waves of weather change from the tropics into the extratropical regions, producing winter rains in southern California and drought in central India, for example.

In northern Australia, the intensity and severity of flooding waxes and wanes with fluctuations in the El Niño–Southern Oscillation system, and I wanted to use the record of floods as a proxy indicator of these climatic fluctuations during the last millennia. After several seasons of fieldwork, however, I concluded that the resolution of the flood record is insufficient to make inferences about a climatic pattern with a recurrence interval as short as two to nine years. Although I fell short of my original goal, I learned many new things en route and shifted the course of my research to focus on the effects of large floods on bedrock channel morphology, a course I still pursue today.

I am glad to be a student of rivers, even if there is much I will never comprehend. Water sustains life and shapes landscapes, and rivers are its finest expression. They epitomize movement and renewal within the stability of a defined framework — a juxtaposition of opposing forces that has fascinated humans for centuries. As Ralph Waldo Emerson wrote, "Who looks upon a river and is not reminded of the flux of all things?"

Walking back to camp through the heat of the afternoons, following the patterns of the broad, shallow potholes slowly carved into the rock by each season's floods, I appreciated the cool river at which I could refresh myself. The river deposited the sand on which I slept and the wood with which I cooked, and the sound of the rapids was a background over which to embroider my life. I hope that I am always a student of rivers. I would know their secret places and silent ways and be privy to their wild days as well as to their common hours. If I could learn the grace of that clear green water as it flows seamlessly past stones, I would be doing well.

2

Seeking a Beach Beyond Reach ~

> Ecstasy is identity with all existence.
>
> Peter Matthiessen, *The Snow Leopard*

Queensland narrows down to the Cape York Peninsula, which points across the coral-studded Torres Strait toward New Guinea. Coming from the south, the paved roads end at Mount Molloy, and 300 kilometers further north at Cooktown, the roads become impassable to all but four-wheel-drive vehicles. The Great Dividing Range runs north-south through the eastern half of the peninsula, covered with impenetrable rain forest reaching down the flat coastal plain to the mangrove swamps at the edge of the sea. The Aborigines live in relative freedom here, and a scattering of national parks ensures the preservation of at least some of the diverse wildlife that thrives away from white civilization. To the east lies the Coral Sea, with the Great Barrier Reef closely paralleling the coast. To the west lies the Gulf of Carpentaria, a huge, land-sheltered body visited only by hunters, missionaries, and prawn trawlers. The peninsula contains the greatest wild stretch of Australian tropical rain forest and is a frontier of the imagination with its legendary history of miners and Aborigines, shipwrecks and lost explorers.

The Dutch mariners Willem Jansz (1606) and Abel Tasman (1644) were the first to explore the shores of the Gulf of Carpentaria, and the great English navigator James Cook (1768–1771) made the first successful voyage along and through the reefs to the east of the peninsula. Cook's success was followed by the wreck of the HMS *Pandora* in 1791. The *Pandora* ran onto the coral at 7 P.M. on the night of August 28 while returning to England from Tahiti with fourteen of the HMS *Bounty* mutineers. Early on the morning of August 29 the ship sank, killing thirty-one of the crew and four of the mutineers. The ninety-nine survivors traveled north in lifeboats to Timor, where they were able to get passage home in a Dutch East Indiaman. This was only the beginning of a long history of shipwrecks in the reef waters. Those who survived the initial wrecks faced starvation and dehydration beneath the tropical sun during their long, difficult journeys to the nearest civilized outpost and were forced to brave the hostility of the native blacks along the coasts. Their triumphs and tragedies are recorded in Hector Holthouse's book *Ships in the Coral.*

Settlement of the Cape York Peninsula proceeded slowly after the disasters that befell Edmund Kennedy's party in 1848, and today the peninsula contains only small, isolated towns like Weipa, Cooktown, and Laura. The effects of the rapidly growing tourist trade of Queensland do not appear until Cairns, at the southeastern base of the peninsula. My travels in northern Queensland extended north from Townsville to Cooktown, and inland to the crest of the Great Dividing Range, and always I had before me the vision of a "beach beyond reach" — a private tropical paradise.

My first view of Townsville, spreading along the coastal plain at the base of the Great Dividing Range, was from the air. A jog in the coastline interferes with the prevailing moist southeasterly winds, and Townsville is drier than the areas immediately north and south. But when I stepped off the airplane into the warm humidity, I knew I was in the tropics.

A city of approximately 100,000 people, Townsville was my base between field expeditions, and I came to think of it as home. The town has a relaxed yet festive atmosphere, as though every day were Saturday. The air is warm and gentle between the blue sea and the rugged, thickly forested mountains. Some days the sea deepens out from aquamarine to royal blue, with white flecking the crests of the swells. Others it is slate gray, with silvery patches where shafts of sunlight break through the low clouds. Along the Strand the sea breezes twine among the trailing roots of the giant old fig trees and gently coax the strolling people. Joggers and lovers, young families with prams, restless teenagers, and gently quiet pensioners all pass among the red-legged seagulls begging for bread along the low seawall.

Inland from the Strand lies the Mall, where the shops and restaurants face each other across an open walkway broken by palm trees and flowers. There are always people on the Mall, stopping for ice cream at the brightly colored stands, browsing in the bookstore, holding up clothes in the shop mirrors. In from the bush, the Mall eased me gently back into civilization with its quiet holiday atmosphere.

The houses of Townsville are built for the tropics, elevated on airy platforms that allow both breezes and wet-season floods to pass beneath. The houses cluster around the open areas like Queens Gardens, where flower beds and green lawns complement palm groves and expansive fig trees. The Australians have mastered the knowledge lost in so many American cities: that the oasis of a quiet corner where people can relax and enjoy the beauty of their surroundings is as necessary to individual and civic health as a well-functioning hospital. The Queens Gardens gave me many pleasant lunchtimes and hours of reading in their green quiet.

Townsville was a place of introductions and new experiences for me. There I saw my first Aborigines, broad-featured people of quiet movements. There I grew accustomed to businessmen in shorts and knee socks and to the pervasive long "i"s of spoken Australian. Coming as I did from the national capital of Canberra, Townsville was my first glimpse of a more insular Australia.

Townsville was founded in 1864. Sydney merchant Robert Towns, with extensive pastoral holdings in northern Queensland, needed a port accessible from the interior and protected yet navigable from the sea. Towns's managers Andrew Ball and John Black found Ross Creek flowing into Cleveland Bay. Within a few months Townsville took shape as a row of bark huts along a muddy track bordered by the crocodile-haunted mud flats of the creek. In the 1880s a breakwater was built at the mouth of the creek, and as the country north of Townsville developed, sugar, bananas, and other goods were brought in by small vessels for transshipment. Mining booms in the interior invigorated Townsville, and railroads went out to the rich mining centers of Charters Towers (shortly before 1886) and, 1,000 kilometers inland, to Mt. Isa in 1924. The copper finds at Mt. Isa led to the construction of a copper refinery and fabricating plant in Townsville.

Terminus of the railroad from ore-rich Mt. Isa in the interior and located on a good harbor from which the sugarcane grown along the coastal plain to north and south can be shipped, Townsville is also the site of a rapidly growing tourist industry based on the Great Barrier Reef and coastal beaches. But the city is still considered the outback by those living in the more populous areas of southeastern Australia. Employees at some government agencies in Townsville receive a free plane trip to Brisbane each year to counteract the effects of living in an isolated community.

When I was in Townsville, I stayed in caravan parks, something of a cross between a KOA Kampground and a permanent trailer park. Plots of land at the edge of the cities or towns, caravan parks have both permanent and temporary trailer sites, as well as tent spaces. For a few dollars a night I got a tent space, access to bathroom, shower, and laundry facilities, and sometimes a pool or TV room. The caravan parks along the north Queensland coast do a booming business. In addition to tourists, many of their customers are pensioners spending their winters in the warmer climate, as well as young families living in them for a period of weeks or months so that the parents can follow seasonal or temporary work. The parks are regular little communities that people enhance with tiny lawn plots and the conveniences of televisions and stereos, but they often struck me as too crowded when I had just come in from the bush, and I silently commiserated with Professor Henry Higgins on "humanity's mad inhuman noise."

James Cook left a wake of names in his 1770 passage through the Townsville area. Magnetic Island he christened for its supposed effect on his compass. Now the island is a national park a half-hour ferry ride east of Townsville. Numerous small, protected bays and beaches are tucked around the edges of the mountainous chunk of the island like jewels on a necklace. Horseshoe Bay, Balding Bay, Arcadia, and Nelly Bay are all flat names for paradise found. Names like Radical Bay hide diamond-white sand beaches, water clear as mountain air deepening gradually from pale turquoise to azurite, opaline sailboats anchored in teal blue water, and emerald green forest spilling down the hills to a fringe of palms at the very edge of the beaches.

Balding Bay was my favorite, a small arc of clean white sand framed on three sides by massive granite boulders and forest ending in stately, symmetrical Norfolk Island pines. Gentle swells of the stunningly beautiful water caressed the beach. I was endlessly amazed by the incredible beauty of water so pure and brilliantly colored that it was a pleasure to be in and a part of it. Sitting on the warm sand of the beach, watching fragile little crabs scurry across my tracks as lightly as sea foam, I looked east across miles of blue water to a boundless horizon. James Cook and his crew must have felt magic at work here.

Hiking across the island, I found the interior rocky and mountainous beneath a cover of open woodland. Several lizards darted across my path, and I gave the courtesy of the road to a small, slender golden brown snake just in case. There are thirty species of dangerously venomous snakes in

Australia, ranging down from the real nasties like taipans, death adders, and tiger snakes to the innocuous-sounding small-eyed snake. They play an important part in traditional Aboriginal culture, where the blood of some snakes is used in initiation ceremonies and snake dances are performed. Aboriginal snake myths often deal with the spread of disease following some improper act on the part of an individual or a tribe, recalling our story of the Garden of Eden.

As I returned from the island, the sun set red and clear behind the line of low, black mountains to the west, and the full moon rose simultaneously in the east. Eastward it was all horizontal lines where the gray-blue sea with a breath of green met the solid, gunmetal gray mountains, and the powder blue sky low on the horizon paled upward through indeterminate white to delicate eggshell blue. Improbably large, a richly golden full moon lay between the blue skies. It was fine sitting on the back of the ferry with a cool wind blowing, watching the moon rise higher and whiter into the blue evening, the lights of Townsville coming up alongside us.

North along the coast from Townsville the Herbert River joins the sea near the town of Ingham, named for sugar plantation owner and merchant W. B. Ingham. Beyond Ingham is Cardwell, a road's width back from the sea, boasting the world's best batter-fried fish. Then in quick succession come Tully, Innisfail, Babinda, the Atherton Tablelands, Cairns, and Port Douglas. North of Port Douglas the settlements stop until road's end at Cooktown, one third of the way up the Cape York Peninsula, beyond Daintree River and Cape Tribulation National Parks.

Following this 500-kilometer route on Highway 1, the Bruce Highway, the vegetation grows denser as the air grows slightly more warm and humid. Pineapple fields and banana plantations alternate with long stretches of bright green sugarcane backed by steep, thickly forested mountains. Beyond Cairns the mountains come directly down to the sea, and the forests are untamed by agriculture. The Bruce is a major highway in usage and importance, gradually outgrowing its childhood as two narrow, bumpy lanes without shoulders. It runs through blackfellow country, and the country of struggling small farmers, of the flotsam and jetsam of international youth who wash up onto the Cairns beaches, of affluent white tourists, of pensioners from the cold south. For the Northern Hemisphere images are reversed here, and people speak of soft northern nights and the deep north.

Narrow, winding mountain roads radiate out from the Bruce. Nervous roads, for though I was careful to drive slowly, I had several near-misses when other cars came swinging merrily around a bend. Such roads led to Mount Spec National Park and Crystal Creek Falls, where small cascades winding and twisting among boulders in fluted bedrock channels were so perfectly arranged that even Ruskin would have approved. At the other end of the spectrum, the cliff of the Wallaman Falls rears up 300 meters from the surrounding rain forest. Plunging over the edge of the falls, water separates into plumes of mist weaving sinuously downward like pure white smoke, and as each plume hits the solid surface of the pool below, it shoots out sideways over the pool's surface.

When night fell, I looked for inviting dirt tracks leading off into the open eucalypt forests, where the white tree trunks rose straight and tall as columns. Supper was cooked over a twig fire as the light gradually dimmed and the night insects replaced the calls of the kookaburras. Each morning began clear and cold, with the sunlight filtering down through the leaves as I breakfasted on rolls and honey. On Sundays I listened to the Australian Broadcasting Commission's morning program *Australia All Over,* featuring "Aussie" folk music of Scots-Irish tunes with lyrics like "I'm bloody well Australian through and through." Combining interviews with country folk, traditional folk music, poetry reading, story telling, and hints for country living, *Australia All Over* became my favorite radio program.

Familiar radio programs take on a peculiar importance when you are alone, providing a lifeline to the comfort of a known past, and a sense of continuity and stability. Something about listening to the chatting of people far distant makes you feel both connected and yet very alone. I remember one night along the coast when I accidentally picked up a broadcast of *Prairie Home Companion* and spent the next hour listening more avidly than I ever have at home.

Wherever I traveled in Australia, I found eucalypts, the Australians' well-loved gum trees. From the snow gums in the Australian Alps, to the river red gums and ghost gums of the interior deserts, and the gums of the rain forest, the ubiquitous genus has settled into every environment on the continent. During a journey inland to Bathurst in January 1836, Charles Darwin described in *Voyage of the Beagle* the appearance of the gums in terms commonly used by those unfamiliar with them:

The extreme uniformity of the vegetation is the most remarkable feature in the landscape. . . . The trees nearly all belong to one family, and mostly have their leaves placed in a vertical, instead of, as in Europe, in a nearly horizontal position: the foliage is scanty, and of a peculiar pale green tint, without any gloss. Hence the woods appear light and shadowless.

In *Rainforests of Australia,* Leo Meier and Penny Figgis explain that modern eucalypts derived from ancestral rain forest stocks under special climatic conditions associated with soils of low fertility. They are drought- and fire-resistant, and the Aboriginal use of fires aided their proliferation. Geoffrey Blainey discusses the effect of Aboriginal burning practices on eucalypts in *Triumph of the Nomads.* In northern Australia, eucalypts shed their seeds in the dry season, most of the seeds reaching the ground close to the parent tree, so that dispersal is slow. Strong bushfires spread the seeds much greater distances because the heat of the fires bursts open the seed capsules, and the seeds are then carried on turbulent air currents. Frequent bushfires also create a surface soil ideal for eucalypt seed generation. It was only recently recognized that the "pristine" landscape found by the first white settlers was actually the product of generations of human control. Bernard O'Reilly vividly described a Queensland bushfire in *Green Mountains:*

At last it came; there was a roar more terrible than anything . . . yet heard; the sun was blackened out, the light faded into awful twilight through which was a sullen red glow; the wind became a hail storm of sparks and fluffy, blazing stringybark. The fire, travelling in great tongues one hundred feet above the tree-tops . . . taking homes at one lick, and leaving only the water storage tanks, boiling like great kettles . . . even the creeks in its path boiled dry.

I had my own little fire show one night along the Queensland coast. North of Ingham lies the Tully River, one of a series of coastal rivers north of the Herbert that flow through deep, narrow gorges from the Atherton Tablelands to the sea. The Tully is dammed for hydroelectric power, but the lower portion of the gorge below the dam remains a turbulent, whitewater, boulder-strewn channel, where the Raging Thunder raft company runs day trips.

Steep walls hemmed in the river. The walls were green and tangled with dense rain forest, though lacking the palms and tree ferns of the wettest areas. Scabs of bedrock showed through in spots. Long, hard columns of dark basalt twisted up from the brown river, and looser columns of white water twisted down the basalt. River's edge, the white falls melted into the clear, swift-flowing, tea brown water of the main flow. It was low water, dry season flow, with boulders sticking up all over like jutting ribs on a starved carcass. Rapids were scattered across the water's path, chutes and falls to tip the rafts and make the water laugh with glee. I looked back at the other boats and laughed myself as one tried to navigate a narrow chute and hung up well above water level. We needed to find a bigger river. But the mischievous little brown stream churned up memories of other rivers . . . big, green rivers with inscrutable depths that flowed along quietly in peaceful boils until they found a boulder pile and suddenly the world was chaos.

There is a certain smell to big rivers, hard to pin down with words, easy to recognize. Mostly I wasn't aware of it, but sometimes, drifting in quiet pools and watching the shore birds, the cool, musty smell worked its way into my brain. I noticed it most in the mornings, crawling stiff and sleepy-eyed out of my bag onto the cool sand, stumbling with sleep-pampered feet down to the river to bathe. Then, before the sun had reached the canyon floor and vaporized the night air heavy with river smells, the air held the mark of the river.

Sometimes I could smell it in the midday shadows after a rapid, too. Drifting quietly, then, almost imperceptibly, the water flowing swift and smooth down a gentle incline toward the point of a "v." Deceptively smooth, and the raft guilelessly follows the gently down-dipping sheet. But a moment to stare in amazed horror at the great hole and backward-curling wave at the base. The raft drops sickeningly downward in a great swoop, bends nearly backward on itself in a senseless churning of white water and violent forces. Spluttering, dripping, blinking we go, as the raft rides the whitewater tails at the end of the rapids with a series of rough slaps. Always then, in the quiet water at the end, all my senses tingling keen, I smell the river.

The rapids on the Tully were fairly small and short except for the raft-eaters, which sucked the boats in greedily and refused to give them up without a valiant struggle. On one abrupt little chute, I was thrown out of the raft — one of the hazards of riding front, where you are the first to see what is coming but unable to do much about it. I spluttered and thrashed about in surprise before managing to swim to shore and then decided to do it again. The whole raft pulled up at the bank just downstream of the falls, and we climbed back up along the bank to go over the falls individually. The falls dropped three meters to a large, deep pool. Most people went over headfirst, lying on their stomachs, but I went feet first, to be plunged underwater, turned upside down, and spit back up to the surface, disoriented from the powerful, roaring chaos of pale green water shot through with bubbles. I got a good noseful of water in the process and came up wondering why I do such things.

We returned along the coast through a sunset, twilight, and finally full darkness spectacular with the lurid glow of cane fires. It was a calm, dry night, and the cane farmers were burning the sugarcane prior to harvesting it. Apparently this practice originated in the days when the cane was harvested by hand, and it was necessary to rid the densely growing stands of snakes and the poisonous cane toads. Eventually machines were developed for cane harvesting that did not require burning, but the practice of burning helps rid the stalks of the dried, sugarless leaves, which facilitates processing and is still common. That evening, the dense palls of brown smoke hanging in the air produced a lurid orange-and-red sunset behind the black mountains. Once it was fully dark, the distant fires looked like great Roman candles, with pieces of burning cane shooting into the air and a pale orange glow reflected in the fires' smoke. At closer quarters, the burning cane crackled and popped loudly, and the air was heavy with the smell of burnt sugar.

North of Tully I discovered Etty Bay, a small crescent of sand shouldered against the sea by steep, forested cliffs ending in black basalt. Low tide exposed the rocks fringing the beach, revealing a variety of creatures: nervous little fish in shallow pools and crabs scuttling hastily into crevices, fragile plants encrusted on the crinkly black shells of the mussels, and anemones tightly curled against the dry air. Snails in spiral shells and barnacles that clamped their parrot beaks shut when I ran my finger over them. The edge of the beach was strewn with tiny, delicate by-the-wind sailors, their blue tentacles hanging softly beneath their iridescent bodies, or spread out like a halo as they drifted along in the shallows.

Sunrise at the bay had a vast backdrop of orange-and-green sky, black rocks framing the foreground, and between sky and rocks, the opaque silver sea, strangely solid-looking. The low clouds turned to molten gold as the sun rose behind them, and the silver eyelash of moon faded away. Out on the water were the black silhouettes of the friendly, practical fishing boats with their green and white lights, nets to each side like arms akimbo. As I passed a fish bone lying on the surface of the beach, a small crab suddenly retreated from it into the sand. We were in the swash zone, alternately exposed and submerged, and I was amazed at how neatly the crab immersed itself (buried seems an inappropriate word), leaving no holes or other signs of its presence. It made me wonder how many other creatures I strode over unawares. I stood very still, and a few bubbles slowly broke the surface of the wet sand, followed by just the tips of the crab's eyestalks, two little beads sitting on the sand. I left it to enjoy its meal, thinking of Rachel Carson's lines in *Silent Spring:* "Most of us walk unseeing through the world, unaware alike of its beauties, its wonders, and the strange and sometimes terrible intensity of the lives that are being lived about us." It was a rare privilege to walk along the beach that morning, alone with the surf and the sunrise, on sand unmarked by human feet.

Later in the day other people came to the beach. Like the Americans, Australians have a high standard of living, never more evident than when they flock to the beaches with cars, radios, surfboards, sun umbrellas, eskies (coolers), and barbies (barbecues). It was a noisy, crowded, typical holiday scene for a while, but when the shadows lengthened across the beach, the people slowly left. With the incoming tide, the sea reclaimed its own. As the sun set, the tiny green and white lights of a ship far out to sea were all that separated sea and sky. The crickets began to sing in the cool, peaceful evening. The future seemed very long on such nights, and I was relaxed in the feeling of time enough. There was no great urgency about anything, after all, and I could merely enjoy the unique moment.

Feeling meditative, I sat in the warm, gentle dark of the deserted beach. But the mosquitoes were having none of that, and I retreated to shelter and my waiting data. As I traveled the Queensland coast, I worked steadily to make sense out of the mass of measurements and observations I had collected on the Burdekin and Herbert Rivers.

I have decided that there is really nothing straightforward about field research. In a historical science like geology, the ideal situation would be to have a time-lapse film of the processes occurring through time at a given site. Barring that, the features created by those processes must be used to reconstruct the processes themselves. But nature is not a very meticulous bookkeeper, and half of the entries may be erased, written over, or otherwise obscured. The field scientist thus sets out to be a detective in a setting where half the clues are missing and the others may be difficult to interpret because of lack of time, tools, or understanding.

Ideally, I would have camped out in the Burdekin and Herbert Gorges for several seasons, actually watching the flood sediments being deposited from some safe vantage point. I would have had large field crews and equipment like a backhoe to gain access to the most deeply buried sediments, and I would have had a much larger budget, allowing me to analyze many more radiocarbon samples. Finally, I would have had a thorough understanding of the climatic mechanisms that cause floods and of the multiple factors that control sedimentation.

Lacking all of these wonderful things, I did my best to develop a story from what I could see and what I did understand. A century ago, Thomas Chamberlin warned geologists against having "favorite children" and advocated the use of multiple working hypotheses. It is human nature to begin to develop a story or an interpretation of evidence as it becomes available. We are always trying to determine causal relations and to explain things, from the mundane details of our daily lives to the great riddles of existence. What Chamberlin cautioned geologists against was becoming too attached to the first interpretation that presented itself. It is only too tempting to begin by developing an explanation that seems to fit all of the observed details and then interpret all subsequent observations so as to support that explanation.

I began my work in Australia expecting to see a non-uniformity in the distribution of floods through time that would reflect non-uniform climatic conditions. I could not begin to test that hypothesis until I received the results of the radiocarbon analyses being conducted at a laboratory in southern Australia. Meanwhile, I performed the mathematical analyses that would transform the survey data into a representation of channel geometry and went over and over in my mind what I had seen along the rivers, trying to develop the most complete and logical story.

~ ~ ~

Inland from Tully lie the Atherton Tablelands, basaltic uplands perched near the top of the Great Dividing Range that combine the contrasting extremes of northeastern Queensland: lush, primeval rain forest and neatly ordered pastoral lands. As in most of Australia, the contrast is reflected in the place-names that are either very British or derived from Aboriginal names. Kuranda, Tchupala Falls, Yungaburra, Malanda, and Millaa Millaa lie peacefully beside Davies Creek, Ravenshoe, the North Johnstone River, and Atherton. Small restaurants

A small stream channel on the Atherton Tablelands.

advertise Devonshire tea (scones with jam and cream), and placid Holsteins graze green pastures bordering ravines filled with wild tangles of vegetation. With time these wild pockets have grown smaller and smaller and are now preserved mainly in a series of small national parks and forests dotting the map in a sparse checkerboard.

Both a highway and a railroad track make the steep ascent from the flat coastal plains to the tablelands. In 1882 construction began on the railroad that would carry the lumber and ore of the interior down to the waiting ships. The route followed the Barron River Gorge up to the town of Kuranda. I took a train up this route, a train now reserved for tourists and serviced by restored cars with wooden interiors and red leather seats. Where I rode in ease and comfort through sheer-walled rain forest gorges and long tunnels, the original construction workers struggled mightily with heat and humidity, insects and fever, deluging rainfalls and landslides.

The railroad line began in the residential areas of the coast, where corrugated-metal-roofed, gaily painted wooden houses on stilts shouldered up to the tracks. These gave way to broad cane fields before the line began to ascend the mountains. From a distance, the thick vegetation covering the mountains appeared an impenetrable wall of tall trees thickly hung with vines intertwined with the understory of shrubs and trees rising to meet them.

The thin red line of the railroad cars advanced boldly into the chaotic tangle of green. Where the track curved, I looked out the window and saw the line ahead as the rhythmic, swaying motion of the train carried me up and inward, away from the scintillating blue sea and the comfort of houses and into the dark mountains. The train pulled steadily on, to be immersed in vegetation. Tree ferns lapping at the windows, palm fronds brushing the roof, fig branches obliterating the sun. Beyond the self-conscious hustling and puffing of the train, the forest lay dark and quiet, rising up steeply into cloud curtains and dropping off abruptly as long, green falls down valley slopes. The motion of the cars condensed sights as I sat motionless, and newly created flower colors flashed out of the undulating greens, fresh and vibrant as the first colors of existence. Bellbirds and whipbirds gave the weird calls of the jungle, undulating between the vines falling from the tree crests down, down, descending into the leaf-cushioned floor. Rivulet waterfalls compounded of tea brown water and sugar white foam flashed spontaneously from the darker shadows. I leaned out the window of the train, unthinking, opening every sense to the strangeness of it. Then we were above the mountains, resting on their quiet back, among houses again.

The line ended at Kuranda, a small town hosting an outdoor Sunday morning market. Rows of wooden stalls held handcrafts like pottery and jewelry, homemade preserves, bakery and dairy products, and a cornucopia of fruits and vegetables grown in the rich soil of the tablelands. Much of the produce comes from small farms settled by Italians who came to Australia in one of the waves of postwar immigration and mixed into the solidly British dairy-farming population of the area. I bought a variety of goodies at the market, including a homemade Cornish pasty for lunch, and continued on through Mareeba to Atherton. The land had a certain European feeling of settled, prosperous age, as well as of altitude. On either side of the road stretched lush green fields and pastures with fringes of forest, and in the distance beyond the gently rolling plateau lay the green mountains — scenery combining wide vistas and the feeling of space with a pleasing greenness and prosperity. If I were a pastoralist, I could be happy there, and the farm women in their Wellingtons looked content.

Pastoral scenery has its drawbacks, however, and I got quite enough of scenic one-lane roads on the Tablelands. Many of the secondary roads have a single, central paved lane with dirt tracks on either shoulder. You drive along in the center until you see another car coming the other way, when both swerve off to their respective shoulders and drive with two wheels off the pavement. Many of these swerves become near-misses, as the roads are often winding, hilly, and narrow, and I saw a huge logging truck that had skidded off the road and down the hillside in one such encounter.

At Malanda, a large dairy center, the older people were coming into the dairy fair dressed in their conservative Sunday best, heightening the European atmosphere. A short walk brought me to Malanda Falls, one of the many falls over ledges of resistant basalt where clear deep-green water flows, delicately framed by the greenery of palms and tree ferns reflected in its pools. Another walking track led to Lakes Eacham and Barrine, old volcanic craters now filled with clear waters that have preserved a 190,000-year-long pollen record of the surrounding vegetation.

Many plants are prodigal in their production of pollen, sowing it broadcast on the winds. Some of these pollen grains reach the female parts of the plants and carry on the life of the species, but many others are entombed in unsuitable sites. Quiet lakes often preserve a record of the surrounding plants, each season's pollen production lying buried in a thin layer of lake sediments. These layered sediments may be cored and dated, either by counting the number of layers back from the present or by measuring the decay of naturally occurring radioactive elements contained in the sediments. The pollen from certain types of plants has a unique appearance when viewed under a microscope, and the number of pollen grains for these plant types in a sediment layer indicates the nature of the surrounding forest when that layer was deposited. Australian scientist Peter Kershaw has carried out this type of analysis for the sediments flooring Lakes Eacham and Barrine and concluded that the rain forest has existed for at least 190,000 years in this region, interrupted only by a short period of drier, sclerophyll woodland between 9,000 and 26,000 years ago.

Eacham and Barrine are associated with another type of history as well, as recounted in *Rainforests of Australia*. The Djirubal tribe of the Tablelands has a Ngadyan story about the time in the days of open scrub when the wrath of the Rainbow Serpent raised great winds, twisting and cracking the earth. The skies filled with clouds of a red never seen before, as though the sky were on fire, and cracks opened in the ground to swallow the frantic people as they tried to escape. There were volcanic eruptions in the region between 10,000 and 15,000 years ago, when the forest was open scrub, and evidence of an increase in fires some 40,000 years ago indicates that Aborigines may have occupied the area since that time. Thus the Ngadyan story may be the oldest recorded oral prehistory of any human culture.

A national park at Palmerston Gorge encompasses the descent from the Tablelands back onto the coastal plain. The pamphlet for the self-guided nature trail to Tchupala Falls explained the competition for space and light in the forest (hence the vines and basket ferns) and noted that some of the three-meter-tall saplings may be thirty years old. Although I kept a sharp lookout for tropical leeches, I never faced anything worse than plenty of tropical mosquitoes. The deeper forest grew progressively darker, and even the rock outcrops became covered with gray-and-black mosses. Lawyer vines, named for their grabbing spines, twined among huge-leaved trees. Leaves in the tropics are characteristically large, sometimes more than twenty centimeters long, with tapering drip-tips to funnel off excess moisture. When paleontologists reconstruct long-vanished forests from a few leaf imprints left in stone, they use large leaf size and the presence of drip-tips to infer warm, wet conditions.

The falls were a series of steps running down a towering rock face into a jumbled mass of large boulders with luxuriant vegetation. From a massive boulder on one of these steps, I reveled in the fine, cool mist coming off the cascades above and gazed in fascination down onto the tops of the trees lining the creek banks below. My first impression of an undifferentiated mass of deep green, distinguished mainly for quantity, slowly resolved itself into details like the spiky serrations of palm fronds curving through the spreading, waxy leaves of an umbrella tree, or the droopily smothering embrace of a clinging vine on a boxwood. Epiphytic orchids perched on the tree trunks and the aerial roots of spreading fig trees hung down like graceful curtains. The symmetrical leaves of the ferns spread like a delicate lace over the forest floor.

The scene was a riot of life in seeming disorder. Under a cloudy sky the forest was a dark and somber place, where enormous fig trees loomed ghostlike, trailing thousands of roots down from their branches. But when the sunlight filtered through the canopy, the forest was filled with lovely shades of emerald, beryl, and malachite, and the details of the plants stood out in the contrast of sun and shade. Still, it was hard to realize

Wallabies on the Atherton Tablelands.

much of the detail. Like walking through a fog, things were really only seen occasionally here and there.

Before continuing north to Cairns, I took a snorkeling trip on the Great Barrier Reef. Picturing the reef as lying very close to shore, I had imagined swimming out to it from the beach, but it takes a stronger swimmer than I am to reach the nearest reef, twenty kilometers offshore. The reef was designated a marine park in 1975, although members of the Queensland government still cast covetous glances on it and wish parks and reserves had never been invented. Sir Joh Bjelke-Petersen, a former conservative Queensland premier for twenty years, at one time advocated mining the reef to provide limestone for paving Queensland's roads. Now Sir Joh sees more lucrative possibilities in the reef and is doing his best to aid international developers, particularly the Japanese, in commercializing the reef. Twenty offshore resorts presently exist, and trendy visitors can fly directly to the island of their choice to eat and drink luxuriously, swim on the beaches or in the chlorinated freshwater pools, and enjoy nightclub entertainment. Once-isolated Dunk Island, immortalized by naturalist E. J. Banfield in his 1908 book *Confessions of a Beachcomber,* now decorates the posters in the Sydney airport and all the southeastern Australian travel agencies.

The Great Barrier Reef is composed of numerous individual reefs and cays. A cay (or key, as it would be called in the Caribbean) is a small sandy island of pieces of broken shell and coral collected by wind and ocean currents in the shallow portion of a reef. The cay forms a nucleus surrounded by reefs and water gradually deepening outward in all directions.

A lot of lip service is given to the idea that modern life is too harried, that we are seekers of sensation rushing from one stimulus to another without ever pausing to think about our lives or to fully experience any one situation. I have noticed this to a certain extent in myself, although I am unsure how much is due to personality rather than culture. No matter what I am doing at any given moment, my mind is almost constantly divided and my attention only partial. There are so many books to read, so many places to see, so much to learn and do that I get caught up in the notion of ticking things accomplished off my mental list — reading a book quickly but superficially so that I have the satisfaction of having it out of the way and can go on to another on the long list of those I want to read.

I try to force myself to be aware of what I am doing and to think about the meanings behind surficial appearances, but to a great extent, I am never fully present at any moment in my own life. I come the closest to living fully concentrated when outdoors, and it is with a rather dismayed amusement that I watch myself go through predictable stages when I return to the wilderness after a prolonged period of urbanized living. At first, delighted as I am to be out, my thoughts are still very much caught up in the existence I have left behind. I am receptive only to the grossest details of scenery and weather, and beneath this my mind still runs on like an animated calendar organizer, reviewing what I have just left behind and plotting out a schedule for what I will do on return.

Over the next few hours, or if my sojourn is long enough, days, I gradually, imperceptibly, slow down and open up. I become more aware of the finer details around me, separating the landscape into components and then building these again into textures that now have more meaning because I am aware of their constituents. I become sensitive to the smell of sun-warmed grass and the sound of wind slipping through pine needles. I sit still long enough to see ants wandering across the design of white and pink crystals on a granite boulder. I feel myself more a part of my surroundings, observing from within rather than looking in through a filtering window. This, I think, is what many people refer to when they speak of the healing qualities of nature. There is healing in this slowing and concentrating of awareness, and perhaps it is more satisfying to be fully aware of one small part of reality than to be dimly aware of a great deal. My times in the natural world prevent me from fragmenting myself so widely that I can never collect the pieces again.

This process of concentration occurs to a certain extent every time I seek the outdoors, but it cannot be forced. I cannot go out, sit myself down on a sun-warmed boulder, and say that now I will make myself receptive, now I will make my mind a blank of the past and future and then see what flows into it from the present. Rather, when this does happen, it comes upon me unawares. And because it is hoped for but uncoerced, it is intensely satisfying. Twice in my life have I experienced the height of this sensation and an accompanying sense of deep joy and well-being. The first time was during a raft trip down the Grand Canyon of the Colorado River.

The Colorado float trip was one of my first noncar camping experiences, and I brought along a tarp in lieu of a tent for protection against the elements. The tarp was not overly effective in protecting me against anything except access to my bed. The second day of the trip, we rode into a stiff, cold headwind that picked up droplets of river water and flung them against us like bullets. By the time we made camp late in the afternoon, I had a severe headache, and I hastily set up my bedroll and tarp and crawled in to sleep without waiting for supper. In my haste and discomfort, I fastened the head of the tarp to very short sticks, so that it hung into my face when I got into my sleeping bag. In too much pain to care, I fell asleep quickly.

Sometime during my sleep I pulled the tarp aside completely, so that I lay sleeping under the open sky. When I awoke a few hours later, the rest of the camp was still. I was lying on my back, and just above me, seemingly within reach of my arm, was the dark, rich sky, full of stars, arching over from horizon to horizon. It was as though I were immersed in space, surrounded on all sides by darkness and stars, and for the first time I was able to conceive of the earth as being immersed in an endless realm of space with thousands of other planets and stars. In that moment, I as an individual, separate being ceased to exist, and the idea of a cosmic harmony was no longer uncomfortable or vaguely sentimental. It felt as though everything was in its proper place and perspective, and I as one tiny part of the whole could never be useless or lonely or truly finite in time or space. This feeling passed gradually, and I once again became aware of the feel of an uncomfortable stone under my left hip and the coolness of the breeze on my face. But the memory of that momentary experience as one of the greatest of my life remains with me.

I lost my sense of time and space again while snorkeling on the Great Barrier Reef. I took a boat to a portion of the outer reef about two hours' travel from shore. When we arrived at Michaelmas Cay, the ship's crew put on a little fish-feeding show, culminating in the feeding of Neptune, a giant grouper. As the first of the passengers over the side a few moments later, I got a good look at Neptune underneath the ship. He was an awesomely large, dark, blunt-nosed fish, and I was glad he did not have a taste for snorkelers.

As I swam off toward the cay in the other direction, I entered a dimensionless, silent world of diffused, pale blue light. Looking down through several meters of perfectly clear water to a featureless, white sand bottom and unable to focus on any colored, concrete objects, I lost all sense of proportion and distance. As I adjusted myself to the power of the long, heavy flippers on my feet and the hoarse sound of my own breathing through the snorkel, I began to perceive shadowy outlines and faint colors below me, and then suddenly I was at the reef.

It was a self-contained world wholly different from anything I had ever experienced before. The coral grew together on the irregular surface of the reef, rising to plateaus and spires, spreading away in plains, or dropping into canyons. I relived an old fantasy of flying out from an aerial precipice, like a bird soaring into space, as I passed over the reef edge and across the depths. But these depths did not inspire the fear that deep water sometimes does, for I could see to the bottom, through shoals of silvery fish. It is only the unknown in the depths that brings fear.

There was an astonishing variety of coral: spreading white fans, bulbous gray brains, giant yellow fungi, red shag carpets waving in the current, purple-blue trees, brown thorn bushes, yellow grasses. Blue starfish and orange starfish draped sensuously over the coral. Giant black sea slugs crawled the sand floor like caterpillars, and bristling sea urchins festooned the coral. I was slightly afraid of touching the unknown coral, so I kept a certain distance between myself and it. But slowly I overcame the fear, and swimming with my face only a few centimeters above the coral, I could observe the intricate beauty of its details.

This was an intimate, small-scale beauty of tiny star and hexagon patterns and gently waving fronds, which only the fish and I shared. And oh, the fish! Dozens of varieties and hundreds of fish. If there is such a prodigality of fish at one small cay, imagine what all the oceans hold. Schools of tiny fish glittered in the sunlight like confetti filtering down from a height. Black-and-white-striped fish grazed on the coral like zebras on a grassy plain. Great fish in the blue depths rolled over on their sides to scan me with one eye as I passed over them. There were shy, nervous fish the color of ripe lemons on a bright Arizona day; fish to inspire the paint of an Indian warrior; fish combining all colors on themselves, so that the light rippled across them like a rainbow against a stormy afternoon sky; fish that settled slowly down to the ocean floor beneath me like brightly colored autumn leaves; ghostly silver-white fish that lost themselves against the white sand bottom; iridescent purple-blue fish glowing as if under a black light. Small reef sharks, the essence of lithe grace, undulated snakelike and smooth below me. Schools of huge, hump-snouted wrasse sailed along majestically, and grazing parrot fish spit out little white clouds of powdered coral. Clouds of fish, mists of fish, shimmering, darting schools of fish. Fascinating as were the corals, it was the fish I loved. They gave life and reassurance to what would otherwise have been a landscape too different and unreal.

I surfaced for a while to warm myself in the blinding light reflected from the white sand of the cay. The cay, a low speck of land in the midst of vast, deep blue water, hosted thousands of sooty and noddy terns. It was nesting season, and the terns clustered thickly where mats of low, tough grass spread across the sand. Each adult bird hunched over a single brown-speckled white egg laid directly on the sand or tended a fluffy young chick. The adults were black and white, all sharp, clean lines and angles. The chicks were fluffy gray toys, unbalanced caricatures without tails, stretching their stubby little wings and squawking. Wheeling, screaming birds filled the air, swooping and darting just above my head. The whole colony was raucous with bird noises — adults arguing with each other, adults and chicks calling back and forth, adults quietly squawking as they hunched over an egg, glancing back nervously at the gawking human. It was a bright, white, loud world, and as I waded back into the water, the wind carried the pungent, fecund odor of birds and their guano. Then I dipped below the water, back into the silent, blue-tinted world of the coral and the fish.

I spent some three hours circumnavigating the cay, staying in the water until my fingernails turned blue, then hauling myself up onto the coarse, white sand of the cay to warm in the sun. Warmed, I returned to the water, where shafts of sunlight filtered into a quiet, pale blue as they

Sooty tern (*Sterna fuscata*) chicks on Michaelmas Cay, part of the
Great Barrier Reef, near Cairns.

passed downward. I hung suspended over chasms where the reef floor
dropped away to a deep blue mystery, effortlessly tracing the edge of the
reef. I swam and swam, tiring but entranced, until gradually the cold crept
into me once more.

Over a shallow patch of coral, I had just decided to return to the ship
for the day when I stopped swimming and held my breath. Hanging
motionless, I heard the rasp of a fish grazing on the coral. Fish surrounded
me closely, unafraid, graciously accepting me into their world, and I felt a
part of that world. I was no longer an alien or a stranger, dazzled and yet
slightly afraid. I hung unmoving in the water, the fish and I swaying back
and forth in the currents. It felt completely natural, and I belonged where I
was, as I was, a member of a community secure in a place. The mask and
snorkel ceased to exist. As in the Grand Canyon, there was a complete
epiphany of my surroundings, and I was unconscious of myself as a
separate, discrete entity, temporarily free from the overbearing
consciousness of self.

Returning swiftly across the blue-green water in the boat,
wind-blown, sun-warmed, rimed and itchy with sea salt, I was tired and
happy. If only Cook and the other early mariners could have guessed at

the beauty beneath the waves. The color of the waves was so brilliant that the water seemed to vibrate with it, to glow of its own accord with a color that was the sea as a whole, and every droplet of it. The little silver torpedo of a flying fish went bouncing and skimming across the water's surface. I thought of what I had just experienced. An old and treasured experience in the history of the race, that of ecstasy. The best description of it that I have ever come across was written in 1167 by Hildegarde of Bingen, a religious mystic and hermit. Listen as she describes her vision of the spirit of the macrocosm:

> I am that supreme and fiery force that sends forth all living sparks. Death hath no part in me, yet I bestow death, wherefore I am girt about with wisdom as with wings. I am that living and fiery essence of the divine substance that glows in the beauty of the fields, and in the shining water, and in the burning sun and the moon and the stars, and in the force of the invisible wind, the breath of all living things. I breathe in the green grass and in the flowers, and in the living waters. . . . All these live and do not die because I am in them. . . . I am the source of the thundered word by which all creatures were made, I permeate all things that they may not die. I am life.

Camped on the shore that night, I took a walk along the beach after dark. Barefoot beside the sea, beneath the stars, I began to dance. Dancing and singing, I celebrated life, fitting the dance to the occasion and the place, sinuous, graceful, relaxed, undulating.

~ ~ ~

Cairns calls itself the capital of far northern Queensland, which seems reasonable: although not by any means a large city, it is certainly the largest within a radius of a few hundred kilometers and the last major outpost before the wilderness of the Cape York Peninsula. Cairns, named after the serving Queensland governor Sir William Wellington Cairns, was proclaimed a port of entry in 1876. Lured by the potential profits of the new goldfields at the Palmer and Hodgkinson Rivers, parties of Townsville and Cooktown businessmen chartered steamers and virtually raced to found the new port, unload their stores, and make tracks into the interior.

Since World War II, Cairns has grown rapidly from a sleepy little outback town serving fishers and cane growers to an international tourist destination with multistory beachfront hotels, a large airport, and offshore resorts and reef cruises. Though still not a rival to the southern resorts like the Whitsunday Islands or the Gold Coast, Cairns is growing rapidly enough to shock people who have not seen it in a few years, and seems particularly attractive to certain groups.

Where do they all come from? Like flotsam stranded on a beach, they wash into Cairns on tides from around the world. The railroad brings them, the highways, the buses, the planes, often to stay longer than they had planned. I call them the international vagabonds. People in their twenties and early thirties taking a year, five years, ten years to travel the world, picking up odd jobs along the way. Cairns snares them with cheap hotels, good nightclubs, and gently curving swaths of sand white as newborn clouds cradled between arched palm trees and warm blue sea.

I believe the sea has moods. At Cairns it was always happy, a happy laughing blue. And the climate, too, was a Mary Poppins kind of climate, practically perfect in every way. So the vagabonds come to Cairns and find it good. I met many in my wanderings through the city: Bente, a young Scandinavian living out of a backpack with the minimum of necessities, for whom a frisbee was also a dinner plate. Keith, at one time of London, most recently from three years of teaching English in Japan via five months in an Israeli commune, bound for home by way of the South Pacific, Australia, New Zealand, and the States. Molly, a businesswoman from Washington, D.C., who opted for a world tour rather than proud possession of a suburban house when her bank account reached maturity. Americans, British, Aussies, Swedes, Israelis, Canadians, French, Germans — a floating population of the newly independent seeing the wide world on a narrow budget. I began to feel quite staid by comparison.

I spent the Fourth of July in the Cairns area beach hopping. Wandering empty beaches, I remembered other Fourths, growing up in Ohio. They all flowed together into one seamless day in my memory: early morning, I put up the small American flag in the front yard, the red and blue sharp against the green grass. I rode my bike around the neighborhood to see the other flags, the soft morning air still cool and dewy beneath the long shadows. Down the street lived the boys with the firecrackers. They took risks I wouldn't, and I was both envious and suspicious. But they had the firecrackers, the smoking cherry bombs, and pinky-sized sticks that exploded in horrendous noises. Scaring and daring each other, we excited in parental tales of manglings and mutilations from careless firecracker play.

My grandparents came for lunch, and we all sat beneath the shade of the big maple in the backyard. My grandparents smelt vaguely of the mothballs they used too liberally, and my grandfather ringed himself with splotches of brown tobacco juice. Hamburgers (extra garlic on Grandpa's), potato salad, watermelon, baked beans, and cookies. I did not realize until later how archetypally American was our private ritual. As the air grew hot, the day buzzed with cicadas and sunlight. The adults played cards and talked, drinking pitchers of iced tea while I set off caps with a toy gun and hammer, engrossed in the loud, quick bang and fierce smell of gunpowder.

When the shadows lengthened again, I pestered my father for the firecrackers, and as the hot sunlight slipped down beyond the edge of the world and the mourning doves gave way to crickets and fireflies, he brought out sparklers and Roman candles and lit the hot, blue-white flames of magnesium tape. In the distance the aerial displays of the community shopping center burst against the dark sky in globs and sprays of color while I stood in the thick darkness at the edge of the yard, swatting at mosquitoes and hopping excitedly from foot to foot until the last rocket's red glare smoldered out.

As I walked the beaches, thinking of home, I also thought of Emily Dickinson and Henry David Thoreau: it is not what, or how much, you see, but how you see it. (Witness Thoreau's "A worm is as good a traveler as a grasshopper or a cricket, and a much wiser settler.") I was trying both to see a great deal and to see it well. The life of constantly traveling and seeing new things was exciting and stimulating, and each day I looked forward to new adventures. Yet in odd moments I regretted the absent routines of home life. I feared seeing things too superficially, and at times I wondered why I was traveling at all. Others have asked the same questions. In his novel *Kangaroo,* set in Australia, D. H. Lawrence answered this way:

> "Then why am I going?" he asked himself. "Wait! Wait!" he answered himself. "You have got to go through the mistakes. You've got to go all round the world, and then half-way round again, till you get–back. Go on, go on, the world is round, and it will bring you back. Draw your ring round the world, the ring of your consciousness. Draw it round until it is complete."

On other days it was easy to understand traveling. From Cairns a spectacular road winds precariously between sheer coastal cliffs and the bright blue sea, north to Port Douglas and Four Mile Beach, where steep green headlands sweep down to the white sand. Walking along the beach, I was envious of my own luck. From the cool, pearl gray of predawn, through the stunning blue, white, and green of midday, to the warm, quiet glows of sunset, the coast of northeast Queensland cast its spell over me. As I moved on to something new each day, neither restricted or rushed, I saw how such a life became habitual and got into your blood so that you became a lifelong traveler with an eternally unsatisfied wanderlust. I was well on my way. Australian author Miles Franklin expressed it eloquently in *My Career Goes Bung:* "Beauty is abroad. Under her spell the voices of the great world call me. To them I give ear and go."

As elsewhere on the Queensland coast, the placid atmosphere of the present day in Cairns obscures the violence that went before, as chronicled in Hector Holthouse's *Ships in the Coral.* The bêche-de-mer fishers operated along this coast, risking death in their daily trade so that Oriental connoisseurs could eat dried sea slugs. The fate of Captain Kane of the schooner *Wild Duck* provides an example.

Kane had an experienced, trusted crew of one white, one kanaka (Polynesian laborer), and sixteen Aborigines. The kanaka, Billy Matlock, was inspired to seek easy riches by the tales of his white drinking companions in the gold ports, and he persuaded the Aborigines to murder Kane and the other white on the ship. They fired the schooner and pushed off in the longboat with provisions and bêche-de-mer, landing on a deserted beach north of Cairns. During the night the Aborigines abandoned Matlock, dead to all sounds in a whiskey-sodden sleep. Undismayed, Matlock sailed the longboat to Townsville, sold the bêche-de-mer, and was still in the nearest pub when news of the burned hull of the *Wild Duck* reached town. Arrested and questioned, he made up a plausible story and got off with two years in jail. While Matlock was in jail, the true story spread from the Aboriginal divers working for Kane's friends. When Matlock was released, he went to Cairns, where he was one day joined by a friendly looking group of white men who had a few drinks with him and invited him out on a pig hunt. He never came back, but his companions, Captain Kane's friends, thought it a successful hunt.

North of Port Douglas I had my car ferried across the Daintree River. Dark and sluggish between banks thick with vegetation and numerous signs warning of the estuarine crocodiles, the Daintree seemed the border of adventure. Beyond lay the cloud-obscured summits of the steep green mountains, the intimidating rainforest wilderness, the real bush. If I had possessed a four-wheel-drive vehicle, I would have gone all the way to Cape York and gazed across the Torres Strait to the truly wild lands of New Guinea.

The rain forest has always been a symbolic frontier for me. In the literature of Western civilization, men and women go out to the extreme places of the world to test themselves beyond the boundaries established in their lives among other people. These extreme places are the great uninhabited spaces, the deserts, the rugged mountains, the polar latitudes. Here, the general attitude implies, you can see into and perhaps beyond yourself more clearly by forcing confrontation with the unknown and unexpected.

The first time I came to the desert, I felt an immediate, instinctive kinship with the landscape. Where others have found the vast open spaces and clarity of line and form harsh or threatening, I have always felt liberated and invigorated by the desert. Eight years of living there have made a well-vegetated landscape claustrophobic for me. Thus the rain forest, the most densely vegetated landscape of all, presents the greatest challenge. Where the desert has traditionally been associated with a visionary, spiritual quest involving simplification of physical needs to the barest essentials, the rain forest has often been viewed as containing dark, primitive, threatening revelations. Joseph Conrad's depiction of the descent of a superficially cultured white man into a state of savage bestiality as a result of his journey into a rain forest in *Heart of Darkness* is only one example of a prevalent literary treatment of rain forests.

Rain forests such as those of the Amazon basin have been the last strongholds of some of the world's most traditional cultures, so that even today they hold the possibility of contact with a way of life totally unlike ours, thus implying danger. And the teeming nonhuman life of the rain forests presents many dangers. The tropics are often associated with virulently venomous insects and snakes, creating a vague image of pythons and fer-de-lances draped from the branches, and with army ants devouring everything in their path. Exotic fevers and diseases wait to seize the unresistant whites and, together with the heat and humidity, beat them into an enervating lassitude.

The desert is very hot, and the sun there may bake your brains, but the popular image of the solitary white in the desert does not involve a slow draining of energy and a sinking into uncaring sloth, as does that of the rain forest. "To go native" conjures a picture of late risings and prolonged drinkings in palm-thatched huts, not in desert fastnesses.

Venturing into the desert, you must endure privation and hardship, but you will eventually reach a state of enlightenment and spiritual purification. You risk defeat in meeting your goal, but the goal is a striving toward something positive. Venturing into the rain forest, the most you can hope for is the maintenance of what you already have, but you risk the erosion of all civilized values, and a degeneration into some primitive, bestial remnant of early humanity.

Many naturalists have approached rain forests with a different attitude, astonished and delighted at the endless variety and abundance of life they contain. Writing during the first half of the twentieth century, William Beebe described in *High Jungle* the "beauty and excitement" of the jungle in Venezuela, and in *Edge of the Jungle,* he wrote of the "sheer joy" of watching insects in British Guiana. In April of 1832, Charles Darwin noted in his journal that he never returned empty-handed from his excursions into the forest around Rio de Janeiro, where the "noble forest . . . completely surpasses in magnificence all that the European has ever beheld in his own country." Naturalist W. H. Hudson even wrote a romantic novel, *Green Mansions,* in 1916 in which the Indian heroine symbolizes the beauty and mystery of the Amazonian jungle, although she is violently killed near the end of the book.

In his 1869 book *The Malay Archipelago,* Alfred Russel Wallace wrote of "delightful hours" in the forest but also described the gloomy atmosphere of thick stands of vegetation where the sunlight never reached the forest floor. This note of ambivalence is sounded by many of the naturalists, who were always foreign visitors to the countries of which they wrote, when they described the thickest tracts of forest. As Francis Ratcliffe wrote in *Flying Fox and Drifting Sand* during a visit to the Queensland rain forest: "With the jungle I found that a little went a long way. For a few hours, a day at most, one is enthralled. After that the over-stimulated senses seem to revolt and become a prey to a growing uneasiness."

The last word here goes to Bernard O'Reilly, who was raised in the rain forest of southern Queensland. His book *Green Mountains* is a love song to the rain forest, which he describes in terms of jewelled valleys with emerald mountains and turquoise skies. I think that the truest words for the rain forests will come from those who have grown to adulthood in them and thus see deeper than we who merely pass through.

The prevailing cultural stereotypes of the desert and the rain forest, like many stereotypes, reveal more about the people who create them than about the subject, but they continue to influence our perception of the world. For me the rain forest thus represented both a cultural and a personal challenge — a result of my acclimation to the openness of the desert — in the sense of a misperception to be overcome. What little I have seen of the world has taught me that every place has value expressed through a beauty and harmony of its own, as well as something of importance to teach. The challenge is to discover the spirit of each new place by defining the individual characteristics that combine to create its uniqueness. This invariably promotes a greater sympathy and appreciation for the landscape, so that I end, to paraphrase Will Rogers, by deciding that I have never seen a place I didn't like. Sometimes, however, the challenge of perceiving enough beauty and gaining enough understanding to feel at ease is very great, as in the rain forest.

It was easy to be intellectually ready to appreciate the rain forest. It is a diverse and beautiful environment and a vital global ecosystem in danger of destruction from unregulated human activities. The rain forest represents tracts of some of the last great wilderness left on earth, and its natural history remains relatively unexplored. If I ventured into it, I would be emulating in a minor way a great tradition I have grown up admiring, that of the intrepid explorer-naturalists who combine (and perhaps justify) personal adventure and danger with important contributions to the shared knowledge of humanity. Thus did I reason with myself. Emotionally, I knew that here I ran the risk of being defeated in my challenge of learning enough about an ecosystem to feel at ease. There was hanging over my head that centuries-old accumulation of dread of the deep, dark forest and of the unknown.

The cultural stereotype of the rain forest as threatening is interesting from another perspective as well. It may help to explain what unfortunately is still a prevalent attitude toward both the rain forest and many other ecosystems — that short-term exploitation is acceptable. If the rain forest is unconsciously regarded as a threat, both to our individual, personal standards of morality and technological competence, and to the progressive tradition of civilization that they represent, then it is easy to justify the destruction of the rain forest. If something threatens to subvert all the qualities you hold most estimable and necessary, it is your duty to destroy it.

In the case of the rain forest, it can not only be destroyed, but converted to something viewed as beneficial. This is the fate facing the rain forests of the earth today, from the Amazon to Asia to Australia.

Whether the justification is recreational resorts or subsistence agriculture, it involves the destruction of the rain forest as a functioning, intact natural system. The situation is not helped by the location of much of the world's rain forest in economically expanding, heavily populated countries with low standards of living, where the view of rain forest as threatening and subversive still prevails. It seems we are developing an increasing awareness of the ecological diversity and fragility of the rain forest just as it is being systematically wiped from the face of the earth. For never before have we had the pressure of such human numbers behind us creating the ability and the desire to alter such large tracts of the tropics. I also carried this knowledge with me in my encounters with the tropical rain forest.

The road beyond the Daintree was unpaved — steep, winding, rutted, and repeatedly flooded by creeks, barely passable in a passenger sedan. I drove first to Cape Tribulation, a name that had been ringing in my mind. It was so named by Cook in 1770 because shortly after passing it he ran aground on a coral reef. Just north of the rocky cape I found a beautiful beach fringed with mangroves and rain forest. Looking up from the beach to the densely forested mountains, I imagined that Cook and his men must have found them formidable and intimidating and stuck to the coast. And how lovely the coast was; close to noon the sun finally shone out clearly, bringing out the blues and greens of the sea and the deeper greens of the forest.

From Cape Tribulation I turned south again, stopping to walk through the weird world of the mangroves at Myall Beach. These mangrove swamps border large stretches of the beaches and are nearly impassible unless there is a trail or, as at Myall Beach, a raised boardwalk. A skirt of supporting roots up to a half meter high and a meter and a half in diameter extend from the mangrove trunks, so that the trees look like they are growing on stilt platforms. The skirts of adjoining trees intermesh to form a continuous network of sloping roots impossible to walk on or through. Sluggish little freshwater rivulets meander through the roots and, together with the daily tides, leave a rich residue of silt, clay, and organic detritus supporting a variety of invertebrates and shore birds.

Like many fine things, mangroves may be an acquired taste. Working in Queensland in 1929, naturalist Francis Ratcliffe described them as "indecent-looking vegetables, the hobgoblins and abortions of the arboreal world." Mangroves produce brown, palm-sized hollow seed husks that float to new beaches suitable for mangrove colonization. The

Aborigines decorate these seedpods by painting, carving, or burning designs into them, and they are now to be found among the woven dilly bags and ochre bark paintings in tourist shops.

Walking through the mangrove swamps, I better appreciated the hardships suffered by Edmund Kennedy. As a tourist, I found the rain forest beautiful and exotic and the mangrove swamps a fascinating ecosystem. I remained in each of them only as long as I chose and required nothing from them but scenic beauty and interest. But Kennedy must have come to hate this coast as he struggled along it, trapped between a thickly vegetated, trackless interior menacing with hostile blacks, sickness, and dangerous insects and reptiles, and an unapproachable blue sea. Suffering from a white man's ignorance of possibilities of food or shelter, Kennedy must have viewed the rain forest and mangrove swamps only as hideous obstacles between himself and his increasingly desperate goal.

Trials and tribulation: are not these the expected lot of any explorer? Ah, but there is a large gap between expectation and experience. I found the small beaches closely hemmed in by vegetation stumbling and sprawling over itself in its rush to the sea. So was I hemmed in, tethered to the blue-and-green sea that lapped easily at the roots of the mangroves. On tiptoe at the edge of the mangroves, I peered in. Better to remain by the sea, given the choice, for this is a restricting wilderness. I could follow the cleared corridor back to the car, and in the car follow another cleared corridor sealed in at the sides and overhead by the hungry plants. Breaking through the seal, I found that the plants continued on and on, only slightly less dense than at the edge, dark and moist and silent, and I turned back. Better not to force too many frontiers in one day. Maybe Kennedy's ghost was in there, curled in its agony among the buttress roots. Where would the ghost of a Kennedy go — to the scene of his death, or to the earlier, thoroughly known, well-beloved places?

I found a large group of protesters in their mid-to-late thirties semipermanently camping out in Cape Tribulation National Park. The Daintree forest has become a symbolic region in the fight to preserve something of the north Queensland rain forest. The main threats to the rain forest are development for commercial tourism and clearing for woodchipping and pasturing. Although Australia created the world's second national park in 1879, the Australian environmental movement developed as slowly as its counterpart in the United States. Australian environmentalism has grown rapidly since the mid-1970s, however, when it was galvanized by the actions of the Tasmanian Hydroelectric Commission in flooding Lakes Pedder and Gordon in Tasmania's Southwest National Park and in proposing to dam the lower Franklin and Gordon Rivers of Tasmania. The main foci of interest are now Antarctica, the Tasmanian and southeastern Australian temperate rain forests, the Kakadu region of the Northern Territory, and the tropical rain forest of Queensland.

The battle over Queensland's rain forest has recently intensified as a result of a 1987 UNESCO decision to add close to two million acres of Australia's tropics to its World Heritage List. UNESCO's 1974 World Heritage Convention Treaty allows signatory countries, of which Australia is one, to nominate significant natural and cultural areas within their borders to the World Heritage List. Upon listing, the nation is obligated to protect the area.

Australia presently has 7 of the 288 World Heritage sites, including the Great Barrier Reef and a portion of Kakadu National Park, but in 1983 commonwealth legislation to protect World Heritage sites passed only over state protests and legal challenges. The commonwealth's conservation role is limited by a constitution that gives states the right to administer public lands and to create national parks and reserves according to their own criteria. Queensland politicians tend to be jealous of the commonwealth government, and Queenslanders are suspicious of the urban southeasterners from the populous Sydney-Melbourne region who often support environmental legislation. Although Queensland has established more than fifty rainforest parks, they are scattered patches focusing on unique features like spectacular waterfalls, which preserve less than 15 percent of the available rain forest. Amidst lawsuits and "greenie bashing," a strong "green vote" helped Bob Hawke and the Labor Party retain office in the 1987 elections, and in December 1987 the government nominated the World Heritage rain forest.

In *Rainforests of Australia,* Leo Meier and Penny Figgis describe the six major types of rain forest that occur on the Australian continent: tropical, monsoon, subtropical, warm temperate, cool temperate, and dry rain forest. The first two types occur in patches east of the Great Dividing Range in northeast Queensland. The appearance of the forest varies greatly due to spatial and seasonal moisture and temperature gradients. Optimum rain forest development occurs in global regions with greater than 2,500 millimeters of rain uniformly distributed throughout the year and constant warm temperatures. The highly seasonal distribution of

Australian rainfall prevents the Queensland tropical rain forest from matching the luxuriance and diversity of rain forests in such equatorial regions as Amazonia, Malaysia, and Costa Rica. In fact, it is cause for wonder that the driest continent, 80 percent of which receives no rain for three months at a time, even has any rain forest.

But Australia contains over one million hectares of tropical rain forest stretching in a band some 700 kilometers long and up to 50 kilometers wide between Townsville and Cooktown. Logging of these forests began in the 1870s, and what remains today is less than half of that existing a century ago, but it still contains 1,160 species of higher plants, including 450 found nowhere else; almost one-fifth of all Australian bird species; and nearly two-thirds of the continent's butterfly species. This is the greatest concentration of rare and endangered species in Australia.

Worldwide, species diversity increases as the equator is approached, but many of these species have very restricted distributions, some occurring on just one or two mountain summits. This is why it is not sufficient to preserve merely a few token hectares of rain forest. One of the great wonders of the tropics is the prodigious variety of life forms thriving there, and any adequate conservation scheme must preserve this diversity.

The unpaved road I was following north through Cape Tribulation National Park had recently been extended clear to the northern boundary of the park, although the new portion remained impassable for the type of car I drove. This road was especially controversial, for environmentalists wanted to preserve a large tract of rain forest intact, whereas developers promoted the road with the intent of using it as a springboard for the construction of future coastal resorts. My impression was that if any of the rain forest or other ecosystems of the Cape York Peninsula are to be preserved, the impetus will have to come from outside Queensland — either from the national Australian environmental community or from the international environmental community. Queenslanders tend to be rural, conservative people and to support their resource-extraction-oriented state government. The people living illegally in the park campground are practicing a form of nonviolent protest against the destruction of the rain forest, but in their own way they are destroying a small part of it, overloading the sanitation and refuse systems and providing no very convincing argument on the stewardship abilities of those who profess to care for the environment.

I camped on a dirt track off the highway that night and thought back over the rain forest I had seen that day. It was beautiful and fascinating, but I was still equivocal about it and was not instinctively and immediately drawn to its beauty as I am to that of some other areas. One of the rain forest's chief merits is its diversity of texture, color, and life. Perhaps so much detail is intimidating, crowded into so little space as to appear at first unresolvable. Certainly the darkness and lack of long views intimidates. Anyway, I continued to reserve judgment.

I pulled out early the next morning, under a sky dark with low-hanging clouds. But the sky soon cleared, and as the road turned north and inland, the vegetation slowly changed to open eucalypt woodland. It was an adventurous dirt road full of ruts and rocks to dodge, cattle and wallabies to watch for, and plenty of dust to swallow, but when there was time left to look at the countryside, it was beautiful. I was inland from the rain forest now, across the orographic divide and in a land of orange-red rolling hills and mountains, a land of dry watercourses with floodways and water-depth markers. Every so often the road passed a jewel-green billabong, well fortified with signs warning of the crocodiles.

Whenever I crested a hill along the road, I had a splendid, sweeping view of undisturbed forest. It was a good land in which to be at play. The usual solitary kookaburras, easy to identify with their squat, ill-proportion-ed bodies, large heads, and thick bills, sat on tree branches or telephone wires. Kookaburras are giant kingfishers that have adapted well to living with humans. Their demonic cry, rising and falling in a long ooh-ooh-ahh-ahh, is the source of the nickname "laughing jackass." As they sit hunched-up on their perches, overlooking the strange sandy spires of termitaria, they have a look of satisfied, ironic knowledge.

As the road turned back toward the coast, the vegetation grew thicker and greener again until I crested a hill abruptly and got my first view of Cooktown. It was hard to make an end when the unknown stretched smoothly onward to the horizon. I have never been one to leave once-glimpsed things for later; there are too many unglimpsed things and not enough laters — fewer laters every year. But now I had to be content with that at hand.

Cooktown lay below me in a magnificent setting of azure water rimmed with white sand, vast green lowlands, and plateaus stretching away unbroken to the north. The town lay on a hillside between a steep headland to the south and the mouth of the Endeavour River to the north, where gleaming white boats rested quietly in the blue water of the estuary. The town consisted of one main street with a few hotels and stores fronting the harbor, and a collection of corrugated-metal-roofed houses straggling around. A casual little gathering of tropical-style white houses set between blue sea and green hill. White boats, blue sky, white sand: point, counterpoint. I sat on the hill overlooking the houses and the bay and stored the bright colors against darker days. Such an extravagant place for colors, all shining and clear. Layers of color built up to form the color of sight, and tucked away behind it all, the knowledge of the dry, opaque, dusty colors back beyond the hills in the desert.

Hector Holthouse has described the founding of Cooktown in *Ships in the Coral.* Cooktown was christened in late 1873 by G. E. Dalrymple, a representative of the Queensland government sent to find a suitable new port to service the gold rush triggered by finds on the Palmer River, 250 kilometers west of Cape Tribulation. He surveyed the town site and left a scene of white tents and busy workmen, which by early 1874 had sprouted sixty-three hotels and was serving both gold diggers and bêche-de-mer fishers. Chinese gold diggers began to arrive in steamerloads of 400 at a time, many to be killed by Aborigines before even reaching the goldfields. In March 1876 gold was found south of the Palmer, and the population shifted, but Cooktown remained a busy port for pearling vessels and bêche-de-mer crews throughout the 1880s.

Dalrymple had good precedent for choosing the mouth of the Endeavour as a safe port. During his 1769–1771 Pacific voyage, James Cook sailed north along the eastern coast of Australia, then through the Torres Strait to Indonesia. As he recounted in *Voyages of Discovery,* on June 10, 1770, Cook was within sight of a headland that he afterwards named Cape Tribulation because "here began all our troubles." Cook by then had sailed 1,000 kilometers inside the inner reef without realizing that the mazework of coral was steadily closing in on him. Late the next night the water depth changed suddenly, and Cook's ship, the HMS *Endeavour,* ran aground on a coral reef. Dumping cannon and ballast, they finally floated the ship off the next night and limped northward looking for a sheltered harbor.

They found it at the river (which they named for the ship), and there they spent two months repairing the ship and discovering the wonders of the local fauna and flora: kangaroos, flying foxes, dingos, possums, and crocodiles all went into the ship's log. Joseph Banks, naturalist for the *Endeavour,* had difficulty in describing the animals the Aborigines called kangaroos, as his journal entry (cited in Graham Pizzey's *A Separate*

Creation) for July 14, 1770 demonstrates: "Our second lieutenant who was shooting today had the good fortune to kill the animal that had so long been the subject of our speculations. To compare it to any European animal would be impossible as it has not the least resemblance of any one I have seen."

I had my lunch at Finch Bay on the south side of the headland bordering town. Finch Bay — just another gorgeous, perfect little beach of rocky green headlands sheltering an arc of white sand and crystal clear, soothingly cool, blue-and-green water, with the dark silhouettes of further headlands to the north beyond the glittering blue sea. I swam for a while before climbing up onto the rocks on one side of the water, little black crabs scuttling swiftly away before me. I especially loved those small, sheltered beaches and knew I could lose myself there for a long, long time without much effort.

But I did not lose myself and eventually turned inland once more. A little distance in and the dry dusty colors of the desert reappeared. The lively greens and fathomless blues gave way to red and stoic olive, and the trees shook themselves and settled apart from one another. More vistas there, and a command of space. I shared the openness gladly with the squat kookaburras and gargled back at them in relief at hints of desert. I was for the open inland now.

3
West to Mt. Isa ~~~

> She was also afraid of the country. . . . But this fear, like certain dreams, was something to which she could never have admitted. . . . "Everyone is still afraid, or most of us, of this country, and will not say it. We are not yet possessed of understanding."
>
> Patrick White, *Voss*

A map of annual rainfall distribution in Queensland gives innumerable clues to the character of the landscape. The trade winds bring the moisture eastward from the Pacific Ocean, but the imposing barrier of the Great Dividing Range snags most of this moisture and prevents it from reaching the lands to the west of the range. Hence, the lines of rainfall distribution parallel the east coast, building up rapidly to a crescendo over the summits of the range and then falling off equally rapidly into broad bands to the west. And it is rainfall that governs the nature of the landscape and its uses: the vegetation, the wildlife, the traditional structure of the lives of the Aborigines, the settlement history and patterns, and the current economy and lifestyle.

Tourism and agriculture in Queensland are largely confined to the moist coastal fringe of reef, rain forest, and coastal plain. The larger cities are located there as well, including the capital city of Brisbane. The interior of the state is the outback, the bush, the back of beyond, popularly perceived as flat, dry, and empty.

The arid interior of Australia is the land of the miners and the station people, cattle and sheep, a place with few paved roads, which Francis Ratcliffe called "the kingdom of the dust." Rivers dry as dust ten months of the year may suddenly flood out of control, inundating hundreds of kilometers of countryside. Or the remaining two months of the year may be drier yet. Precipitation in the Australian drylands is among the most variable in the world. The mean rainfall at Alice Springs, in the center of the continent, is 270 millimeters, but no rain has fallen in every month of the year. Years may pass with annual totals of only 50 millimeters, to be followed by a total of 650 millimeters in a year, or even a single month, setting the landscape awash.

Many regions of the Australian outback have annual precipitation means similar to those of the Sonoran Desert in the American Southwest, but the Sonoran precipitation stations cover a much more limited range. Floods on the Sonoran rivers will cause damage, like the floods in Tucson, Arizona, in 1983, but the floodwaters don't overrun the countryside as in a wet year in Australia. One result of the larger-scale flooding of Australia is a much greater fuel load when the sudden spurt of vegetation dies back after the rains cease. This facilitates the tremendous bush fires unknown in the Sonoran desert. Unlike Sonoran plants, the Australian eucalypts and acacias are adapted to these fires.

Another result of Australia's highly variable precipitation has been to make life rough for the stockmen and -women. In order to survive they had to have major financial or land reserves, like land baron Sir Sidney Kidman, who bought out so many smaller stations that he ended up with enough land to ensure at least some pasture in a bad drought. The smaller stockmen went bankrupt during the dry years and had to sell cheap. C. T. Madigan discusses this in *Crossing the Dead Heart:*

> Annandale [an interior station] was a typical example of what is often called the Kidman blight on the country, and indeed it did seem as though some plague had descended upon it, or some invader despoiled it and driven off the inhabitants. . . . the stations closed and all the cattle gone, yet here were water in abundance, an artesian bore half completed, and luxuriant feed for countless miles around, enough for many thousands of cattle within reach of the existing waters. How can these things be? Well, firstly, before Kidman took up the stations the previous pioneers and owners had probably failed and been forced off the holdings. . . . But this was a very exceptional season. There might not be such another, or such a succession of two or three, for another ten years. In the following summer the annual plants would die down and soon blow off the sandridges altogether.

Today the remaining stockmen still operate on a vast scale, with the size of operations being dictated by the aridity of the landholding.

I made a long loop through the arid interior of Queensland, out to Mt. Isa at the edge of the Barkly Tableland in far western Queensland and down through the central highlands of Emerald and Springsure along the diffuse ridges of the Great Dividing Range.

A highway follows the railroad route inland from Townsville to Charters Towers, built during the great gold rush of the 1870s and 1880s. Orange-red hills covered with open eucalypt forest and grasslands roll low between larger, scattered ranges, and creeks like Chinaman, Pinch Gut, and Kookaburra wind among the hills. The road swells and shrinks from highway to track, always punctuated by one-lane bridges, and huge "road trains" of multiple supply trucks linked to one cab barrel along in clouds of dust and cinders.

Set back from the road are the stilt-legged station houses with their peaked metal roofs, surrounded on all sides by a shaded porch open to the breezes. Men working outdoors wear low-crowned, broad-brimmed hats, short-sleeved khaki shirts, short corduroy or heavy cotton shorts, and ankle-high, elastic-sided boots. The women sometimes wear pants or shorts, more often loose cotton dresses.

Miners who had seen the touch of Midas in the Wild West of California first found gold in Australia in 1851. Their discovery was like a match to a powder keg, and for the next fifty years Australia was rocked by continual gold rushes that sent people surging from one end of the continent to the other. The mining of gold from quartz veins began in Charters Towers in 1872. By 1886, 9,000 people worked the goldfields, mills were operating, and British capital flowed in. Between 1891 and 1896 Charters Towers was Australia's most productive goldfield and the second largest city in Queensland. But when gold production there peaked in 1899, the gold seekers began to look elsewhere, and the rush was finished by the time of World War I.

During the flush days, its proud citizens constructed impressive Victorian banks and public buildings like the town hall, today the chief charm of the main street. Small, false-front shops rub shoulders with imposing civic monuments along this street, epitomizing frontier architecture. After gold slumped, Charters Towers hung on as a focal point for the surrounding stations, with a boarding school, an old men's home, a little leftover mining, and, today, gradually increasing tourism.

As with almost every town in Australia, the Charters Towers's ANZAC memorial stood in a prominent position. Australia lost a huge proportion of its young men fighting far from home in defense of the British Empire during World War I. According to F. K. Crowley's *A New History of Australia,* of a population of 600,000 men of military age who described themselves as fit for duty in 1915, 417,000 enlisted and 60,000 were killed by war's end. This was the highest casualty rate of any British Empire army in World War I. Today each small town has its silent white statue of a "digger" from the ANZAC, or Australia–New Zealand Army Corps, mute testimony of a sacrifice slowly being forgotten by younger generations.

East of Charters Towers lies Ravenswood, a collection of memorable old buildings in various states of disrepair, its chief attractions being the two pubs. I chose the pub at the Railway Hotel, entering the cool dimness slightly blinded from the mid-afternoon glare outside. Where Charters Towers has tree-lined residential streets and a main avenue bustling with cars and pedestrians, Ravenswood teeters on the brink of being a ghost town. My dominant memory of it is of its burnt redness — bare red soil stretching flat and uncluttered to the horizons, decaying red buildings slowly blending into the landscape. Gold was found at Ravenswood in 1868 and its mining briefly revitalized by the use of cyanide on the tailings in 1891, but Ravenswood was always overshadowed by nearby Charters Towers. Today the two pubs glean a living as a collection point for the widely scattered people of the bush and for stray tourist flotsam like myself.

The bar of the Railway Hotel resembled the old-fashioned kind seen in cowboy movies — a wood and marble-topped counter with an ornately framed mirror behind it lined with bottles. Old photographs and advertisements lined the walls, giving a picture of Ravenswood in its heyday. The hotel itself was a staid Victorian building with interior stained glass partitions, a dining room, billiard room, and bedrooms upstairs.

I ordered a beer, negotiating my way through the subtleties of outback slang, where beers come as tinnies (cans) or stubbies (bottles). This was one of the frequent reminders that Australians and Americans do not speak quite the same language. My travels in the British Isles were my first exposure to a variant of the language I speak, but nothing had prepared me for the richness of Australian speech, where accent only accentuates the obtuseness of slang. Even after being in the country for six months, I sometimes found it difficult to understand people over the telephone.

The Aussies have a penchant for shortening words and adding a long "e" sound to the end. A postie delivers your letters, unless he is feeling under the weather and has taken a sickie. If the postie is really ill, he may

A typical outback hotel and pub, Mt. Morgan, Queensland.

chonder (vomit) or do a Dan McGrew (rhyming slang — in this case, spew). After working flat out or flat tack for a while, you may be stonkered and ready for a smoko or a breakie. On a beaut day you pack up the eskie with tinnies and stubbies and have a barbie in the park. If you're a bit peckish, you have a bickie (biscuit). When nature calls, you use the dunny, assuming it's not all grotty. If it's a bonza day, you greet your mates with "G'day." Being a true citizen of Oz, a didgy di or fair dinkum Aussie, you don't concern yourself overly with details — it's "no worries" or "she'll be right." And when you approve of someone's actions, you tell them "Good on ya."

I heard a lot of "good on yas" that day in the pub after I was drawn into a four-hour talk with a bloke and his three mates. As we sat in the bar listening to American country-western music, they told me their life stories and bought me more Foster's than I was quite prepared to drink. Mick and John were telephone workers from Charters Towers, and Jan and Brian were Irish tinkers doing some gold panning in the area. They had all reached that slightly drunken stage of easy camaraderie and seemed pretty contented with life. The Irish maintained that Australia needed more people in order to adequately support the roads and other infrastructure of the vast country, whereas the Aussies were content to take things as they were.

Mick was a short, fat fellow whose boisterous friendliness reminded me of one of my grandfathers. He had no hesitation in evaluating me as natural (down-to-earth), pretty, and very tan after my outdoor work — this latter quality seemed to especially impress him. He was fascinated by my activities in Australia and eager to know what I thought of the country, as were many of the Australians I met. I, too, find myself casually asking foreign visitors how they like the States, as though the welter of conflicting impressions you receive from a new country could adequately be summed in a few pithy phrases.

I left the pub late in the afternoon and returned to the Burdekin dam site for a hongi being held by some of the construction workers I had met briefly on my way to and from the field sites. A hongi is a New Zealand pit roast, and this one was orchestrated by Frank, a Maori worker at the dam. I first met Frank while he was duck hunting along the river upstream of my sites. Frank was a stocky fellow in his early forties whose jolly brown face lighted up whenever he saw his young daughter Elk. He was anxious that I participate in all aspects of the hongi, and as he took me through the various steps, he kept up a running banter about my being his caddy at a mythical golf tournament the next morning.

The hongi began with a huge bonfire to heat large chunks of metal from construction machinery that were being used in lieu of the traditional basalt boulders. The ashes were raked out when the metal was a glowing red, and the chunks were lightly covered with sand in a large pit dug into the riverside sandbank. A large woven metal crate lined with aluminum foil was filled with successive layers of dismembered pig and chopped potatoes, cabbage, and pumpkin, then covered with wet sheets and layers of thick wet burlap and buried in a pit to steam for several hours.

The guests began to arrive in a steady stream at dusk. The hongi was held in the large clearing behind Peter and Willie's trailer, overlooking the river. Peter worked as a truck driver for the dam project, and the trailer he and Willie shared was the last outpost of humanity above the Burdekin Gorge. I had made my debut on their stage by inadvertently scattering gear across their yard. After getting permission to park my car in their lot during my stay on the river, I intrepidly set off with my pack. Unfortunately, I had a rucksack rather than a backpack on that first trip, with various pieces of equipment tied on to the outside like a tinker's wagon. I did not even get across their yard before my sleeping bag and tent fell off. Although I'm sure they considered me the Aussie equivalent of a greenhorn, they were polite enough not to say so, and they gave me a ride partway into the gorge in their battered old truck.

Peter's real name was Vivian, not an uncommon male name in Australia, and Willie was actually Wilhelmina. They had come from the coastal town of Mackay about 300 kilometers to the southeast and lived simply and contentedly in a small trailer shaded by river gums. When they learned that I was a geologist, they told me of the placer gold Willie had found in the river and then thrown back in ignorance. She didn't regret it, though: "I don't need gold. Some people have it in their blood, but I don't." They also did not seem to have exploration in their blood, for their trip with me was the farthest extent of their adventuring into the gorge despite having lived beside the river for months. In this they seemed to be like most of the fifty or sixty people at the hongi.

While the food cooked, they set up another bonfire and started the radio blaring. There was enough liquor to set up a store, and I watched people stagger off to sleep in their cars as the night progressed. Everyone was very friendly, and I got a good collection of life stories over the next few hours. There was Delphine, a twenty-year-old secretary from Cairns with a talent for telling funny stories about the horrors of dragging the lead line on a prawn-fishing net, of a surprise visit from Jehovah's Witnesses when she was nude sunbathing on her back deck, and of flooding from a tropical cyclone in Cairns during the Christmas barbecue. I met another Mick, a former Londoner who had come to Australia six years ago by way of Southeast Asia and India. He missed the English pageantry of history but liked the unstratified social life of Australia. And then there was Linnette, Peter and Willie's short, plump, submissive neighbor. Linnette was a pretty young woman in her mid-thirties married to Bill, who apparently had a tendency to be abusive when he got drunk. Linnette and Bill had come to the Burdekin from his uncle's sugarcane farm, and I wondered what kind of psychological scars they were passing along to their newborn child.

My attention was taken over for a while by Scrooge, a fast-talking man in his fifties who described himself as a compulsive worker with no outside interests. He did things like seeing how many shifts he could go without sleep just to find out what his limits were, which undoubtedly endeared him to his co-workers and family.

And of course there was Willie. She had always wanted to cut men's hair, but at seventeen she went to work as a barmaid in her aunt's bar and quickly married quiet, steady Peter. A feisty, brash little woman with the loud manners of a barmaid, Willie was exceptionally kind to me, perhaps pitying the shyness I often have trouble hiding. Willie had a running skirmish about the radio volume through the night and into the early morning with some of the more drunken partyers, but she won in the end after threatening to use the shotgun she normally reserved for crocodiles.

The others are less clearly differentiated in my memory. Their main pursuits seemed to be work, drinking, and duck hunting, and they called their head boss "God." Many of them had come up from New South Wales and Victoria to enjoy the more relaxed atmosphere of the north, and they were certainly relaxed at the hongi. I finally went to sleep at one in the morning, waking just in time to have the finally cooked pig for breakfast. It was delicious, and I set out on the road soon after, enjoying the soft morning light on the landscape.

When I stopped to take a photograph, an elderly couple slowed down to see if I needed help. This was a frequent occurrence in outback Australia, where the frontier spirit of neighborliness is alive and well. We shared a "cuppa," and they told me of their travels up from Melbourne. They had just spent a week on his sister's station near the Burdekin and spoke of the "wild hillbillies" there. I didn't think it necessary to tell them that I had just spent the night with the hillbillies.

From the Burdekin I turned west on a highway lined with names like Homestead and Prairie, Barenya and Kynuna, Quamby, Kajabbi, and the Waggaboonyah Range. I was beyond tourist country now, and at night I joined the other travelers camped beside their cars at rest areas on the road. The route was the Flinders Highway, after Matthew Flinders, who charted much of the Australian coastline between 1797 and 1803. Here the Great Dividing Range was just a series of gentle hills cresting at 550 meters, and as I continued inland toward the town of Hughenden, the land began to flatten and open, the trees growing more stunted and sparse. The occasional small towns looked as though their buildings had dropped from the sky as they sat forlornly on the flat, barren ground, bearing no relation to the surroundings.

Finally the route entered an area of absolutely flat, treeless plains stretching endlessly to the horizons. The gray-green edges of the plain folded and rippled where they merged with the pale, dusty sky, and I was locked to the liquid black road, undulating and melting beneath the

The featureless plain along the road to Mt. Isa.

glaring sunlight. The road parted the plain in a thin black line, and on either side the flat land flowed on endlessly. Passing drivers waved to establish connections. I thought of the early explorers who had crossed that way, and wondered how they possibly found water, or how the Aborigines and animals survived there.

Mirages rose up from the shimmering plains, undreamed-of beasts. Wallabies: deer heads matched with small, suppliant front legs and overgrown hind feet. Emus: prehistoric birds with skinned heads and wingless bodies. Scintillating swarms of jade green budgerigars and fluttering clouds of sunset pink galahs. I was disembodied, detached from all that had come before or would follow, slipped into a warp of space and time where the horizon forever receded and no changes marked progress. Then the car radio brought me back again, and I understood the importance of the radio to the people who drive through, and inhabit, these areas. It is literally a lifeline, reminding them that the plain is not endless and that time has not stopped. For the inhabitants the radio is entertainment, news, school, clinic, and telephone.

Together, the radio and the airplane have done much to make these vast inland distances inhabitable. They were brought to the interior mainly through the devotion of the Reverend John Flynn, whose

Australian Inland Mission first provided inexpensive wireless sets for the outback stations and developed the famous Flying Doctor Services and the Bush Hospitals. Australian author Ion Idriess shared Flynn's love and knowledge of the outback and its people, and in *Flynn of the Inland* Idriess traces the thoughts that led to Flynn's inspiration:

> It could be such a happy land but . . . He was thinking of mothers, and fathers, with aching hearts sending their children a thousand miles away to school. . . . If the wife gets sick! If . . . That "If" of the Inland spoilt the security, the strength and happiness of Inland life. . . . He brooded on the distances necessary to bring medical help when in pain or to travel stock to market — that twenty days' rough travel necessary to transport a sick person from Alice Springs to Oodnadatta railhead, for instance. Even then a hospital was six hundred miles farther south. . . . No wonder the sick ones seldom arrived. Distances — distances — distances.

This is what Baldwin Spencer called "Australia's Great Lone Land."

A flock of brilliant green-and-yellow budgerigars *(Melopsittacus undulatus)* flashed across the road. These "budgies" are commonly sold as pets, to be kept singly or in pairs in small cages. After seeing them in the wild, their use as pets seems an abomination. A flock will suddenly appear out of nowhere, darting and turning together through the air in deftly coordinated movements, the whole mass of birds moving as if acting on a single mind, the sunlight flashing off their brilliantly colored feathers. Presumably, it was this habit that gave rise to their specific name, *undulatus*. In *A Separate Creation,* Graham Pizzey notes that budgerigars are highly nomadic in response to varying inland rainfall and make regular southward and eastward movements each spring to breed in areas of higher rainfall near the coasts. Preferring open woodland, they have been favored by clearing of trees and the establishment of stock dams and tanks and are now more widespread than when the first whites reached the continent.

There were wallabies on the plain as well, their tails pumping them along as they fled at my approach. Others lay dead at the road's edge, providing a feast for the kites. And I saw my first emus, large, ostrichlike birds that suddenly made the whole setting seem even more exotic, as though I were in Africa. The emus resembled a child's drawing of a bird: stick legs, a great feathery lump of a body, a stick neck, and an incongruously small, naked head. But the emus' long, thick feathers looked softly luxuriant when ruffled by the wind. Their legs were long and powerful, ending in strong, three-clawed feet, and their heads had an odd raw, plucked look. When accustomed to people emus become quite tame and bold at stealing campers' food, but when I stopped my car, these took off across the plains at a swift pace.

Emus *(Dromaius novaehollandiae)* belong to the ratites, a bird group including New Zealand kiwis, African ostriches, and South American rheas. Although they occur over much of Australia, emus prefer open terrain. The eggs are incubated for eight weeks by the males, who then care for the young for up to a year and a half. Emus are wide-ranging in pursuit of their omnivorous diet of grasses, leaves, flowers, fruits, and insects, and they can attain speeds of fifty kilometers an hour. Their speed has served them well in their struggle to survive the animosity of farmers, who have often viewed them as pests, as recounted by Clifford and Dawn Frith in *Australian Tropical Birds.* In 1932 the Australian army was involved in a ludicrous campaign to exterminate the emus in certain areas, herding them with trucks to fences where they could be machine-gunned. Several thousand rounds of ammunition were required to kill a few hundred birds before the attempt was given up as a failure.

The land began to grow more hilly again around Cloncurry, an active copper- and gold-mining district. The neighboring towns all sprang up as a result of mining between the 1870s and the 1950s, for the whole region is rich in lead, copper, silver, uranium, and phosphate. By 1877 Cloncurry slumped, only to be revitalized by the demand for copper during World War I. The town could not be described as booming today, but the gas station attendant told me that it is still rocked by daily mining blasts.

Beyond Cloncurry the colors of the landscape became more vivid, scrubby white gum trees scattered among vermilion termite hills, with great red buttes and mountains beyond. The red rock outcrops and semiarid vegetation made me feel as though back home in Arizona, and the scenery continued mountainous until I reached Mt. Isa. With no advance warning, I suddenly found myself in a modern, flourishing town that seemed to have appeared magically from its desert surroundings.

Mt. Isa was founded as a silver-copper-lead-mining center in 1923, growing slowly and fitfully until the discovery of uranium in the 1950s. In *The Rush That Never Ended,* Geoffrey Blainey has chronicled the dramatic history of Australian mining. The story of Mt. Isa's discovery is one of those improbable tales of a rugged, determined man with an eye open for any good thing he stumbled on. John Campbell Miles was the son of a London printer, the sort of background that could easily imply narrow shoulders and familiarity only with city ways. But one detail alone of his story counteracts any impression of limitations: after arriving in southeastern Australia, he reached Queensland on a bicycle with grass-stuffed tires, a journey that today would surely qualify him for an article in *National Geographic.*

Miles spent fifteen years in the hot, dry, flat, unforgiving Gulf Country, working on stations and shooting wild pigs. His big break came in 1923 when he recognized sulphide of lead at Mt. Isa and pegged a claim for sixteen hectares, starting a lead rush. Other claims sprang up quickly around his, with names like Last Hope, Black Duchess, Ace of Diamonds, Durban Angel, Collar and Pockets, Edge of Beyond, and, my favorite, No Tin Lizzie. Once it was grubbed up out of the earth, the ore had to be hauled 3,000 kilometers to Port Kembla in New South Wales for smelting. The subsequent history of the field, like that of most mines, was a series of booms and busts. The mines closed in the 1930s, reopened for the copper boom of World War II, slumped again, and finally prospered under the current demand for uranium.

One final note on Mt. Isa's history: according to David Baird in *The Incredible Gulf,* the first mission undertaken by Australia's Flying Doctor Services, which has saved the lives of so many in the outback, was to move a miner with an injured leg from Mt. Isa to Cloncurry in 1927.

Today the Mt. Isa mine supports a city of 30,000 people, with neatly planned, green-lawned suburbs and an indoor shopping mall. The largest underground mine in Australian history, it now concentrates and smelts its ores on the field. Its stability has attracted a higher proportion of married men than most fields, hence the modern town. I bought some groceries at Mt. Isa but found little there to interest me. It had a feeling of modernity and prosperity that seemed to preclude a sense of history, and in its appearance it could have been any new small city in western Europe or the United States. An acquaintance in Cairns had told me that because of the Greyhound schedule, she was forced to spend six hours in Mt. Isa - five and a half more than necessary.

Having reached my farthest western point, I retraced my route eastward, angling to the south. Through a landscape of white-barked gums stark against red termite mounds and hills of great red boulders, I entered the southern half of the Burdekin River drainage basin. Driving that way, I began to appreciate the vastness of the land and the sparsity of its population — the western United States writ larger. The land was flat or gently rolling, with immense vistas empty of any sign of humanity. This is the reality behind the facade of the coastal cities, which are but a slim fringe of development. With the vast, open land behind them, they are like individuals standing at the edge of the sea.

The immensity of this continent was intimidating to the early overland explorers, and the psychological effect on the first settlers and their modern descendants appears in Australian literature and poetry. As in the United States, some viewed it as an invigorating challenge. They saw a chance to found a personal dynasty and to create a settled society like the one left behind in Europe. For others the solitude and space were a horrid torture that killed their souls and left them embittered or insane.

Ernestine Hill has written eloquently of the people of the outback in *The Great Australian Loneliness.* She writes of "men half mad with loneliness," of places named Mount Hopeless, and of Madman's Corner on the north coast, named from the fact that the first three pioneers of a neighboring solitary station were ultimately found and "taken south" to civilization. As late as 1935, a police trooper of the north told her that death from natural causes meant delirium tremens for a man, childbirth for a woman.

Yet there were also men and women who cherished the solitude of the bush. In *No Man's Land* and *Australian Pioneer Women,* respective authors Barbara James and Eve Pownall tell the stories of the many women who ran the large outback cattle stations while their husbands were gone. These women throve on the physically demanding work of driving and mustering cattle. After spending thirty-five years living with the Aborigines in the outback, Irishwoman Daisy Bates, as quoted in Elizabeth Salter's *Daisy Bates,* wrote:

> A glorious thing it is to live in a tent in the infinite. . . . There was no loneliness. One lived with the trees, the rocks, the hills and the valleys, the verdure and the strange living things within and about them. My meals and meditations in the silence and sunlight, the small joys and tiny events of my solitary walks, have been more to me than the voices of the multitude.

In the Central Highlands the land grew more personable again, gentling into easy hills covered with grassy woodlands, the colors varied in the more generous moisture. The landscape invited human presence, and fences, telephone lines, and station houses spread along the road.

Somehow between here and farther inland lay an invisible gradient creating a barrier beyond which human dwellings, if they existed at all, clung together for comfort and support. Here, in their confidence, the houses spread serenely out over the hills among the eucalypts and oddly swelled bottle trees. A few surviving giant prickly pears provided reminders of an introduced pest that had temporarily become a plague. Australia has had a disastrous history of plants and animals introduced accidentally or purposefully that have run wild in the absence of natural checks and balances. Foxes, cats, pigs, goats, donkeys, camels, rabbits, mice, and water buffalo have all taken over portions of the continent in the past and been brought under grudging control after protracted struggles.

The history of human colonization shows a strong conservative tendency to replicate, where possible, the appearance of the home country left behind. Settlers from the low-hilled coniferous forests and meadows of Scandinavia brought their red-and-white barns and log cabins to the low-hilled coniferous forests and meadows of the Wisconsin region. Moors brought their screened wooden balconies to Spain, and the Spanish carried them to Peru. The English brought roses and rabbits to Australia. The rabbits bred as they are famous for doing and literally overran the country. I saw 1930s newsreels of station people driving thousands of rabbits into pens and clubbing them to death in a desperate effort to stem the tides.

Specifically, rabbits were first released in Victoria in 1859 by the wealthy British-born landowner Thomas Austin with the well-intentioned, if ecologically ignorant, aim of providing both sport and poor men's dinners. The rabbits did well in the new environment, covering the 1,800 kilometers from southern South Australia to northwestern Western Australia in sixteen years, for example. Veritable armies of people were recruited to hold back the surging hordes. Some of the large pastoral firms had more than 100 men shooting, trapping, and poisoning the beasts, but still they spread. As explained by Geoffrey Blainey in *A Land Half Won,* Austin was a high-profile individual who was blamed for much of the subsequent disaster, but he was merely the most conspicuous among many landowners who released rabbits in the mid-nineteenth century.

Francis Ratcliffe has written in *Flying Fox and Drifting Sand* of the ecological disaster for native plants and herbivores produced by the rabbit plague, but the situation probably would not have provoked such furor and concern if the rabbits had not caused economic damage as well. The rabbits competed with the sheep for vegetation in a land where sheep are a primary resource for human existence. By 1955, forty-five million rabbits were killed annually, in addition to those that died from the effects of the 1950 introduction of myxomatosis virus. The virus worked fairly well for about ten years but slowly lost its effectiveness. Although the rabbits are not as great a problem today, they are still present, kept in check by the use of sodium fluoroacetate (compound 1080) baits, which indiscriminately kill other animal and bird species and remain in the environment as a deadly residue.

Similarly, prickly pear cacti, introduced as natural fences, throve on the badly overgrazed rangelands of the semiarid regions, and within forty years ten million hectares of Queensland and New South Wales were so densely covered with prickly pear as to be impenetrable. In 1925 moths that feed on the cacti were introduced from the prickly pear's native Argentina and were largely able to bring the cacti under control. The fight against other pests continues: flies, the scourge of my existence while in Australia, grow fat and fecund on the droppings of cattle. Introduced dung beetles, which rapidly decompose and bury the dung in which fly maggots grow, are helping the problem, but there remains much room for improvement.

Near Springsure, I followed a side road to the Old Rainworth Fort, imagining an American-style log stockade. It turned out to be a station house built of stones and lime mortar in 1862 as a result of the nearby Wills Massacre in which nineteen white people were killed by Aborigines. According to the interpretive signs at the fort, this was the largest single killing of that sort in Australian history, for the Aborigines never had the population density or the resources to support the type of armed resistance that the American Indians mounted.

As explained by Josephine Flood in *Archaeology of the Dreamtime,* there were at least 300,000 Aborigines in Australia at the time of first contact with whites, although estimates are uncertain. They lived throughout the continent, with the greatest population concentrations along the southern, southeastern, and northern coasts. Never practicing agriculture, they nevertheless had an extensive trading network, and as nomadic hunter-gatherers they enjoyed a varied, nutritious diet and plenty of leisure. Australian historian Geoffrey Blainey, in *Triumph of the Nomads,* has favorably compared the Aboriginal standard of living in 1800 with that of the lower classes of Europe on the basis of diet, health, comfort, and leisure.

The Aborigines first arrived in Australia from the Indonesian area approximately 40,000 years ago, spreading across the continent rapidly. Using Stone Age technology, the Aborigines were limited as to the resources they could extract from the land in order to support themselves. Epidemics killed many Aborigines, and they kept their own population low through abortion, infanticide, warfare, and the killing of feeble aged, so that their population rose slowly and they rarely starved. The Aborigines also established a type of game preserve in many of their sacred sites. Describing the hunting practices of the Aborigines in the central deserts of Australia, for example, T.G.H. Strehlow in *Journey to Horseshoe Bend* writes:

> No game or wildfowl could be killed by hunters within a radius of about two miles from the hill containing the sacred cave. Irbmangkara [a water gap in the Krichauff Ranges] had hence been, according to ancient traditions, a game and wildfowl sanctuary "since the beginning of time". Its ti-tree and bulrush thickets afforded magnificent breeding grounds for several varieties of ducks.

The Aborigines had reached a good equilibrium with the land on which they lived, and a sustainable way of life, but the arrival of the first Europeans in 1788 upset the balance catastrophically.

The British government sent the First Fleet to Australia in 1788 with the intent of occupying only one or two points on the Pacific coast. Rather naively, the government assumed that the marines and convicts could peacefully coexist with the Aborigines. It might have worked if the whites had been confined to the coast, but it was quickly discovered that sheep — jumbucks in Aussie slang — thrived on the Australian grasslands. As the wool industry boomed, inland pastures became a prize, and trickles of squatters swelled to a flood, multiplying contacts and clashes with Aborigines. There were few representatives of the law in the bush, and when sheep and Aborigines competed for the same grass, the sheep owners took their own measures. Aboriginal grass fires killed sheep and cattle. Whites hunting kangaroos and possums decimated the meat supply of the Aborigines. The Aborigines acquired a taste for flour and sugar, breaking into isolated huts to obtain them. Lonely white men raped or kidnapped Aboriginal women. For the first few years bloodshed was averted, but eventually pressures reached the bursting point, and the killing began.

In *The Tyranny of Distance,* Blainey notes that the Aborigines were weakened by their linguistic differences and inability to cooperate or choose large-group leaders. In some areas, like Tasmania in the 1820s, they waged short-term guerilla war, and in Queensland they learned to steal large herds of cattle and horses. Against firearms and the occasional gift of poisoned flour, the Aborigines had spears and nulla-nullas (clubs); few bush Aborigines acquired guns. Eventually, superiority of numbers, organization, and firepower triumphed. In 1876 the last full-blooded Tasmanian Aborigine died, and the other groups fared only slightly better. Not surprisingly, the largest numbers of Aborigines live today in the tropical north and arid interior where the whites never settled heavily.

Old Rainworth Fort is now maintained by two sisters in their fifties who own 4,000 hectares of the surrounding land, used mainly as grazing for cattle, with a little farming. Their grandfather homesteaded the area in the 1860s. I especially liked Kath, who looked like a true ranchwoman with her weatherbeaten face, beaten and sweat-stained hat, work-hardened hands, and ranch dogs trotting at her heels. She expressed pity for my generation, who have not had self-discipline forced on them by a war as have previous generations.

On a morning that dawned clear and cold, I set off for the next set of intriguing names on the map: Goomeri and Wondai, Nanango, Yarraman and Kilcoy, Caboolture and Caloundra. The very essence of Australia resonates through these words. They are words to be repeated, lingered over, savored. I hear them, and an image of place is conjured up quite apart from any personal experiences in these towns. Solely by the sounds of the rolling vowels, I hear Australia, just as I hear the ruggedness of impenetrable mountains in Kathmandu or the sweep of the sandstone plateaus in Uncompahgre. I hear these names, and in an instant I am halfway round the world, keen on the track of those who first recorded the names and gave the boundless world a new tongue.

I collect names as I go, symbols of both inner and outer travel. For the outer journey, the names are the signposts of new physical environments, and their syllables contain all the new customs and creatures. Inwardly, the names lodge themselves in my brain, which grows to make room for the new acquisitions. Here they are the signposts of expanding realization of the world's potential. The echoing names are two-faced, elusive; in their strangeness they express the change of travel, yet the process of naming tames and confines the new, rendering it accessible.

Feelings like these must have been at work among the early explorers. Look at James Cook, spattering the landscape in place-names with a wild abandon. Cook discovered so many islands, capes, promontories, and passages that he ran out of names for them. After honoring even the most junior officers on his ship, he named Lindeman Island in the Great Barrier Reef after his wine merchant. Those names Cook left behind brought convenience of reference, but also possession. Naming was the first step in taming the wild southern continent and containing it through identification. And it was also his means of stamping his own actions on the landscape. Cook's explorations are indelibly tracked along the Australian coasts in the names on a thousand maps.

As I continued southeast to the coast through the seaward portion of the Great Dividing Range, it gradually clouded over and began to rain. The land rose into a series of mountainous ridges thick with forests and fields growing the rich, sweet fruit of the tropics: pineapples, bananas, and pawpaws; avocados and passionfruit; custard apples, ginger, sugarcane, and macadamia nuts. It was pineapple season, and I gorged on the lusciously sweet fruits being sold at roadside stands for a dime. Late in the morning I reached the flat, wooded coast scalloped by innumerable small estuaries. The Queenslanders have tagged each stretch of their east coast, presumably for tourism, with names like the Gold, Sunshine, Capricornia, Sugar, Hibiscus, and Whitsunday Coasts. I was in the Sunshine State during the dry season, driving the Highway of the Sun along the Sunshine Coast, so of course it was cloudy and drizzling.

From overlooks I could gaze down onto the rain forest, where the tops of the palms looked like tufts of green feathers as they fell softly out and away from a center point. At one, a bewildered young opossum temporarily separated from its mother stared at me from great dark eyes set in a round, blunt face. Opossums, wallabies, and kangaroos are the most visible forms of the enormously diverse marsupial fauna of Australia.

One of the dominant factors of Australian natural and human history is the geographic isolation of the continent. According to the theory of plate tectonics, the great unifying theory of geology developed in the 1960s, the crust of the earth is composed of approximately twelve plates that ride on the underlying, partially molten mantle like log rafts on a lake. These plates move over the earth's surface at rates ranging from one to ten centimeters per year, jostling and bumping each other as they go.

We are still uncertain what causes the plates to move, although one major hypothesis involves convection currents in the mantle. The interactions between plates moving in contrary directions depends on their relative speeds and densities. Continental crust tends to be less dense than oceanic crust and will usually override it in a collision. When two continental plates collide, their edges often crumple against one another and deform into great mountain ranges like the Himalayas, which lie between the Indian and Asian plates.

Two hundred million years ago all of the continental plates were joined in a universal landmass, Pangaea. Pangaea broke up into Laurasia, comprising the northern group of continents, and Gondwanaland, a southern group consisting of South America, Africa, India, Australia, and Antarctica. Over the next 150 million years, South America, Africa, and India all broke away and moved northward, eventually making contact with a northern continent, so that evolving plants, wildlife, and peoples interchanged freely among the continents. The early marsupial mammals that had evolved on the southern continents were often displaced by the placental mammals from the north, with the exception of the American opossum, which colonized North America.

Other than Antarctica, only Australia remained isolated by sea from the other continents. In this isolation, marsupials evolved to fit a variety of ecological niches, flourishing in the mild, humid climates. Their story is told in Josephine Flood's *Archaeology of the Dreamtime,* and Michael Archer, Suzanne Hand, and Henk Godthelp's *Uncovering Australia's Dreamtime.*

Australia reached its present position approximately fifteen million years ago, and the climate cooled and dried in a trend culminating in periods of extreme aridity over the last two million years. The climatic change favored grasslands and woodlands over rain forest, and the former began to spread some five million years ago, to the advantage of one type of marsupial, the macropods — kangaroos, wallabies, and euros. Probably descended from possumlike ancestors, the macropods radiated explosively, filling niches from the rain forest to the desert and ranging in size from a mouse to the two-meter-tall red kangaroos. Marsupials that today bear musical Aboriginal names arose as well: koalas, wombats, possums, bandicoots, numbats, and quolls.

Flying insects, birds, bats, and a few floating reptiles colonized Australia from the north, but mostly the Australian biota were endemic, or unique to this one place on earth. Unlike North America, Australia was not invaded by fauna from the outside during most of the Tertiary Period (66 to 2 million years ago). The first major changes came with the entry of rodents during the Miocene-Pliocene Epochs (approximately 4.5 million years ago), the second on the watercraft of the Aborigines some 50,000 years ago.

The first Aborigines encountered a variety of large animals often called the Pleistocene megafauna because they lived during the Pleistocene Epoch (2 million to 10,000 years ago), becoming extinct within the last 30,000 years. In Australia, this group included sheep- to rhinoceros-sized browsers called Diprotodontids; the Dromornithids — the largest birds ever to evolve anywhere in the world; marsupial lions; three-meter tall giant kangaroos named Procoptodons; and large pythons named Montypythonoides (no, I'm not joking!). Their equivalents in North America included mastodons, mammoths, saber-toothed cats, and camels. The megafauna of both continents died out rather suddenly toward the end of the Pleistocene, about the time that human hunters appeared. Their extinction has been attributed to climatic change, overkill by hunters (the "blitzkrieg" theory of Paul Martin put forth in Martin and H. E. Wright's *Pleistocene Extinctions*), and habitat alteration by manmade fires and is probably due to some combination of these factors.

The Aborigines greatly increased the incidence of fire, and their lethal spears probably speeded the end of the giant marsupials. Introduction of the dingo about 5,000 years ago probably destroyed the larger native predators, the thylacine and the Tasmanian devil, on the mainland. Thylacines (marsupial wolves) survived in Tasmania until the coming of the Europeans, and Tasmanian devils still live on the island today.

The changes wrought by the Aborigines were minor compared to those associated with the European whites, as detailed by Eric Rolls in *A Million Wild Acres* and Francis Ratcliffe in *Flying Fox and Drifting Sand*. Cattle and sheep, grazed too heavily, destroyed the grasslands by compacting the soil and changing the species composition, with terrible consequences for the endemic fauna. The introduction of house cats, those wily hunters of birds and small animals, may have speeded the decline of bandicoots and other small marsupials. And the shift from a regime of frequent, low-intensity fires to one of infrequent firestorms altered the nutrient balance of the soil and stressed the flora and fauna that had evolved under the earlier regime. Seventeen species of small macropods have vanished since the coming of the whites, and twenty-eight more are endangered. In this, as in the preservation of the rain forest, the Australian people are at a crossroads. They must decide, and swiftly, whether they will develop a new land ethic or whether it will be business as usual. As naturalist H. H. Finlayson wrote in his 1936 book *The Red Centre:*

> The results of all this [economic development] are hailed by the statistician and economist as progress, and a net increase in the wealth of the country, but if the devastation which is worked to the flora and fauna could be assessed in terms of the value which future generations will put upon—them, it might be found that our wool-clips, and beef and timber sales have been dearly bought.

~ ~ ~

Farther along the Capricorn Coast I found the Singing Ship, a large metal sculpture on a high point designed to vibrate in the wind as a memorial to Cook. The sea was a sullen gray-green beneath the cloudy sky, and a cold wind sang through the Ship. I felt close to Cook as I stood looking across the choppy water to the dark offshore islands. There must have been many days like this when he stood on the deck of the *Endeavour* and looked to unknown lands that he was the first to discover and chart. Damp, stuffy, gray days, as well as days of brilliant blue sea and bright clear wind. I understood how one could give a lifetime to such adventures, always following the horizon to the unknown, filling in the blank spaces on the maps and the holes in the mental geography. Fame and fortune were an added benefit for the first comers, I imagine; the main thing would have been to see for themselves what was there. And for those of us who come after, the map is still full of blank spaces and always will be until we have personally seen each place, drawing D. H. Lawrence's ring of consciousness around the world.

There is a world map published in 1578 in connection with Martin Frobisher's Arctic explorations that perhaps sums it up best. Across the top of the map lie a series of islands labeled Meta Incognita, or Unknown Destination. Even more than the familiar Terra Incognita, these words contain the lure that pulls men and women from the comforts of home halfway round the world. What could be more enticing than an unknown destination, with all its possibilities of travel and discovery? Although I often followed a road to a specific point on a map in Australia, I seldom really knew where I was going or what I might find en route.

Beach-hopping northward, I reached the Whitsunday Coast, named for Cook's Whitsunday Passage, made through a clear area among muddy shoals on the day the Anglican Church commemorates Whitsunday. One of the major tourist centers of the Whitsundays is Shute Harbour and Airlie Beach, busy with marinas, shops, resort homes, and hotels. The steep, rocky bottom produces good harbors, and each little cove is filled with pearl white sailboats set in the sparkling blue sea. The pale blue water is clear as an aquarium, and slowly flapping rays cruise the shallows.

The Whitsunday Coast was not always such a safe place for geologists, as explained by Hector Holthouse in *Ships in the Coral*. In October 1854 a scientific expedition traveling on the ketch *Vision* stopped at No. 2 Percy Isle, about twenty kilometers in circumference and covered with gum trees. Four men, including the government geologist Frederick Strange, went ashore to look for water. They met a party of Aborigines from the mainland who had come to the island to fish. The details are unknown, but a coastal directory published in 1859 contained a footnote to the effect that nine Aborigines were taken prisoner on the island in February 1855 in retaliation for the murder of the four whites.

This was no isolated incident; in August 1861 two seamen were murdered at Shaw Island, and six months later the crew of the ketch *Dundas* were ambushed and murdered one night. In February 1864 the schooner *Nightingale* was wrecked by a cyclone on the coast of Long Island. Warned by the earlier attacks, the captain set up a defensive structure on the beach, which the natives reconnoitred but did not attack. The crew built a boat from the schooner's wreckage and headed for Bowen, but a gale took them in tow, finally beaching them at Magnetic Island, 100 kilometers farther up the coast. Lovely Magnetic Island, with its jewel beaches. The castaways had just begun to look for water when a war party of Aborigines attacked. The whites barely escaped, battling back toward Bowen against wind, starvation, and thirst before finally being rescued.

The last recorded attack by the Whitsunday Islanders was in 1878, when the schooner *Louisa Maria* was boarded while a shore party was searching for water. The schooner was fired, but the captain escaped by diving overboard and swimming ashore to the boat party, which was rescued en route to Bowen by another schooner. I doubt that most tourists to the Whitsundays today think of these things.

Camped that night at a caravan park, I struck up a conversation with Jim, probably in his sixties, tanned and lean, with a shock of white hair and bright blue eyes. He traveled in a small, well-appointed van, with barely enough room for a stove, small refrigerator, and bunk. He invited me to supper, and we sat on the bunk, hungrily scooping up fried scallops, fresh from the bay that afternoon, with thick bread, and drinking XXXX beer. I had earlier learned to appreciate the subtleties of the Queensland brew XXXX, Castlemaine's Bitter Ale.

Jim filled the deepening night with his own talk, I glad to listen. A wanderer himself, he liked to strike up acquaintances with others. He began his story with his time in the Aussie navy, teaching merchant marine ships the use of guns in the waters off Indonesia and New Guinea. Long, soft tropical nights giving place to hot, still days over pale blue coral seas, pulse of the sun broken by the booming of the great guns. Then, for a time, he had solitude and the tempests of the Roaring Forties. Caretaking on a small island south of Tasmania, at the ends of the world, he re-collected himself, felt his blood quickening again, and eased into civilization at Melbourne.

Now the winters grow colder, and he shelters from them in the tropics once more, casting Bowenward to test himself against the younger men in the tomato fields. No break, 8 to 3, sixty cents a pail, keep your own daily tally, shortage from the total count deducted from each. He manages 250 buckets a day, claiming the young men don't have the backs for the constant bending. In the paddock, ego drives him as he unconsciously notes his neighbors' progress. Two weeks he'd stood a factory, lived by a clock with furtive glances at 3:30, mad rush out at 5, and always the time cards. Enough of that and tomatoes looked good. Jim didn't have to pick, but he needed the feel of life streaming around him, carrying him with it, and he saw no sense seeking the backwater when his muscles could stand the current.

But Bowen had its troubles, too: the local people couldn't get jobs, farmers paid $6.70 a crate from setting seeds to marketing, then sold for $5 while grocers marked up by more than 100 percent. Southern demand for fresh vegetables dropped off under the chill of a southern winter just when the crops were in, then rose for summer salads when the north was floundering through monsoon. Jim felt the climate was changing — not a good monsoon for eight years and irrigation salts riming the soil. He smiled apologetically. "Ah well, I'm an old sailor, and I just like staying around the beach, meeting people."

~ ~ ~

And so my travels in Queensland came to an end. Back in Townsville buying airplane tickets and making last trips to various Queensland agencies to gather statistics and verify facts, I began excitedly to study the maps of the Northern Territory. At last the Red Center, the most remote outback, of which I had read and dreamt so much. I was eager for the desert and the vast open spaces. I was getting the humidity blues, and my tent and sleeping bag smelled like something dug up from the dark, dank earth.

Yet I had had some memorable experiences in Queensland and was sorry to be leaving, though I carried with me my photographs, journal, and mental images. As I packed my suitcases, some of these images passed through my mind: the vast, dry interior of gray-green-leaved eucalypts, tan grasses, and red-orange soil; the stunning colors of the far northern coast with its bright, deep green, impenetrable-looking mountains, searingly blue sea and sky, and white sand; the exotic shapes of tree ferns and palms among the waterfalls of the rain forest; the kookaburras sitting squatly on telephone lines and the grass-colored wallabies leaping away into the gum forest; the men of the bush, with their low-crowned, wide-brimmed hats; the relaxed, colorful, holiday atmosphere of the tourist towns like Townsville and Cairns; the silvery sheen and gracefully symmetrical outlines of the sugarcane; the small towns with their two-storied hotels bearing beer advertisements and their ANZAC memorials; and the Southern Cross standing out from a multitude of stars each night. I had within my mind an overall image of the landscape, a progression inland from the dense green wetness of the coast, over the crest of the mountains, down and out into the spreading dry redness of the desert. It was a mental geography like that which the Aborigines followed in their songlines, chants of place that carried them across the land. Now I, too, had a knowledge of place and of the fitness of things. What had come before, what was now, what might be. I was ready for the next frontier.

Part II
The Northern Territory: Australia's Outback ~

There were men who said they had explored Africa; they had written books about it. But I knew the truth. I knew that, for myself, the country had not yet been found; it was unknown. It had just barely been dreamed.

Beryl Markham, *West With the Night*

I dreamed of the land long before I saw it. It was a mythical, magical place, a completely new environment for the great adventures of existence, unknown plants and animals, strange peoples. The myths emanating from it primed me: giant saltwater crocodiles, dark and silent beneath the thick tangle of mangroves where the fresh water met the salt; clusters of bulbous red spires where termite mounds reared up from the flat plains; small stations punctuating the vastness, giving rise to men and women still living the frontier tales; a red center of rock and sand, dry, hot, and bright as only the desert can be. I believed that there were magic places on earth.

The second area I had chosen in which to study paleofloods lay in the northern portion of the Northern Territory. Comprising approximately one-sixth of Australia's landmass, the Territory has a human population of 155,000 spread thinly over 1,360,000 square kilometers, with 50,000 of that population collected on the northern coast in the capital city of Darwin. The Territory is generally regarded as Australia's outback and boasts of such on its license plates, although Queensland, South Australia, and Western Australia have areas as remote and rugged. The Territory has been immortalized in fiction like Mrs. Aeneas (Jeannie) Gunn's classic Australian novel *We of the Never-Never*. Gunn's romanticized account of life on a turn-of-the-century cattle station in the Territory has done much to shape the perceptions of the outback held by the urban majority in Australia. Gunn followed the Victorian style of writing, emphasizing the good and touching only lightly on the bad. She wrote a hopeful, happy book, inviting the reader to experience the life described but ignoring the psychological difficulties and physical and sexual violence of a situation in which white males forcibly mixed with a disintegrating Aboriginal society. Later twentieth-century novels such as *Capricornia* and *Poor Fellow My Country* by Xavier Herbert more realistically portray the racial tensions and often harsh lifestyle of the Territory.

As in Queensland, a trip from the coast of the Territory into the interior is a climatic and ecological progression from coastal swamps and monsoon rain forest to arid desert. The Territory lacks Queensland's luxuriant rain forests, however, for the southeast trade winds lose much of their moisture by the time they reach the north-central coast, and the monsoon winds coming across the Arafura and Timor Seas from the Indonesian region are not as regular in their rain bearing. During the winter dry season of May to October the rains come seldom, and even the wetter coastal fringe assumes a parched, brown appearance. As in Queensland, the rainfall distribution parallels the coast, dropping off rapidly from 1,000 millimeters a year to 200 farther inland. But during the summer Wet, the land blooms. A carpet of tiny annuals flowers in the red sands of the central desert, and the northern coastal plains become an almost continual billabong sprouting water lilies and head-high grasses.

From the coast to the center, all life-forms adapt to the wet-dry season cycle, and water dominates existence. As residents of the driest continent in the world, the Australians recognize the importance of water, their fascination reflected by everything from the early exploration for a mythical great inland sea to the prominence of Lake Burley Griffin in the center of the national capital at Canberra.

In 1928 an English publisher brought out one of the most comprehensive accounts of Australia's dry inland published to date, Baldwin Spencer's *Wanderings in Wild Australia.* Spencer began exploring the inland as the zoologist on the 1894 Horn Expedition and became so entranced with the region that he returned repeatedly over the next thirty-five years. He described the seasonal fluctuations in water:

> In the dry season, and this may lengthen itself out so as to extend over a year or two, you can travel hundreds of miles and scarcely see a living thing, except here and there a bird and ants innumerable. In the wet-season all is changed. The trees and shrubs burst into fresh leaf and blossom, the desolate plains and even the sand-hills become

green with grass. . . . Animals of all kinds, birds, lizards, frogs and,
worst of all, myriads of flies by day and mosquitoes by night, appear
as if by magic. For a short time the rivers actually run, and great
stretches of country, once impassable through lack of surface water,
are covered with flood and quagmires that make travelling
impossible. This does not last for long, and in a week or two . . .
silence and desolation reign everywhere.

Describing the importance of water to the inland Aborigines, Spencer
wrote:

> Everything concerned with water is of great importance to them,
> so that they have distinct names for different kinds of water-holes.
> Quatcha is water, and, whilst the general name for water-hole is
> Quatcha laia, each different kind of water-hole is recognized. A clay
> pan is Underappa; a soakage dug-out in the sandy bed of a creek is
> Quatcha nunja; a spring is Quatcha peinda; a large water-hole is
> Quatcha inianga oknirra; one with small reeds is Quatcha kullbera;
> one with tall bullrushes round it is Quatcha tmorldidja

and so on, through ten more names.

Much of the Territory is flat, and there is no single dominant
topographic feature like the Great Dividing Range of Queensland. There
are isolated areas of higher relief, such as the sandstone escarpments of
Arnhem Land or the Katherine region, but by and large, a route bisecting
the Territory from north to south cuts through sandy plains with
occasional low mountain ranges and plateaus. Such a route follows one of
the few paved roads in the Territory, a thin black line connecting Darwin
to Alice Springs, 1,500 kilometers to the south. Another 1,600 kilometers
south of Alice Springs lies Adelaide on the south coast.

The land of the Territory is divided into private stations, national and
territorial parks, towns, and Aboriginal reserves. Among the largest of the
Aboriginal land reserves are Arnhem Land on the northern coast and the
Petermann, Haasts Bluff, and Lake Mackay reserves north of Uluru
National Park in the center. One of the first victories in the Aborigine's
struggle for land rights came in 1983, when they were granted the lands
of Uluru. They now rent these lands to the park service, maintaining a
voice in park management.

The commonly used symbol of the Territory is a large
black-and-white stork, the jabiru, flying into the setting sun. Jabirus are

common in the northern portion of the Territory, and I lived in the town of Jabiru for three months.

~ ~ ~

I left Cairns late in the afternoon, flying west-northwest over the rugged Dividing Range and into the more arid, subdued topography of the land beyond. In the United States, much of the present landscape is only a few hundred thousand years old, due to reworking by the great glaciers of the Ice Ages or to volcanism and mountain building associated with the active tectonism of the western Cordillera. Northern Australia, by contrast, has been tectonically quiet for millions of years and has not been extensively glaciated since the Permian, 245 million years ago. Thus much of the Australian landscape is old, preserving surfaces initially created as long as sixty-five million years ago.

My travels in the steep, green mountains of coastal Queensland never made me feel as if I were surrounded by ancientness, but I had such a feeling during the flight to Darwin, looking down on the subdued north-south ridges. The land appeared compressed like a great accordion, with the sharp edges of each fold worn away. We crossed the scroll plain at the edge of the Gulf of Carpentaria, rivers and the scars of old rivers snaking across the flat land. As the sun set across the gulf, I looked down into a pure, rich blueness without depth or definition until an island appeared ahead like a dark oil stain on the water, fixing the distance of the earth below me. The island had an outline like the scraps leftover when cookies are cut out of a sheet of dough, appearing out of balance like a land newly flooded.

The sky held a band of violet visible on both sides of the plane long after the pastels of sunset faded. On the Arnhem Land coast west of the gulf the coals of occasional bushfires glowed in the blackness below, as if the surface of the earth were ruptured and a new volcano being born. We landed in the midst of the pale-colored lights of Darwin and entered the pleasant, open-air airport cooled by ceiling fans. Travel light! Wonderful maxim, I thought as I dragged, pushed, and heaved my heavy suitcase along. Wonderful maxim, but it means living less comfortably between moves, and objects just seem to accumulate around me.

I spent the night stretched out on a bench in the airport and took an early flight the next morning from Darwin to Jabiru on a four-seater Air North plane I shared only with the pilot. Seen in the daylight, Darwin was a small collection of commercial buildings on a peninsula of land, with modern residential districts sprawling away to the east. Going east from

Darwin we flew over the vast swampy areas and regularly meandering rivers of the northern coastal plain. The plain was obscured by a flat layer of haze and wispy cloud that formed a shell around the earth so that we flew in silent isolation above it, part of another realm. As we descended to Jabiru, I saw the parallel sandstone ridges of the Arnhem Land escarpment to the east, pale pink in the early morning light. At the airport in Jabiru East I lugged my suitcase across the road to the Office of the Supervising Scientist (the OSS) at the Alligator Rivers Region Research Institute, my host while I worked in the Territory.

The portion of the coastal plain bordering the eastern margin of the Arnhem Land escarpment is one of the most controversial areas in Australia. Various factions throughout Australia are closely watching the struggle as three active uranium mines, a World Heritage national park, and an Aboriginal reserve meet in Arnhem Land, often acrimoniously.

Arnhem Land is a vast sandstone plateau of approximately 100,000 square kilometers, comparable in size to Ohio. The plateau reaches heights of 385 meters but is deeply dissected by narrow canyons and the drainage net of the East Alligator River. The region is held as an Aboriginal reserve, with restricted entry for non-Aborigines. Access to the more rugged portions of the plateau is by foot, boat, or helicopter, but a few four-wheel-drive roads wind through the coastal plain adjoining it to the north.

The caves and alcoves of the plateau are rich with ceremonial meaning and rock art, and the adjoining flatlands with fish, plants, and game, allowing some of the local Gagadju Aborigines to follow a traditional hunter-gatherer lifestyle. Most of them pick and choose from both cultures, using trucks and two-way radios while "living bush" and spending part of their time in European-style houses. They have a community social center in Jabiru East, and some of the women have formed the collective Daluk Daluk, which prints traditional designs on fabric. But there is a great deal of concern among both Aborigines and whites about the Gagagdju culture because most of the traditional stories and ceremonies are held in the memories of a few old men, and the younger men are not interested in giving a lifetime to learning the oral inheritance of their tribe.

Kakadu National Park is a tract of more than 13,000 square kilometers and is among the Australian parks listed as World Heritage sites by UNESCO. The park lies at the border between the sandstone plateau and the plains, with a few outliers of the plateau rising like islands from the flatlands. Many of these outliers have Aboriginal rock art, each site containing layers of paintings of different ages, perhaps going back to the dawn of Australian prehistory 40,000 years ago. The plains around the art sites abound with life: kangaroos and wallabies, fresh- and saltwater crocodiles, goannas and frilled lizards, bandicoots and sugar gliders, death adders and green pythons, barramundi, sea eagles, whistling kites, whistling ducks, palm cockatoos, jabirus, magpie geese, egrets, and literally thousands of waterfowl crowding the billabongs. The present tally lists approximately 50 mammal, 275 bird, 75 reptile, 25 frog, 55 fish, and 4,500 insect species. The Territory economy is increasingly emphasizing tourism as the market for raw materials declines, and Kakadu is yearly growing into a larger and larger drawing card.

And finally, the mines. Uranium was discovered east of Kakadu at Rum Jungle in 1949 in a lode so large and rich that by 1954 an intense hunt was on for more. In 1970 uranium was discovered at Nabarlek, Ranger, Jabiluka, and Koongarra — a chain along the western border of Arnhem Land forming one of the most important uranium regions yet found in the world. Inflow of foreign capital accelerated exploration and discovery, shares boomed, more companies were floated, and excitement mounted. In 1971 shares crashed, reducing mining and exploration to a more reasonable level. Today three mines are active in the area, mostly producing ore for export to France (which is ironic in light of Australian protests of French nuclear bomb tests in the South Pacific), and the miners are vocal in defending their presence and their livelihood. Equally vocal are the environmentalists and the Aborigines, who view the mining as a desecration of one of Australia's special places through both the activities of the miners of this generation and the continuing threat of the radioactive tailings they leave behind.

In the midst of this controversy, the national government established the OSS as a neutral body to monitor the environmental effects of the mining and to minimize those effects. The OSS presently has some forty-five scientists, technicians, and administrators working in fields from physics and chemistry to ecology and geomorphology. The two geomorphologists concentrate on research related to the containment of the large quantities of low-level waste produced by the mines.

Because of their remote location, the rivers of Arnhem Land have few or no gauged records of discharge. The East Alligator River, one of the major rivers near the uranium mines, has sporadic records going back to 1971. In order to design catchment facilities for mining wastes, the OSS scientists need some idea of the largest floods likely to occur along the East Alligator River during the design life of the facilities. These large floods occur seldom, and the probability is low of one being recorded during a short, discontinuous period of discharge gauging. Therefore, the OSS sponsored me to develop a longer record of floods based on flood sediments preserved in the bedrock canyon along the upper reaches of the river.

I met Dr. Jon East, the senior research scientist in the geomorphology section, the morning I arrived at the OSS. He told me a bit about the area and about the OSS, a rather motley, temporary-looking collection of trailers and sheds grouped behind a more imposing administrative building. But the unprepossessing exteriors conceal a facility rich in personnel and high-tech equipment, where valuable research with wide applications is being conducted.

The staff of the OSS were most generous in providing me with technical and logistical support, giving me the use of a field vehicle and equipment, and a donger in which to live when not working in the field. *Donger* is an Australian term for a semi-permanent trailer set on a cement foundation and covered by an open roof. My donger seemed unbelievably luxurious after two months of camping in Queensland, having an air-conditioned bedroom (a real bed!), bathroom, kitchen (refrigerator! stove!), and living room/dining room. The OSS maintains several of these dongers for visiting scientists, complete with bedding and a few basic kitchen supplies.

I shared my donger with a brightly hued green, blue, and pale pink frog that jumped out of the toilet when I flushed it and a very pale little gecko that crawled out of the kitchen sink the first time I ran the water. The frog was particularly disconcerting, as not all Australian frogs are innocuous fly-eaters. I have seen films of some of them waiting at the entrances of bat caves, scooping up any young bats unfortunate enough to fall during the nightly exodus and laboriously stuffing the squeaking, flapping creatures down their capacious green throats. But fieldwork makes you nothing if not adaptable. I spent several days in that donger before I began fieldwork, and no matter how many times I flushed it down, the frog was always there next time to be flushed down again.

Jabiru East consists of the OSS, the small runway and trailer that constitute the airport, the large shed housing the Aboriginal community center, and a few dongers. Seven kilometers away lies the town of Jabiru, housing miners, park service employees, and OSS personnel. Jabiru is

My donger in Jabiru East.

one of the Territory's "tidy towns," a planned, neatly laid out community of suburban-style houses and lawns; shopping complex with post office, bank, and library; school, health, and police facilities; social club; and athletic fields. The residents live in a modern, rather sterile setting that could as easily be anywhere else in the world. The nearest city is Darwin, 250 kilometers to the east, so the national government provides incentives for OSS employees to brave the isolation: tax breaks, paid moving expenses, an allotment of free commercial flying, a high salary, and government cars. Yet most people remain at the OSS for only three or four years, either because they personally grow tired of the place or because their spouses and families find it intolerable.

In spite of the prevailing stereotypes of the vast outback and the self-sufficient station family, Australia's population is highly urbanized and concentrated in the major coastal cities. Jabiru could be a hard place to live without challenging work to absorb one. When I arrived midway through the dry season, the air was heavy with heat and humidity, and it grew more oppressive until we reached the "suicide season," when pressure builds just before the monsoons. During the monsoon wet it rains sporadically and heavily, flooding anything not elevated. The numerous termites eat anything left sitting in place very long, including the rubber of car tires. Ants and cockroaches are present, and, as the Australian writer Henry Lawson noted, the mosquitoes start at sunset and leave off at daybreak, when the flies get to work again. You move within a limited community of people, seeing your co-workers at all public social events, and unless you are a bushwalker or enjoy the natural outdoors, there is no place where you can escape. Pets, except for dogs, are not allowed in Jabiru in order to prevent the introduction of feral species.

Against these conditions there are the advantages. For all its physical discomforts, the far north is one of Australia's most fascinating regions, with a rich human and natural history and a definite aura of romance and adventure. A surprisingly large number of Australians never even visit the north, and to say that you have lived and worked there is like saying that you have worked or homesteaded in Alaska. Numerous clubs are active in Jabiru, and television does much to ease the cultural isolation, as the Australian Broadcasting Commission carries a good selection of musical and dramatic offerings. Most people drive to Darwin every four to six weeks and fly to southeastern Australia at least once a year. And, as in many isolated settlements, there is a sense of community. I joined this community for the three months I worked in the Territory, and I found its residents most generous in sharing with me their unique home. But while settling down to life in Jabiru I had one last stint of fieldwork, this time on the East Alligator River.

4

Unknown Water ~

I am helping to clear a track to unknown water

Judith Wright, "Unknown Water"

Unlike my experience on the Queensland rivers, I made only one working trip to the East Alligator River, which was in many ways the most intimidating of the rivers on which I worked. The East Alligator flows through the trackless, largely unvisited interior of the Arnhem Land plateau, where the crocodiles are not merely imagined or glimpsed occasionally, as on the Burdekin, but are readily evident. I worked on the river toward the end of the dry season in late August, when the heat and humidity were building to nearly unbearable levels. Each day I started work at first light, collapsed in exhausted sleep for a few hours at midday, and then resumed work in the afternoon. My morale and stamina were also wearing down by the time I reached the East Alligator after nearly two months of fieldwork in Queensland, and I was ready for a change of pace. Instead, I faced the greatest challenge of all.

The first recorded sighting of the northern Australian coast by whites was in 1623, when Jan van Carstensz and Willem Joosten van Colster cruised the Arnhem Land area in the Dutch ships *Pera* and *Arnhem*. This was the great age of Dutch exploration, when the tiny, water-logged country at the edge of Europe sent its ships around the globe, bringing all the world's treasures to enrich the coffers of the practical Dutch burghers. In 1644 Dutchman Abel Tasman sailed southeast from Jakarta and charted the northern coast of Australia from the tip of Cape York Peninsula to North West Cape in Western Australia. Martin van Delft followed in 1700, but the Dutch found little there to lure them back, instead veering north to the wealth of spices and silks in the East Indies.

For the next 100 years the region was unvisited, until 1802, when Matthew Flinders sailed up the eastern and northern coasts of the Territory as part of his epic charting of the Australian coasts. Naturally anxious to best their English rivals in all fields, the French began to take an interest in Australia. But their interest quickly waned when Louis de Freycinet pronounced the coast of the Territory horrible and sterile.

Beginning in 1817, the English captain Phillip Parker King took up where Flinders left off, conducting a series of quick coastal explorations. He was responsible for the misnomer Alligator Rivers region, naming the West, South, and East Alligator Rivers in 1818 for the enormous saltwater crocodiles he saw along their mouths. Following King's voyages there was a forty-five-year-long struggle to establish a white settlement along the coast near Darwin, but the region inland from the coast remained largely unknown.

Ludwig Leichhardt's party were the first whites to cross the Arnhem Land region on foot in 1844, and it was another forty years before the wilderness was mapped. There were no conveniences of remote sensing or aerial photography then; in 1883 David Lindsay spent five months surveying Arnhem Land, surviving Aboriginal attacks by spear and fire. Lindsay worked in the area again in 1917, but as late as 1948 a Royal Geographical Society expedition felt that it was entering unexplored wilderness.

Topographically inaccessible Arnhem Land has long figured as a menacing challenge in the minds of white explorers and settlers. The plains surrounding the plateau are flooded in the Wet and smothered by heat in the Dry. The oppressive climate fosters tropical fevers and rots stored food. The insects, snakes, and crocodiles and, above all, the hostility of the local blacks have made the region a place to be respected and feared. Viewed from the air, the plateau is a massive block of stone gashed by the intersecting hatchet marks of deep, narrow gorges filled with vegetation. Entering Arnhem Land from the east on November 11, 1845, Leichhardt recorded in his journal his despair as he realized what lay before him:

> At a distance of four miles I came to a rocky creek going to the westward, which I followed. From one of the hills which bounded its narrow valley, I had a most disheartening, sickening view over a tremendously rocky country. A high land composed of horizontal strata of sandstone, seemed to be literally hashed, leaving the remaining blocks in fantastic figures of every shape; and a green vegetation crowding deceitfully within their fissures and gullies and covering half of the difficulties which awaited us on our attempt to travel over it.

Arnhem Land takes on a different perspective when viewed through the eyes of the traditional owners, the Gagadju Aborigines. To them it is their country, a place rich in the necessities of life and a repository of their long cultural record where the features of the landscape record the adventures of the ancestors in the Dreamtime. The canyon of the East Alligator was created by the ancestral spirit of the large perch, or barramundi, Nanarkol, as he wound his way through the hills and plains down to the sea.

People have lived in the Kakadu region for at least 40,000 years as hunter-gatherers, shaping the environment with such practices as seasonal burns. Though they altered the environment, they did not exceed the carrying capacity of the land, rarely staying in the same place for more than a few weeks as they responded to the seasonal climatic and vegetational changes. Where Europeans recognize the Wet and the Dry, the Aborigines designate six major seasons, as described in *Kakadu Man,* a series of interviews conducted by Stephen Davis and Allan Fox with Aboriginal Big Bill Neidjie. The seasons are Gudjewg (monsoon season), Bang-Gereng (knock-'em-down storm season), Yegge (cooler but still humid season), Wurrgeng (cold weather season), Gurrung (hot dry weather season), and Gunumeleng (premonsoon storm season).

The Aboriginal association with place is both tribal and personal. As described by Baldwin Spencer, "in the Kakadu, like most Australian tribes, every man and woman has his, or her, totem name, that is, the name of some object, most often an animal or plant, after which he or she is called and with which he or she is supposed to have some special close connection." After obtaining the necessary permits to enter the Arnhem Land Aboriginal Reserve and work on the East Alligator River, I loaded my field gear, a canoe, and a motorized dinghy onto a four-wheel-drive Land Cruiser and, with Jon East and Roger Cull of the OSS, set off for the river.

The paved road ended at Jabiru East, and we continued east on dirt tracks across the floodplain of the East Alligator's tributary Magela Creek, then southeast up the East Alligator to the beginning of its gorge at the northern edge of the Arnhem Land escarpment. The sandy woodlands and billabongs were quiet beneath the hot sun of a mid-August morning. Kapok trees stood apart like saplings in winter, their branches bare but for clusters of large yellow flowers at the ends. The seeds develop in large pods filled with silky fibers similar to the milkweed, and these fibers are used in kapok material. My family had kapok sleeping bags when I was a child, and the smell of kapok brought back long-gone camping trips. Clumps of pandanus gave the landscape a prehistoric appearance where their thin, spiralling trunks capped with palmlike leaf clusters rose from the plain.

Crowds of birds frequented the billabongs. White egrets and jabirus stalked among the water lilies near the shore. Pelicans, magpie geese, spoonbills, and ibis thronged the shallow waters. In the trees above, white-breasted sea eagles and black palm cockatoos with brilliant scarlet tails kept watch. The beautiful black palm cockatoos *(Probosciger aterrimus)* bring a good deal of money when smuggled out of the country for the pet trade, but they have the same raucous cries as their white relatives. They are the largest species of cockatoo, occurring in New Guinea and northernmost Australia, with thick, sharp bills adapted to their diet of tough fruit and nuts.

Spencer described the Aboriginal uses of the billabongs:

> The men, but more especially the women, wade in, often breast high, pulling up stalks [lily] and roots. The former they eat, the latter they bake in hot ashes. . . . The pools also are associated with one or two interesting customs. When a man or woman has a front tooth knocked out [as part of a ceremonial ritual], it is buried by the side of a lagoon to make the lilies grow, and when a native dies, his body is first of all laid on a bough platform in a gum tree, but, when the flesh has gone and the bones are bleached, then . . . they are put in a wooden pitchi [hardwood trough] and buried in a hole on the lagoon bank in order, so the natives say, partly to keep them cool and partly to make the lilies grow.

Water buffaloes grazed on the plains. Dark gray to roan beasts about the size of domestic cattle, water buffaloes have large horns curving up and back to sharp tips. The "buffs" are descended from a shipment of buffalo from Timor brought in in the 1820s to sustain the starving colony of Port Essington, whose southeastern-bred cattle and sheep died shortly after arrival in the hostile environment. The new introductions escaped and prospered, and *Bos buffelus,* the Indian water buffalo, has been a familiar element of the northern part of the Territory ever since.

Too familiar, perhaps. According to Ernestine Hill's account in *The Territory,* the buffs were numerous enough by 1885 to sustain hunters. Buff shooters on foot, or sometimes on horseback, left trails of dead bodies behind them for the skinners, usually Aborigines or half-castes.

The hides were picked up along the coast, taken by lugger to Darwin, and then on to Singapore and London, where they made sturdy boots and saddles. It was a dangerous, isolated life, and the buff hunters were as colorful a group as the mountain men of the American West. With the introduction of reliable machines, the buff hunters moved to trucks, hanging precariously off the top and sides while shooting "on the run" at a moving target, as described by David Baird in *The Incredible Gulf.*

We drove through a buff hunters' camp in the midst of the forest; it was a motley collection of small portable trailers, tents, discarded machines, and garbage. Today there is pressure to eradicate the buffs, which radically alter the floodplain and billabong environments, fouling the water for other species and creating wallows that gradually enlarge until the plains look like a cratered battlefield. But the buffs probably will not be completely destroyed, for they are attractive to tourists, and buff burgers and steaks are increasing in popularity.

Being geologists, we stopped to examine relict laterite. Laterite is a characteristic soil produced by the heavy rains and rapid weathering of the tropics. This was a reddish black material similar to lava, with black iron concretions that reminded me of meteorite fragments. In 1941 Hans Jenny codified the relation that generations of students have since memorized when he listed the five basic factors controlling soil development: climate, biota, topography, parent material (source rock), and time. Because of these controls, a well-developed soil profile reflects the environment under which it formed, allowing pedologists to infer the history of a region. A soil may become relict or inactive by sudden burial (for example, by a lava flow or an avalanche) or a change in the conditions under which it was formed. These relict soils can be preserved for thousands of years, serving as indicators of the environment existing at the time of their formation.

Lateritic soils are formed in the tropics under conditions of high rainfall and temperature. Under these conditions organic materials such as dead leaves falling to the ground are rapidly destroyed, so that the rich, black organic layers of prairie or humid temperate woodland soils do not develop. The heavy rainfall also leaches and oxidizes the minerals contained in the soil, breaking down all but the most resistant. The end product is a concentration of iron and aluminum oxides, the iron oxide giving the soil its characteristic rust red color.

When removal of the natural vegetative cover exposes lateritic soils to the drying effects of the air, they harden to the consistency of bricks.

Removal of the natural vegetation also destroys the fertility of the soil. Because of the continual leaching by downward-percolating water, the soil has little ability to support plants unless a thick forest cover insures constant recycling of nutrients. It is this lack of stored nutrients and hardening upon exposure that make the clearing of rainforest vegetation for slash-and-burn agriculture or other purposes such a tragedy. Once the delicate equilibrium that has been building for thousands of years has been destroyed, the land becomes sterile and barren.

We had lunch on the banks of the East Alligator River, boiling a billy of tea where the river flowed between high, sandy banks. Immediately upstream the vertical sandstone walls of the gorge encroached on the channel. We launched the dinghy and canoe and followed the river up until the water grew too shallow for the boats. The river and its canyon were much larger than I had expected, the water all smooth flowing, slow and quiet, its murky green obscuring the sand bed in all but the shallowest places. There were many stretches so shallow that we had to get out and pull the boats, while at others the river formed pools deeper than the reach of our two-meter-long paddles. Throughout its length the canyon remained broad enough to allow sandy banks vegetated with eucalypt and pandanus thickets broken by an occasional stand of tall melaleucas or palms. The sandstone walls rose vertically beyond, broken up into pillars and ridges. As we proceeded up the river, splendid new vistas kept appearing, and I delightedly took picture after picture.

The canyon was vibrant with life. Water buffaloes snorted in the thickets, and the sandy banks held traces of crocodile slide marks. Jabirus and egrets perched silently above the water, and sea eagles soared on swift, strong wings. White-breasted sea eagles are hunters and scavengers of fish and small animals. In February 1802 Matthew Flinders, as quoted by Graham Pizzey in *A Separate Creation,* described a pair, of "fierce aspect and outspread wing," seen on an island in Spencer Gulf off the southern coast of Australia:

> Another bird of the same kind discovered himself by making a motion to pounce down upon us as we passed underneath; and it seemed evident that they took us for kanguroos [sic], having probably never before seen an upright animal in the island, of any other species. These birds sit watching in the trees, and should a kanguroo come out to feed in the day time, it is seized and torn to pieces by these voracious creatures.

The East Alligator River seen from a channelside cave.

Explorers sometimes have vivid imaginations; the sea eagle on the East Alligator made no attempt to tear us to pieces.

Jon and Roger dropped me off about ten kilometers up the river from where we originally put in, and returned to the OSS. Jon offered to leave me the motorized dinghy, but I preferred the quiet, unobtrusive canoe. I balanced precautions in setting up a campsite: I had to be on a high terrace away from the river in order to discourage the odd wandering crocodile from visiting during the night, I had to avoid the buff tracks that thoroughly crisscrossed the banks, I had to camp away from the rock wall to minimize the chances of my food stores being discovered by rock wallabies and various nocturnal marsupials, and I had to avoid the ant nests and preferred tracks. I finally found a suitable location and practiced my daily required radio call to the OSS. I am afraid they had harrowing visions of marauding crocodiles or inept, ankle-breaking falls, but luckily my stay was without accident.

As the echo of the last burr of the retreating motor lost itself in a crevice of the canyon wall, silence settled down like a thick blanket muffling breathing. Beyond the thicket of paperbarks and pandanus, I sensed the blue-green river still lying quietly vibrant in the sunlight. Possibilities there of adventure and discovery, but also the omnipresent tense fear of crocodiles. Around me it was cool and dark, late afternoon shadows slowly oozing from the rock wall. I looked up the valley to the dark fortress of brooding rock on the horizon. Rock cut and twisted, hardened into mazes where I'd lose myself and everything I'd ever known.

The rock walls reared up in towers and spires, thick walls and thin walls laced with holes dark and earth-smelling, where the air buzzed with the wing sounds of flies. The river flowed out of there, slowly at first, gathering drops of moisture from crevices and pools and all the unknown, hidden seeps until there was enough water to face the sunlight and it flowed brassy gold and green over white sands. Fish and turtles haunted the dark pools, and pandanus trees leaned down to drink, dipping their long, rooty fingers into the flow. Reserved mussels clasped themselves tightly in the current of the shallows, and where the river flowed wide and deep into the sands of the lowlands, the crocodiles waited, far down the slow twistings of its path. Ahead lay the land of the rocks, unknowable around the small entrance carved by the river.

My gear lay piled around me on the white sand grizzled with clumps of dried yellow grass, looking haphazard yet expectant. I bustled about, filling up silence with activity. Strange how that silence was so difficult fresh from the bustle of people. I am always aware of the presence of people, even quiet ones. People have a way of distracting the senses even when they try not to intrude. Listen for it sometime — the unceasing, beneath-the-pulse rustle and hum of life we exude, intimate or detached, the tides of life. Live with people long enough, and you're no longer conscious of it. Now what I felt was absence, though I knew from experience that soon all the sounds and tides of the other life around me would fill my senses with their presence. But for the moment I was suspended in transition between two states and ill at ease in the lack of context.

Within a day I settled in to my new life, growing accustomed to the sounds fitted to that place, as when a herd of water buffalo plunged noisily across the river, or the mosquitoes began their ferocious whining just outside the netting beside my ear each night. That particular sound always kept me slightly tense throughout the night, careful not to let my head touch the netting. But before I got into my sleeping bag, there were a few peaceful minutes to watch the seemingly unmoving river in the moonlight, the water's tranquil surface broken only by the splash of jumping fish. Busily working bats filled the night air, occasionally swooping low over the river to almost dip a wingtip in passing, the river remaining unrippled.

The static appearance of the river deceptively hid fluidity. We look with too short a glance; with the perspective of time, the earth itself would flow swiftly in change. Those water droplets peacefully joining to make a river had been everywhere and seen everything, like a Hindu on the endless wheel of reincarnation, and were not yet done with being. A handful of river water slipping through my fingers represented more than I could imagine in 100 years of dreaming. Like the heroic sand grain of the Herbert, each droplet had noble antecedents, condensed from the first elements, collecting on the raw hollows of the newly formed earth after raining down the black silence of space in the murky ice of comets or belched up like an after-dinner indiscretion from a smoking hot volcano. They were borne through the endless recyclings of a frugal nature, slithering through the cold, groping flesh of creatures deep in the dark night of the ocean; sizzling in the sudden shock of balled lightning shredding through heavy gray clouds; slow and silent for long millions of years, trapped in small slots between grains far down from the light, then quickly swept bubbling up from a spring, rushed and jostled down a rocky bed and sucked up again through long thin rootlets then tissued xylem up to escape through stomata, round like fish mouths, into the breezy air; up and up to the cold lightheadedness; down again as warm, fat drops soaking into a pink and green frog; around and through guts and blood vessels; out again, up and aloft to the top of the world; frozen immobilized like a pinned bug in a museum, beauty and permanence falling down silently to coat the great shoulders of a polar bear with a lattice of lace; sublimated by the sun; carried again and drunk down neat by a man with a sun-blonde mustache; breathed out as he slept; escaping out the window; rained down again onto a rocky plateau at the middle of the earth; floating cautious past knife-toothed reptiles; scooped easily through careless fingers; on again.

I spent my days, as on the Burdekin and Herbert, digging into and describing flood sediments and surveying the river. The stratigraphy along the East Alligator presented one of my major challenges because of the depositional style of these flood deposits. The flood sediments along the Burdekin formed high, continuous levees along the channel banks. Wherever these levees were cut by a tributary to the main channel, I had a ready-made section through the deposits that I could merely enlarge. Along the narrower Herbert Gorge, flood sediments were preserved only as terraced deposits on the inside of meander bends, again partly exposed in tributary gullies. But along the much broader East Alligator Gorge the flood sands formed low, continuous levees rarely exposed along tributary channels. Therefore I had to dig down into the sediments, creating downward-stepping pits up to two meters deep and three meters long. Because I was working with a small shovel, these pits took on something of the nature of an epic project, particularly when the loosely consolidated sand walls collapsed repeatedly as I dug. It was a short-lived epic, though, for I knew that the first flood of the next wet season would completely obliterate them.

Unfortunately, the low levees that I examined consisted of sands reworked during most wet seasons, and the flood record from the East Alligator does not have nearly the accuracy of those from the Burdekin and Herbert Rivers. I also had trouble with the surveying along the East Alligator, where the low channel gradient and subtle bank topography were difficult to measure accurately with my instruments.

I had changed my surveying technique to sighting on a point and then pacing off the distance, keeping my eye on the designated point as I walked. Consequently, I kept brushing against green-ant tree nests as I traveled, with negative consequences for my temper and the accuracy of my surveying. Ants were plentiful in the area, and the green ants were by far the worst of the ant tribe.

Oecophylla smaragdina are about a centimeter long, pale green and yellow, and, like most ants, never come singly. In his book *Kakadu,* Derrick Ovington explains how the ants build nests in trees by cementing a bundle of leaves together into a ball about twice as large as a softball, which they defend vigorously by biting and squirting formic acid at intruders. The nests are bound together with silk threads secreted by larvae brought from other nests by worker ants. The bite of a green ant is not to be taken lightly, for it literally throws itself into the job, standing on its head as it bites to increase its effectiveness, then squirting formic acid on the wound. Naturalist Francis Ratcliffe, working in Queensland in 1929, described them in *Flying Fox and Drifting Sand* as "little green devils" and cited botanist Joseph Banks's description of their "revengeful dispositions." The ants swarm on certain trees and are quick to drop off and bite when the leaves are brushed. Once green ants begin biting, it is impossible to simply dislodge them by brushing them off en masse; each ant has to be individually plucked or pinched off. The ants also form bands on the ground and seem to avidly seek human legs. I often performed that trendy new dance, the Green Ant Stomp.

Beyond the technical difficulties of the site, my greatest problems were the enervating heat and all of the discomforts, crocodile fears, and cumulative tiredness and loneliness that made me ready to quit. I think the only things that kept me going on this last leg were a sense of pride both in the science and in the adventurousness of the project, and a continued appreciation of the natural environment. At times when I found myself standing waist-deep in a tea-colored tropical stream overhung with pandanus, nervously watching the shadowy banks for crocs while flies and mosquitoes swarmed ceaselessly over any exposed flesh, I knew that Indiana Jones had nothing on me!

The long, hot days were broken by the sights and sounds of the river world, as when the budgie squadrons screeched by, executing their complicated aerial maneuvers en masse. Rainbow bee-eaters *(Merops ornatus)* watched me at work and inspected my camp. These extraordinarily lovely birds have all the colors of the rainbow flashing iridescently over their plumage: orange head, green shoulders, blue back, black tail, yellow face with black eye mask, and copper wings. They are the only Australian representative of the twenty-three species of bee-eaters, though they also occur in the Lesser Sunda Islands, the Bismarck Archipelago, the Solomon Islands, and New Guinea, where many of the Australian residents migrate for the winter. In *The Malay Archipelago,* the pre-eminent Victorian naturalist Alfred Russel Wallace described the bee-eaters as "one of the most graceful and interesting objects a naturalist can see for the first time."

Crossing dry sandbars, I noted a variety of tracks, from the delicately arcuate tracings of grass stems blown in the wind to the undulating trace of a goanna dragging its tail between its footprints. Several species of goannas, lizards that may be more than a meter long, live in the region and provide good bush tucker (food gathered in the wild) for the Aborigines. At one point, fumbling along through the brush back from the river, I came to the canyon wall and climbed up it a few meters to explore a shallow alcove. In this I found the high-water marks I was looking for, along with Aboriginal drawings and grinding hollows. The drawings were simple stick figures in red ochre, but it was pleasant to think that I was probably the first white person ever to see them.

Exploring the canyon walls in search of these high-water marks, I found a region of caves and tunnels resembling a ruined city. Entering through a long, dark cave in which I had to walk nearly doubled over, I emerged into the space between two walls. Solutional, or karst, erosion of the escarpment had created the walls, each of which was riddled with tunnels and caves like a raised rabbit warren. I stayed until an approaching storm turned the eastern sky purple blue beyond the sunlit river, and distant rumbles of thunder echoed in the caves. Racing the storm back down the river in a stiff headwind, I saw a cockatoo struggling to fly against the wind, startlingly white as the last of the sun shone on it before the storm-dark clouds.

The high-water marks I was searching for took the form of silt, scour, or driftwood lines. Silt lines are essentially bathtub rings. As with the dirty water in a bathtub, the finest silt and clay carried in suspension by floodwaters will adhere to the rock walls of a canyon, leaving high-water marks as the floodwaters recede. In protected areas like alcoves or overhangs, these marks may be preserved for hundreds of years. Similarly, the driftwood and other debris carried by floodwaters may be deposited on the valley slopes as the waters recede. In channel reaches where the flood flow is turbulent and erosive, soil or colluvium along the valley walls may be scoured away below the water level, leaving a scour line. All of these high-water marks are more accurate water-level indicators than the silts and sands that accumulate from suspension, for the latter usually have some depth of clear water above their highest point. By adjusting my measurements of floodwater depth from these other indicators, I hoped to obtain a more accurate estimate of flood magnitude.

Below the alcove with the Aboriginal drawings, I surveyed a long stretch across a flat, unvegetated sandbank scorched by a wind blasting up little clouds of sand. At its far edge, I quickly passed through a band of scrub and into a patch of rain forest vegetation. A narrow, dry channel ran along the base of the canyon wall, a place of quiet and cool shade beneath the graceful palms and gum trees towering up through the canopy. Climbing vines covered the talus blocks at the base of the wall, and I felt as if I had discovered an ancient lost civilization that no one even knew existed.

It was another world, wholly different from that of the rest of the river and in marked contrast with the searing sandflats just 100 meters away. I noticed most of all the cool silence, and I listened carefully. It was actually no more quiet in the shadow than in the sunshine, for the air resonated with the sounds of cicadas, birds, and flies. But there was a psychological effect of sun versus shade. The tropical sun was so intense that the air throbbed around me, my head and eyes throbbing in response. The very leaves gave off a rapid vibration so high-pitched I had to listen closely to hear it. In the shadows things were stilled in limp relief from the sun. The blood beat more slowly through my head, knocking more softly about my ears, and the diminution of sound was palpable.

Although each day began sunny and hot, pleasantly cool breezes kept life bearable for a few hours. By midafternoon I usually found it difficult to do anything under the intense sun of twelve degrees latitude, and I could only wonder what the sun was like at the equator. It would have been wonderful to take a cooling swim in the river, but I never dared. My anxiety about crocs was not as high as on the Burdekin because I had a boat, but I still examined the water warily whenever I went to the river's edge to drink or wash.

During the few days I spent at the OSS before coming to the river, I had heard plenty of crocodile horror stories. The worst concerned a woman named Val Plumwood from Sydney's Macquarie University, who had been attacked while canoeing on the South Alligator River the year before. It was during the nesting season, and she had apparently gone too close to a croc's nest. Pulled from the canoe and taken for a "death roll," she barely escaped with her life and had to crawl a long distance for help. She survived only through her own courage and common sense and through the alertness of a ranger who noticed that there were no lights in her donger that evening. Yet her story, as told in Hugh Edwards's book *Crocodile Attack,* is strangely inspiring. Plumwood is a dedicated and understanding bushwalker, and she bears no grudge against the crocodile despite her ordeal. She realizes the responsibilities of humans in a large predator's natural environment and accepts the risks accordingly.

The water buffaloes also kept life from growing dull on the East Alligator. I was awakened in the middle of one night by a noisily grazing

Freshwater crocodile (*Crocodylus johnstoni*), lower East Alligator River.

water buffalo coming slowly toward my camp. He stopped about six meters away, and in the bright moonlight we stared at each other for a time. Having just awakened, my sleep-fogged brain formed the dubious plan of hitting him over the head with my small shovel if he charged. Fortunately the buff had other intentions and to my great relief continued on around me.

One night the moon rose just after sunset, the sky to the northwest still flushed with a pale rose color and the rocks on the opposite side of the river holding a pale tangerine afterglow. The moon was full, so bright it seemed hardly credible that it only reflected and produced no light of its own. As I lay back looking at the few stars still visible beyond the moonlight, a series of black shapes passed overhead. They appeared suddenly above me, then faded like phantoms into the blue-gray twilight moonward, passing singly and in small groups until I counted close to 100. At times they flew so low I could hear the swooshing of their wings, but they uttered no cries. At first I thought them birds, but then realized that they were the large fruit-eating bats called flying foxes. Black flying foxes feed on the fruits, flowers, and leaves of trees, particularly species of ficus, eucalyptus, and melaleuca. They are important pollinators and disperse viable seed through their excrement, playing a vital role in the perpetuation of some plant species. Watching these flying foxes, I wondered where they roosted during the day and where they were all going, then wished them good hunting and rolled over to sleep.

I enjoyed taking a few moments from whatever I was doing to watch the canyon and the river change during the day. The colors of the canyon walls were richest at midmorning and late afternoon, falling into a gray shadow at midday when the sand along the river blazed dazzlingly golden white and was too hot for bare feet. The river itself remained quiet and dark until the sun reached its zenith, when the wind ruffled up green and gold patches. A few birds sang at midday, and a hawk circled slowly, or I startled an egret from a sandbank by the shallows. Late afternoons when the heat was overpowering and the air was heavy with the faintly nauseous odor of the flowering melaleuca trees, I sat in the shade reading and writing letters. Often I was accompanied by double-barred finches pecking about in the sand, the black rim around their faces coming down into a "v" between their eyes that made them look owlish. I was always accompanied by flies, which I learned to mostly ignore, while remaining subconsciously alert for the different sound of the wings of the slow-moving, biting horsefly. I took great satisfaction in killing the horseflies. I must be good eating, since something was always biting me — horseflies, mosquitoes, big green ants, little brown ants, big red ants.

At the start and close of each day, when the sand along the river was luminously white, every bird in the area spoke up, from cockatoos to the iridescent green-and-copper kingfishers. The buffs roared from dusk into the evening, and from up the river there occasionally came an unknown, spine-stiffening scream. Evenings after supper, I liked going down to the river just as the sun set beyond the canyon rim. The blazing orange of the opposite wall reflected in the still water. There were usually a few cumulus clouds off to the north, hovering above the dark silhouettes of the buttes and spires forming the broken outline of the canyon, and in spite of all the little discomforts, it was good to be there.

When the sun set, the river was so still that it seemed to cease flowing, its surface glass smooth but for the dimples of feeding fish spreading rippling circles. The cliffs down the river became dark silhouettes, and at the end of the valley a faint rose-and-purple haze brushed across the lower part of the sky was reflected in the still water. As it grew slowly darker, more stars appeared in the sky until the faint haze of the Milky Way formed the backdrop for a brilliant show that, Warty Bliggens-like, could have been put on solely for my benefit.

Watching the river, I wondered. It seems unbelievable that such a large quantity of water should be ceaselessly flowing by, away. The hydrologic cycle notwithstanding, it would seem that the earth would be sucked dry and would collapse in on itself. The river, endlessly moving yet on my time scale changeless, confronted the rock walls, mute and unchangeable beyond imagining. The rock walls were the skeleton of the place, as the river was its blood, and between themselves the rocks and the river held all the quicksilver life of the plants and animals, seemingly too rapid to be held down even to count its pulse. I passed through all this as a water strider across the river, hardly touching it and leaving no trace of myself. Yet the river, and the rocks, and the quicksilver life, all left their marks upon me, crisscrossing etches of various depths and hues scarring my memory and slowly changing the aspect they first wore, as time flows on more surely than any river of water.

As on the Burdekin and Herbert, physical, outward life on the river was gradually reduced to the bare essentials. I missed the comforts of cleanliness, good food, shelter, and passive amusements, yet I was glad to have the opportunity to live simply, to appreciate the daily comforts I generally take for granted, and to think of things too easily put off during the bustle of the daily routine. On the river desires were simplified, and the tempo of existence slowed. Sitting in the shade of a tree at the hot, still noontime, there was nothing I wanted so very badly, nowhere I had to go. I simply existed, feeling the heat envelop me. Only to think, or not even that. Time ceased to exist, for there was no forward or backward motion.

The world existed only as I perceived it, and when I closed my eyes, it vanished. This was the peace I had sought through all the harried days and nights at school, all the hours of anxiety at things that must be accomplished before . . . before. On the river there was time enough. I accomplished what I could, and the rest did not matter. At dusk and moonrise I could smile good-naturedly and come up with a solution, at dawn I could act hurriedly and purposefully on surface thoughts, but at noon I did not care and neither thought nor acted. Willa Cather captured the mood perfectly in her novel *The Song of the Lark,* describing a sojourn in an Anasazi ruin in a canyon of the southwestern United States:

She used to wonder at her own inactivity. She could lie there hour after hour in the sun and listen to the strident whirr of the big locusts, and to the light, ironical laughter of the quaking aspens. All her life she had been-hurrying and sputtering, as if she had been born behind time and had been trying to catch up. Now, she reflected . . . it was as if she were waiting for something to catch up with her. She had got to a place where she was out of the stream of meaningless activity and undirected effort. . . . And now her power to think seemed converted into a power of sustained sensation. She could become a mere receptacle for heat, or become a color, like the bright lizards that darted about on the hot stones outside her door; or she could become a continuous repetition of sound, like the cicadas.

As the river rhythm came to dominate, I began to think of life lived at different levels. In the leisure of contemplation, I recognized the transitions, some so abrupt as to be breaks, like the college years. The phrase "college years" had a hollow ring to it from overuse by people unable to look beyond the surface for their divisions. But for me the phrase designated a span of time during which I had upset all the old timekeepers of my life and snuggled dreamily into a burrow of intellectualism, where there was no time.

As a child, I had begun with a simple acceptance of nature's rhythms, courting the first frost, the first thaw. Aware and attuned, the diurnal and seasonal rhythms had marched in and through me, and alienation was unknown to a small soldier in a great army. It was a childhood and adolescence close to nature in presence and in understanding, which must have been one of its strengths.

Then the great walls of the university swept me in on the strength of a vivid imagination not yet too old to believe in a community of ideas and a search for truth. I ran wild there, rioted in the collected inspirations of thousands of years. Reading the words of earlier thinkers set off little explosions in my own mind as ideas dimly perceived came home to roost full-fledged. Even so had I rioted on snowy crests and over green meadows in another life. There was little time for that in the new life. Nodding acknowledgments came at odd moments, in the form of weekend walks or between-term vacations, but my real life lay among all the books tantalizing me on the library shelves. My life became timeless as I wandered giddily among the centuries, and my perception of self changed. When I came to time again, I marked it by myself, by artificial standards of progress set up to mark advancement along the path of a career. The turnings of the wide world stopped, and when I came up periodically, like a swimmer from the depths, I was startled by change.

Several years moderated my pace without slaking my thirst, and the lovely books stretched on. But beside the books I began to recognize a need and an imbalance in my life. I puzzled over it and realized I was reaching maturity without knowledge of the tides propelling this irritating change, this time. Within the rigid confines of an apartment, I dreamt longingly of the strengths of the earlier life of space, of rhythms external to my own driving, of knowledge and patience born of understanding those rhythms. The dream was barely begun, only lightly formed, when I found myself half a world away, with a job to do and rivers to study. Doing the job and feeling again the outer rhythms, the newness of place focused my attention on the natural world. New seasons called for new adjustments, and in the adjusting I remembered what had gone before and came full circle in realization, resolving never to live so completely divorced from the wellspring of existence again.

Finishing my work, I broke camp one morning and headed down the river. The moon still hung in the sky above canyon walls lightly flushed with the early morning sun, and portions of the river steamed in the cold. The rock of the canyon walls had weathered into stacked, horizontal slabs, as though it were artificially-built-up brick or stonework. In many places, the crumbling of the wall produced spires like the towers of an old, ruined castle.

The spires of these walls represented a much greater antiquity than those of any castle, though. Arnhem Land is essentially a huge, fissured block of Kombolgie Sandstone that has been gradually crumbling over millions of years, leaving behind fragments like Nourlangie Rock as it shrinks inward on itself. The sandstone was deposited by shallow seas and rivers two billion years ago, vanished currents preserved in the dipping beds and ripples traced out by its quartz grains. It is rough rock, cracked and split, and scratchy as sandpaper where wind and water have pitted its surface over millennia.

Below it lie even older rocks, spouted from volcanoes or forced up into the earth's crust as granites when the planet was just beginning its long journey. Now the rocks are old, eroding at something like a meter per 1,000 years as the cliff edges are imperceptibly undermined and suddenly give way with a massive crash. Lying at the base of the escarpment, the fallen blocks slowly disintegrate into sand grains again, and the streams flowing from the plateau bring more sand grains, spreading them across the plains in sand sheets, readying them for the next great round of rock building.

Roger and Jon were not to meet me until the next day, so I spent the day exploring the river and moved camp down to the rendezvous point. I passed safely through the "Great Dismal Swamp," a small side channel that I had named on the journey upriver. Where most of the river was open and sunny, the swamp was a narrow, murky stretch thickly overhung with pandanus, vines, and eucalypts, seemingly the perfect setting for a crocodile. Beyond that point the river opened out again, and I suddenly wished to follow its windings all the way to the sea as I watched new vistas unfold.

At lunchtime I experimentally collected several mussels from the river, made a small fire, and boiled them until their shells opened. Apparently I am not really cut out to live off the land. Freshwater mussels have a lot more intestine and other organs than they do foot, and these were so revolting looking that I could not force myself to eat them. After cutting them apart and picking and poking at them for a while, I finally dumped them out and gave them a decent burial.

My last morning on the river, the air was thick with smoke and the sun rose as a glowing orange sphere through a haze of brown. I looked forward to escaping the flies and mosquitoes and to being clean again; my hair and clothes had grown filthy because fear of crocodiles kept me from bathing completely in the river. I packed up my gear and read while I waited for Jon and Roger, who arrived just after noon with their families. We spent the afternoon on the river, motoring upstream to look at my sites, and had a wonderful lunch of sandwiches, fruit, tea, and chocolate cake. Late in the afternoon we left the river, getting back to Jabiru in the evening — civilization!

5

A Tremendously Rocky Country ~

Surely the world we live in is but the world that lives in us?

From the notebooks of Daisy Bates,
as quoted in Elizabeth Salter's *Daisy Bates*

White-trunked gums grow in open, easy stands beside the sand flats and billabongs of the coastal plains. Mirages shimmer in the heat waves there, and kites spiral slowly upward in the long afternoons. In the buildup at the end of the dry season, fat thunderheads heavy with rain press down on a panting earth. In the wet season the land turns to water, and as in the flood of old, the creatures of the land cling desperately to floating bits of stick and leaf, catching at the overhanging branches of trees as they sweep by.

The plains stretch along for hundreds of kilometers, at their back the abrupt escarpments and gorges of Arnhem Land, the tremendously rocky country of Leichhardt. The cross-bedded sandstone and conglomerate of the rocky country weathers into massive blocks crisscrossed by thin stringers of tiny, rounded white quartz pebbles. Time and the rains streak the rock with gray, pink and orange, red, tan, and black, perhaps the inspiration for Aboriginal rock art. I came to know both the plains and the plateau during my stay in Jabiru, wandering from the low forest of Kakadu National Park up into the rough-hewn blocks of the plateau.

It seems a changeless landscape, beyond time, but the seas have shifted across it in the millennia since humans came to the southern land. The spread of the plant communities, and the soil in which the plants set their roots, preserve a mute record of changing ecological conditions. In the sediments of the Alligator Rivers region coastal floodplain lies the story of sea level rising and falling as glacial ice levels half a world away rose and fell. When the glaciers swelled fat on new snow locked in ice, the supply of liquid water free to circulate in the world decreased, and the oceans shrank inward, back from the land. When the great ice sheets melted and thinned, the seas rose again, lapping at the toes of the land. Eight thousand years ago the north Australian coastal plains were a mangrove estuary, with a thousand minute forms of life sheltered in their tangled skeins of roots. By 500 years ago they had taken on the appearance of today: thicket-studded grassy plains set with billabongs.

Inland from the coast lies the progression of tidal flats, floodplains, lowlands, and the plateau, each with distinct vegetation communities. Dense tangles of mangrove forest edge the tidal flats, the mangroves arranged in zones according to the salt tolerance of individual species. Alternately submerged and exposed, the mangroves prop themselves up on a knotted, spaghetti-like understory of aerial roots.

Beyond the reach of the sea, the plants open out to the dune forest and all but disappear under the baking sun of the salt-encrusted samphire flats. Where the freshly fallen storm waters flood the plains each season, sedgelands covered by dense mats of sedges and grasses greedily absorb the moisture, impeding drainage and waterlogging the soil, providing home and shelter for a variety of birds. Shaggy-trunked melaleuca trees sprout from the sedgelands, epiphytic orchids clinging to their limbs.

The lowlands, despite their name, are higher and drier than the floodplains, and the vegetation communities spread themselves out according to conditions of rainfall and drainage. Monsoon forests flourish in areas with permanent underground or surface fresh water. Here trees climbing to thirty-five meters throw out masses of large, dark green leaves, blocking the sunlight from the quiet, shadowed world below, where gnarled old fingers of buttress roots creep out along the forest floor and aerial fig roots hang down like abandoned ropes. These forests resemble the rain forests of Southeast Asia, with a relatively continuous tree canopy and a highly developed community structure of trees, vines, epiphytic mosses, lichens, ferns, and orchids. But the Kakadu monsoon forests are isolated relicts of past climatic conditions and have lower species diversity than their Asian counterparts. Where water is scarcer, there are woodlands dominated by evocatively named eucalypts: woollybutt, stringybark, bloodwood, ironwood, ghost gum. Here the forest is open and sunny.

Finally come the sandstone scrub and woodlands of the plateau, stunted trees and grasses twining their supple roots into the fissures of the rigid rock. It is an exposed, desiccated environment, completely alien to

A billabong near Nourlangie Rock.

the escarpment rain forest that may lie a few hundred meters away at the base of the rock.

Trying to fit the pieces together was like working a great jigsaw puzzle, where the clues lay not in the forms or colors of the pieces but in the moisture controlling their placement. Again, water. Everything here came back to water in the end. In flights of fancy, through time or space, you could trace everything in the landscape to the slow, sure water: the rise and fall of the seas across the feet of the land, the advance and retreat of the water-swollen monsoon clouds across its head. Even I, godless humanist of the twentieth century, the age of manipulation and materialism, danced to the tunes of the water music.

When the waters again recede from the land at the end of each wet season, they leave behind the black jewels of billabongs set among shining green meadows and trees. White egrets stalk among the water lilies *(Nymphaea gigantea)* named as though they were giant water nymphs lying disguised as they wait to seize the unwary. The billabongs focus life in the dry season, harboring a myriad of birds. Nankeen night herons nest among them in a rookery of 2,000 birds. Big-beaked jabirus stalk fish, and brolgas step and dip through their elaborate courtship dance. Rare water species like Burdekin ducks, magpie geese, and water whistling ducks flourish there in their thousands. Small birds, flashes of pure color, roost in the overhanging trees. Egrets immobilize themselves in an attitude for minutes at a time, as if they were egret memorials. And of course the billabongs host bunyips (creatures of Aboriginal myth), which snatch bad children from their homes and eat them!

And beyond all this — outliers and billabongs and forest — lies the escarpment of Arnhem Land, towering up like the walls of an impregnable fortress. Numerous canyons provide at least limited access to it, but from the plains it appears impenetrable, and the phrases of long ago come to mind: the dark heart where the "savages" run wild.

The Aborigines are at home in this varied world, moving seasonally from one plant community to another. Bush plums, figs, yam tubers, palm shoots, lotus lily seeds, melaleuca leaves, and herbs provide food and flavoring. Paperbark sheets form cooking receptacles, rafts, and roofs. The poisons in Barringtonia leaves stun fish. Sedge stems are chewed into paintbrushes, and Banksia seed cones make combs. Fig leaves act as sandpaper to smooth wooden spears, pandanus leaves are plaited into baskets, and so on, indefinitely. Forty thousand years of living with the land have taught the Aborigines much. Baldwin Spencer described the lifestyle of the Kakadu Aborigines early in this century:

> Right through the Alligator Rivers district there are favorite camping grounds by the side of great billabongs. As long as they get lily seeds and roots in abundance, fish and wild fowl, there they stay, each family with its own Mia-mia [shelter]. . . . All day long the women and children are in the water, gathering lily "tuck out" [food], while the men spear fish and catch water-fowl, climb trees after flying-fox and honey-bag or hunt larger game such as kangaroos and emus. When they have thinned the lilies out . . . they move on to another camp, where the same round is gone through . . . all the year round.

In addition to eating their way through the existing plant communities, the Aborigines have also actively shaped and managed these communities, both in the tropical north and in other regions of the continent. The Australian landscape was subject to lightning-caused fires before humans arrived, but the Aborigines greatly increased the fire incidence and thereby reduced fire intensity. Frequent fires favored the fire-tolerant eucalyptus trees, which came to dominate much of the landscape as the less burn-resistant plants died off. Hunting birds thrived as fire followers, feasting on the small life flushed by the heat and smoke. Numerous fires destroyed the protective covering of bark, opening trees to termites, and the mounds of termitaria spread in the wake of the fire-starters. Where natural fires tended to occur late in the dry season, when sufficient tinder had accumulated, the Aborigines scorched the countryside early in the dry, forcing the flora and fauna to adapt or perish. The effects of Aboriginal burning practices are discussed by Eric Rolls in *A Million Wild Acres,* by Geoffrey Blainey in *Triumph of the Nomads,* and by Jeremy Russell-Smith in a summary of archaeological research in Kakadu.

During the Dry, regular, controlled burns are conducted in the Kakadu area in the tradition of the Aborigines to prevent an uncontrollable conflagration. When I arrived, the landscape around Jabiru East was still parched-looking from the last burn, and a couple of weeks later a patch close to my donger was burned. Driving along the road beside the burning area, I felt the heat through the closed windows of the car and watched kites diving for grasshoppers through the smoky air. During the Wet that same road turned into a green tunnel, with grass two to three meters high growing thickly along either side.

I arrived in the Northern Territory about midway through the Dry and stayed until the first rains of the Wet, experiencing the buildup between. I returned from my fieldwork on the East Alligator with a series of sediment samples on which I wanted to perform thermoluminescence (TL) dating. I had cavalierly assumed that the dating of my seven samples might take perhaps two or three weeks, but during the course of my first day back in Jabiru, my projected stay increased from two weeks to one month to two months. I stayed for another three months.

TL dating measures the last time a buried sediment was exposed to sunlight — in the case of my work, the time of the flood that deposited the sediments. Buried mineral grains accumulate energy from the decay of naturally occurring radioactive elements in the environment, and when the grains are exposed to ultraviolet radiation, such as sunlight, this stored energy is released as light. When all of the stored energy is lost, the process is called a zeroing event. If the rate at which the grains accumulate energy is known, then the total amount of energy accumulated can be divided by this rate to give the time since the last zeroing event. Sediments are collected so as to minimize exposure to sunlight and are then artificially heated in a special apparatus that measures the light released during heating, and hence the amount of accumulated energy.

TL dating is a time- and labor-intensive technique, and the TL lab at the OSS was being computerized. Computerization was both good and bad because it meant that as a pioneer I had to work out all the bugs in the system, but also that toward the end I was able to accomplish quickly and easily tasks that took many hours to do manually. Some of the TL apparatus was also malfunctioning during my work, and in an isolated laboratory such as that of the OSS in Jabiru East, malfunctions of complicated machinery mean on-the-spot patch-ups or weeks of delay, sometimes both.

When things got particularly frustrating, it was tempting to regard the computers as sentient, malevolent beings. There were times when I was sure the computers hated me, and the feeling was mutual. The various OSS computers were hooked up to a central system, so that everything worked more slowly when many people were using them. As a result, I took to working early in the morning and late at night when no one else was around. Being barely computer literate, this schedule created problems of its own, which led to Wohl's Law: When the experts are away, trivial problems will cause major delays, and when the experts are present, major problems will cause major delays. When I got frustrated and was unable to make a program perform as I wanted, I often resorted to blindly trying all of the commands that came into my head, like Ali Baba's brother shouting "Open, rye! Open, caraway!" Luckily, I escaped his fate. However, as OSS computer programmer Col Mackintosh said, "When you're a pioneer, you have to be prepared to get arrows in the back." After a while my back bristled like a porcupine.

I had hoped to use the TL ages for the East Alligator River flood sediments as an addition to the radiocarbon chronology, which was sparse for that river, owing to difficulty in finding sufficient organic materials in the flood sediments. However, the TL ages were uniformly older than the radiocarbon ages from the same depositional units, often by two orders of magnitude. In this situation I assumed that the more standard, accepted radiocarbon technology was yielding the ages most representative of the time of the floods. The TL ages were probably too old because of incomplete zeroing. When floodwaters erode sandbars that may have been stable for hundreds of years, the individual sand grains may not be completely zeroed during their transport downstream because of the floodwaters' turbidity. The flood sediments thus may be deposited with residual stored energy, making their TL ages older than the time of the flood that last deposited them.

As my work proceeded, I became more familiar with the natural and human environments of Jabiru and Jabiru East. I got used to living indoors again and to dealing with the limited selection of high-priced goods featured by the single local supermarket. I moved to another donger when I returned from the East Alligator, and although my new home did not have a resident frog in the toilet, it did have a population of geckos, small lizards with pale, lavender-white skins, big dark eyes, and long toenails. The geckos had a startling habit of popping out from behind curtains at unexpected moments, but they kept the ant and cockroach populations to a manageable level.

I soon got used to the new donger's other vagaries, such as the violence of air trapped in water lines of the shower, and I grew to quite enjoy reading and writing at the sturdy little square wooden table standing before the kitchen window. Periodically the OSS would send in cleaners and change my linen, leaving me free to concentrate on science until I was sick of it. There were few clothing stores in Jabiru, and what little I had with me grew progressively more threadbare. I was reduced to using pieces of the pocket lining of my shorts as patches for holes in the seat, which made me appreciate Australian Henry Lawson's poem "When your pants begin to go," which directly correlates self-respect and the state of the seat of your pants.

My donger was a few minutes' walk from the OSS, and I usually saw a variety of birds in the course of my daily walks to and fro. Several times I walked home under circling kites, their wild, piercing cries calling to mind the freedom and wilderness of high, windswept mountains. One of the last entries in John Gilbert's diary, as quoted in Graham Pizzey's *A Separate Creation,* dealt with kites. Gilbert accompanied Leichhardt's first expedition for the chance to fill in the gaps in John Gould's coverage of Australian birds. Gilbert was killed in an Aboriginal ambush at the western base of Cape York Peninsula, near what is now the Gilbert River, but Leichhardt saved his diary and sent it to Gould. This entry was made the day before Gilbert was killed:

> Friday 27 June, 1845. In the afternoon while sitting at the entrance of my tent skinning birds I had a tin case with specimens between my legs, the lid of which I had opened to air the specimens enclosed, among which was the only specimen of my last new

Honey-sucker. This was lying on the top and had deceived the bird [a black kite] so much that he darted down, and to my surprise and vexation fairly carried off my specimen, and flying into a neighboring tree instantly plucked it to pieces, whether he swallowed any I–could not tell, but at all events I should imagine that the Arsenic will not at all agree with its stomach although they display a little nicety in what they pick up.

My kite companions in Jabiru East were fork-tailed kites, *Milvus migrans,* scavengers ranging throughout Europe, Asia, Africa, Australia, and Indonesia to New Guinea and surrounding islands. The kites have benefited by human settlement, which provides food and water in otherwise unsuitable areas.

In addition to working in the TL laboratory, I had many opportunities to explore the Kakadu region while I was in Jabiru, visiting Nourlangie Rock, Barramundie Gorge, and other sites.

The Aboriginal rock art for which the Kakadu region is famous occurs in the alcoves and overhangs of Arnhem Land and its outliers. As one of the largest of these outliers, Nourlangie Rock forms a huge sandstone island set in the sea of a flat plain. The place resonates with the Aboriginal tongue: Nangaloar, Koongarra, Nawulandja, Anbangbang Billabong. Here where the heat and humidity settle down like a shroud, the Aborigines have immortalized their culture.

The rock paintings in the park range from an estimated age of 22,000 years to the Blue Paintings done in 1964. They are mostly in white, orange, tan, black, and red-brown, tones from the earth. The most striking are the intricately detailed x-ray-style depictions of people and animals, particularly the barramundi. Silver barramundi may grow to more than a meter and a half in length and sixty kilograms in weight, providing a hearty meal for a hungry fisher. They spawn and breed in the coastal waters and mangrove swamps, and the young fish follow silt-laden, slow-moving rivers inland. Trapped in billabongs as the Dry progresses, the barramundi await the rising river levels of the Wet before returning to the coast to breed. To the Aborigines, they are power and fascination, endlessly repeated in intricate but unvaried designs. Unlike European art, where the individual creator is celebrated for originality, this art is celebrated for the culture that produced the creator, who remains unknown. But where I could get close enough to see individual brush

Abroriginal rock art that we nicknamed "Mosquito Man," Nourlangie Rock.

strokes in the paintings, I felt close to the artist, and the art grew from a curiosity to a significant expression of personal and cultural vision.

Most of the sites have several layers of paintings, the older still faintly discernible beneath the newer, in a visible demonstration of the passing of time and the slow progression of change in the style of painting. George Chaloupka has worked out a relative chronology for the paintings, based on superimposition and stylistic changes, and in a summary of archaeological research in the park, he defines three styles of painting. Pre-estuarine (35,000-8,000 B.P., or years before present) art is characterized by positive prints of hands and plants, stick figures, and yam figures of humans and animals with the outward shape of yam tubers. Estuarine art (8,000-1,000 B.P.), created during a sea-level rise that surrounded Arnhem Land with a broad salt marsh, is characterized by x-ray-style descriptive paintings displaying the internal structure of animals. The final, post-estuarine period (1,000 B.P. to present) is divided into freshwater art of decorative x-ray paintings where internal spaces are filled with crosshatching, and contact art of the last 300 years, depicting European and Indonesian invaders and their strange ships and horses.

Most people who visit the famous rock art galleries at Nourlangie Rock see only a portion of the base of the rock and miss much of the deeper sense of place that comes from exploring beyond the surface and seeing the whole. I was more fortunate and spent a day exploring the hidden interior of the rock with four scientists from the OSS. We began in the stillness of early morning, the heavy air pressing the damp shirts onto our backs and shoulders. We didn't say much climbing up, breathing heavily, grasping for handholds among the rocks and trees. A brown rock wallaby hesitated a moment, started violently, then fled at our approach. At the top the distances were hazed with moisture. The flat coastal plain spread monotonously north, south, and west to the horizons. The soil was a pale orange-red, the gray gum trees rising from it carefully spaced and uncrowded. East lay the great rocky mass of Arnhem Land, dark in the early light. Nourlangie itself was a maze of caves and deep, narrow gorges at our feet — a smaller-scale Arnhem Land, and we lesser Leichhardts.

Scrambling down great cracks fluted and grooved by running water, I looked up through chasms so narrow that the sky, thirty meters up, was only a small, pale blue patch or not there at all. Climbing, "chimneying," belaying down ropes, I found the hard, abrasive rock roughened my palms and fingertips, scraped my knees. Down in the gorges it was cool and still, the air musty with growing plants, fungi beside rotting wood. Swarms of large, golden Arnhem blowflies buzzed resonantly in the alcoves, where flakes of stone from old Aboriginal quarry sites littered the ground. In the dry, bright heat on top of the gorges, the pillars and walls of rock below seemed separated by channels only a few meters deep, the darker depths hidden by vegetation and the turnings of the rock walls. Clumps of spinifex bristled from the upper rocks, pincushions of flexible pins that snagged and broke off in tender flesh.

We lunched at a wider spot in one of the canyons, where a slight draft slipped quietly through the cool shadows. The roots of a giant fig growing on the canyon rim fell over the rock face like rivulets from a waterfall. The billy boiled quietly on a fire of twigs, an essential Australian ritual. At the edge of the rock the canyon ended, and I could just see through a screen of pandanus trees to the bright sunlight on the plain below. We talked of various things; it didn't really matter what. Talk would soon be forgotten, but the place itself would sink into memory through fragments of sights, sounds, smells, textures. The ease of leaning back against the cool rock in a sweat-soaked shirt, feeling thigh muscles heavy with good

Stilt roots characteristic of trees in the monsoon
forest. These were found in a crevice at the top
of Nourlangie Rock.

use. The sudden cooling through wet, matted hair when a hat was removed. The feeling of being somewhere hard to reach, special, reserved.

Squirming through tiny crevices smooth from other bodies, we studied silica dripstone and entered dead caves dark with the darkness of light unimagined, silent as though sound never existed. Our voices fell flat and disappeared quickly. A small bat flew into me in sudden confusion, squeaking its alarm. Giant cave geckoes blinked in the artificial light of our flashlights, accustomed only to emerging at night from the fissures and caves of the plateau to eat insects, spiders, and other geckoes. Or people, as my companions said. Anything is believable in a soundless, lightless cave.

Coming back down the rock, dropping on ropes over sudden lips of stone, we brushed a green ant nest, and the inhabitants swarmed over it in alarm, squirting formic acid. The sun was setting when we emerged again at the base of the rock, and the still air was heavy with heat and moisture, colors fading into grays as at early morning. Time might have stood still while we disappeared into an enchanted world.

Two months later, the monsoon rains beginning, I found the changes of the progressing season in the rock. Ferns sprang up fresh and green along the walls from the dried brown remnants of previous seasons. Seeps and springs along the rock flowed into clear, cool rivulets of fresh-tasting water. Chestnut quilled rock pigeons nested along the ledges, some already with hatchlings. During a short rainstorm, I looked up from the labyrinthine channels cut into the top of the rock to see the individual raindrops falling through the long, deep space between the narrow gorge walls, each drop shining with the light it was bringing down to the earth from the sky. Then the sun came out, and the leaves of the trees shone and sparkled in their coats of water.

Other days I spent wandering the coastal plains. Those were hot, muggy days, when the world lay stifled and torpid beneath the tropical sun. Mazes of dirt tracks cross the plains, winding among shaggy-trunked paperbarks and spike-leaved pandanus. Where the bamboos grew in feathery clumps, buffaloes and wallabies fled at my approach, and black-and-white cockatoos screamed in displeasure at the intrusion. The billabongs were lush with ducks and egrets, and I glimpsed the subtle orange-brown form of a dingo slipping into the deeper shadows.

Before the shallow billabongs of the last Wet had dried into heat-cracked plains of short, sparse grass, the buffaloes had wallowed in the cool mud, leaving the land so pocked that it resembled the cratered remains of a battlefield. I warily circled a large buffalo bull with great sweeping horns, my camera at the ready, and he as warily eyed me. Near Yarilan Billabong I parked the car and walked through the forest to the edge of the water, perspiring heavily and irritably waving away the flies. When I reached the billabong, I forgot the heat and the flies, for before me lay one of the earth's great wildlife spectacles.

It was like an illustration of the fabled wildlife of North America before the coming of the whites, or of Africa in the last century. Several

Termite mounds on the low coastal plains along the south Alligator River.

hectares of shallow water were filled from edge to edge with magpie geese, whistling ducks, herons, egrets, and other birds. Individual birds were distinguishable in the foreground, but those beyond them rapidly merged into a brown mass that looked solid, and the black-and-white geese filled the air with the sound of their honking. As the waters of the billabong slowly shrank inward during the dry season, the soft mud of the shallow edges was exposed, providing the geese easy digging for buried tubers. I have never seen so many birds at once, but these birds, too, like those of North America or of Africa, are but a remnant. Magpie geese once flocked in the millions over most of Australia, including the southeast, where they are now very rare. We have inherited a poorer world and will impoverish it still more before we go.

Farther along the coastal plain lies Barramundie Gorge, a tributary of the South Alligator River favored as a picnic and swimming spot by residents of Jabiru. I visited the gorge on one of the endlessly hot, heavy October days. The road to the gorge wound through an exotic terrain of giant yellow-orange termite mounds scattered across a plain greened by a recent rain. The termitaria seem fit landscape components in a land called "the Never-Never," which hosts bunyips and flying foxes. The giant mounds create a fantasy landscape, where it would be appropriate to round a bend and come face-to-face with either Stegosaurus or R2D2.

Giant termites *(Mastotermes darwiniensis)* are unique to northern tropical Australia and have the distinction of being the continent's most destructive insects. Other species also occur, the grass-eating termites *Nasutitermes triodiae* probably being responsible for the mounds along the South Alligator. The termite mounds, or termitaria, of these regions reach four to five meters high, with rounded knobs and hollows like slightly eroded sand castles. According to Derrick Ovington in *Kakadu,* the mounds are believed to persist for more than 100 years. From the outside they are rock hard and appear to be abandoned, but inside the silent walls masses of the grublike, translucent, milky white termites swarm and seethe. The termite colony is an expert architect, keeping the internal temperature and humidity of the nest constant year-round. Termitaria present a special challenge to the disposal of uranium tailings in this area, because the uranium wastes occur in the particular grain size that termites favor for building their mounds and bring up to the surface from great depths. Frogs, reptiles, and echidnas all feast on termites, and other insects, birds, and lizards use the termitaria for nests. As I drove among the termitaria, goannas scrambled away from the track, and a pair of brilliantly colored lorikeets flashed by among the trees.

I parked near the end of the gorge and walked upstream alongside a channel full of still, emerald green water overhung by pandanus and paperbarks. The cool shade was a welcome relief from the hot, bright atmosphere of the open plain. The channel became progressively rockier, until the path ended at a large pool enclosed on three sides by high, steep rock walls over which a waterfall flowed. At my end of the pool, fish hung suspended in the clear water over a white sand bottom. I stood waist deep in the water for a while, watching the fish and building up my courage. Barramundie Gorge was supposed to have only freshwater crocs, but the pool was perhaps thirty meters long and fifteen wide, and I was alone. A small striped fish grazed at the sand around my feet, gently nibbling my toes. Other slender, striped fish with long, thin snouts slipped by. Perhaps the elusive archer fish was among those hiding in the green shadows under the overhanging vegetation at the pool's edge.

Archer fish hang just below the surface of the water and spit drops of water up at insects on the overhanging vegetation, knocking the insects into the water to be eaten. These fish have been found only in Irian Jaya and the South Alligator River. I had first read of them in a childhood book by Leonora Hornblow called *Fish Do the Strangest Things* and had been trying to see one ever since learning that they occurred in northern Australia.

I stood in the clear edges of the water, comfortable with the sight of the bottom and the small fish, sun warm on my shoulders, feet in cool water. Sometimes I do things because I am unable to imagine alternatives, dignifying the action as courageous or resolute. Courage at the sticking point, I struck out across the pool toward the falls. In the cool water my limbs felt suddenly stiff, and I swam in jerks. The bottom dropped off quickly. The water was green-black beneath the shallow transparent surface layer in which my white arms struck out ahead as I swam, and I imagined a swimming human seen from below by a crocodile: luminously white, tender, vulnerable. People do the strangest things. I remembered Steinbeck writing in *The Log From the Sea of Cortez* of swimming in the ocean, "expecting at a moment to be devoured by the monsters we no longer believe in."

I clambered onto the rock ledge opposite the falls, where I rested just above the water but no longer a part of it, momentarily safe. No sign of the crocs, which were, after all, "just" freshies. The sun warmed my wet skin, smoothed out the goose bumps. I sat watching the falls for a long time, absorbed by the endless fascination of moving water flowing on ceaselessly yet repeating the same patterns and shapes. At the falls, the frothy white mixture of water and air gliding over the slick, black face of the rock was more viscous than mere water. The white traced out figures against the black, juxtaposing motion and fixity, sound and silence. As George Santayana wrote, "Repetition is the only form of permanence that nature can achieve." With a little shake I slipped into the water again, practicing minimalism in motion, bidding the darkness stay peacefully below until I again reached safety.

~ ~ ~

While I was at the OSS, I had an opportunity to fly over the Kakadu and Arnhem Land regions in a small plane and see how the integral parts of the overall region fit together. I flew with Bob Buchanan, a maintenance man at the OSS who owned a four-passenger plane and loved flying so much that he charged his passengers only enough to cover petrol expenses. From the Jabiru East airport we headed north down the floodplain of Magela Creek, the major tributary of the East Alligator River. To the west, the late afternoon sun set through the smoke of bushfires, its light silvering the water splashed across the coastal plain. To the east lay the outer rampart of the fortress of Arnhem Land, dull orange and gray in the fading light.

We flew low over the floodplain, where flocks of white egrets dotted the emerald green patches of swamp, and resting buffalo made gray humps in the lighter green meadows. Ireland is not more of an emerald color than the Magela floodplain in the generous hues of the wet season. We followed the waters up from the coastal plain where they meandered widely among billabongs and swamps, along the tightening gorge, to the cascade where all the springs and seeps of the plateau collected to plunge over the precipice. From the Magela, we made a broad turn over the lower reaches of the East Alligator, the tidal section where the river almost doubles back upon itself as it winds through the flat, open coastal plains. Large crocodiles, small plastic toys at that height, lay on the broad clay banks exposed by the low tide.

Turning up the East Alligator, we flew along it past my field area before turning back to Jabiru. There were magnificent views along the East Alligator gorge into the endless maze of deep, tree-filled canyons, but heading back over the escarpment the light faded fast as sunset brought an approaching storm. Sheets of rain veiled portions of the cliffs below us, and the plane was tossed about by turbulence, which I could have done without just then. Bob was a very obliging pilot — too obliging. Every time we saw anything of interest, he turned and dipped and circled, and I was soon sick. Fighting nausea in the cockpit's heat, I watched the horizon gauge at the front of the plane go through all sorts of horrible angles, unable to watch the real horizon anymore unless it was level. This was a time for mind over matter, and through the interminable end of the flight I willed myself to hold out. Matters reached the crisis point shortly before we landed, when I emptied my camera bag and prepared for the worst, having neglected to bring any other suitable container. Luckily for my pride and my camera bag, I managed to hold back. The rain began as we landed, and for the next two hours a tremendous thunderstorm shrieked and banged at the world.

During the latter part of my stay the monsoon rains began to fall regularly in the late afternoon and evening. The rains lasted a few hours at most, but I have never seen rain with such intensity. The first hard daytime rain, late in October, gave new meaning to the old saying "the heavens opened up and a deluge poured down." A mid-November storm was preceded by a morning overcast and steamy as a sauna. A torrential downpour began during morning tea, and the rain pounding on the metallic roof made such a roar that I had to shout to the person sitting next to me. The air had an opaque whiteness like fog, and the rain such force that it appeared to be hurled down from the sky rather than simply falling of its own accord. The ground quickly saturated, and puddles appeared everywhere, their surfaces constantly changing relief maps as miniature spires and buttes leapt upward in response to the raindrops. I was amazed that the plants tolerated the extremes of months of scorching sun and no rain, followed by months of inundation.

I simply sat and watched the rain smother everything, streaming in sheets and shoots off every elevated surface. I had been having a frustrating morning due to equipment breakdowns, and I felt the legendary effect of the tropics, where time slows down as human ambition bows to the overpowering force of climate. As I let the rain gradually overwhelm me, I thought of how Western civilization has always measured progress by the ability to overcome obstacles and limits. Dry deserts or flooded tropics have been simply environments to be manipulated to fit our wants. Yet somehow the tropical rain was comforting, and there was nothing defeatist in my acceptance of it. I imagined the greater, subtler challenge of living within a place, rather than reshaping it to a homogenized standard. We are impatient, and like children supported in a frail gossamer web, tear out blindly in all directions, shredding the web before we have begun to see its wisdom and beauty. As Francis Bacon wrote, "Nature is a labyrinth in which the very haste you move with will make you lose your way."

It was slightly cooler walking home that afternoon, and the sky was stretched and twisted into gray and blue-black clouds. The evening storms were equally violent, sometimes literally shaking my bed and lighting my windows through the curtains with lightning flashes.

From October onward, a spectacular massing of thunderheads occurred each evening toward sunset whether it rained or not, and I got into the habit of taking an early evening walk to enjoy the cloud displays. Each night the scene changed, and my journal entries record my impressions:

> 2 October: Massive thunderheads piled up in the east, for the most part blue-gray above the pale green gum trees. In the center of the sky a mass of clouds glowed a soft rose color, as though they had

their own foot and stage lights in the darker clouds surrounding them.

4 October: Rain hanging in purple blue sheets on the horizon late in the afternoon.

5 October: The moon rose through a wine red dusk. Only a thin crescent at the moon's base was illuminated, but I could see the whole spherical outline as a faint gray shadow. The glowing base was like light shining from beneath a closed door.

9 October: An enormous thunderhead on the eastern horizon, glowing pink in the last light, periodically illuminated to a bright white by lightning flashes from within. The flashes erupted here and there across the cloud like strobe lights, or rippled across the whole face in a wave.

29 November: One of the stunning Territory sunsets, a searing ball of sun descending through a tangle of gray-trunked green-leaved trees and pale green grasses — fire and ice. Flashes of dry lightning skittering across the eastern sky.

About a kilometer from my donger was a shallow retaining pond built for the mines. Overgrown along its edges by vegetation, it had taken on a natural aspect, and I enjoyed passing it on my longer evening walks. Generally I started out just after sunset when the air was still full of the day's warmth, like a sponge just soaked in water, and vibrating with the dusk sounds of crickets, frogs, and cockatoos settling in for the night. Slowly, a soft breeze began to stir, soothing and gentle as a caress, the earth breathing a sigh of relief.

At the pond, the water was a mosaic of soft pastels. A reserved white egret quietly stalked the shallows, surrounded by whistling ducks. The last light just showed the dark shapes of water lily pads silent in the gray water at the near end, and the trees growing at the other side were black masses beneath the distant rose-and-tan face of Mt. Brockman.

To the west, the sky was strewn with clouds: puffy, piled clouds; solid, sculptured clouds; wispy, twisted clouds; dragged-out sheets of clouds. So much violent, passionate movement caught in each unchanging moment. I watched the setting sun burn the clouds to smoldering red. To the east, a tumultuous jumble of pearl white clouds glowing against the calm blue sky pulsed with lightning. An almost-full moon rose at their edges, its glow diffused through their tatters. As I continued, a violent thunder-and-lightning storm flared in the western sky, and lights went dancing across the horizon. I sat for a long time and watched the lightning flinging itself about inside the clouds, half expecting to see the clouds split open and release some miraculous force.

I turned west, heading down a slight incline, the land stretching out before me as the leaves of the trees became more distinct and black against the sky. I felt as if I could walk forever, down and on to the smoky clouds, watching the stars appear one by one and breathing in the cooling breeze. At last I turned back when the eastern clouds were dark gray, indistinguishable against the sky until the lightning erupted within them and left a light scar trail across my eyes. When I got back to my donger, I opened the door and sat without lights for a while, unwilling to lose the gentle darkness.

The air cooled wonderfully, and the night vibrated with the croaking of frogs — big frogs, small frogs, fat frogs, thin frogs — the whole frog tribe by the sound of it. Above an overall frog-mass noise rose the unique songs of individual frogs, some like engines revving up, some like taut rubber bands being plucked, others shrill and insistent as cicadas. Kakadu has twenty-five known frog species: green tree frogs, marbled frogs, carpenter frogs, saxicoline tree frogs, dwarf rocket frogs, and a host of others share the varied microenvironments of the region, breeding and reaching their noise crescendos during the Wet.

A storm blew in as I sat drinking tea and reading later that evening. A fierce wind that shook the donger cooled the air rapidly, and cold, hard drops slashed down between the tree branches shuddering in the wind. Thunder vibrated through the ground beneath me, and the lights flickered on and off until the storm slowly gentled to a steady rain and the croaking of frogs. Then at last there was the dark night air, cool but heavy and enveloping with moisture, tiny prickles from an occasional raindrop striking my surprised skin. The sky was loaded with faintly luminous clouds teased by flashes of light to the west and, filling the dark air, the monotonous, always-farther-away croaking of the frogs. Nothing insistent, just a soft, gentle, soothing dark.

Beginning the walk, I had been lonely for an old friend to talk to. Then the peace of the evening seeped quietly into my mind. A traveler wandering the far lands of the earth must be all in all to herself. There must be sufficient pleasure in the experiencing, the telling confined at one remove to a pen and paper. I had read Zora Neale Hurston and knew that I was the world and the heavens boiled down to a drop.

~   ~   ~

The OSS is visited throughout the year by consultants from various Australian universities and government agencies, and I spent much time with Drs. Bob Wasson and Robin Clark of the CSIRO (Commonwealth Scientific and Industrial Research Organization) while they were at the OSS. On one of our trips we took a boat down the lower, tidal East Alligator from Cahill's Crossing. We got an early start to take advantage of the morning high tide but discovered on arrival that we had miscalculated and were faced with an expanse of sticky gray clay surrounding a shallow thread of gray water.

While we waited for the tide to rise, we followed a short trail that wound among small rock outliers with termitaria built up along their sides like wasp nests and had cold drinks at the store bordering the Aboriginal reserve. The Border Store was a small counter with a roofed patio and a few tables. I had ginger beer, a more pungent version of ginger ale, and listened to the stories of Pat, a beefy woman in a sarong who ran the store with her husband. They had to sell their yearly stock of t-shirts, sarongs, and posters during the dry tourist season because the goods got moldy if they sat in the store over the Wet. Pat passed the time by watching a large croc named Fred that frequented the crossing. She had come to regard him as something of a combined pet and tourist attraction, but during the next Wet a croc like Fred killed a local fisherman who foolishly waded into the river.

We put the boats into the river at midmorning, struggling through the tenaciously sticky fine gray clay of the bed. In launching the boat, I sank into the clay over my knees and fought my way out of the mire through the false crocodile alarms of the splashes of jumping fish. The banks were alive with mudskippers, hilarious-looking little "missing links" with long fishy bodies and great bulbous eyes. They skittered and jumped about in the shallows, now below the water, now on "dry" land.

A short distance downstream, we found the water still too shallow to proceed. As we sat in the boats beneath the broiling sun, scraping the mud off ourselves and waiting for the water to rise, Bob and Robin composed a verse in honor of the occasion:

> Here we sit
> Covered in shit
> Waiting for the tide on the East Alligator River
> Not even a Scotch to ruin our livers.

This was chanted against the background of the droning cicadas and an occasional sudden eruption of jumping fish ricocheting across the water like a splashing fountain. Groups of these slender, pale silver fish a few centimeters long skip along the water surface in bursts covering up to a meter. I never figured out how they did it, as they seemed to barely touch the water with the lower third of their bodies between skips. Groups of the little spotted sunfish congregated near the banks.

Baldwin Spencer lived with the Cahills at nearby Oenpelli from June to August 1912. Following the East Alligator River up from the coast, he described the water as

> pea-soup in colour. There were flocks of white cockatoos, cranes and ibises. Every now and then an ugly crocodile slithered down a bank and fell with a plop into the muddy water and a great black snake glided by, carried down by the stream. Once we passed a clump of bare trees, literally crowded with Nankeen night-herons.

At last the tide came in, quickly raising the water level. We started off in high hopes but wasted a good deal of time on malfunctioning motors and were only able to go a few kilometers downstream before the now-falling tide forced us to return. We had a fascinating trip nonetheless. The banks of the river were a thickly lined jungle of vines, undergrowth, and tall trees, some of which overhung the channel. The water had a slightly salty taste, and small boils of sediment spread out across its surface. In spite of the noise from our motor, as we proceeded downstream, we saw curve-billed ibis and copper-colored Nankeen night herons glistening in the sunlight. Two small crocs lay sunning themselves on an exposed clay bank. One slid into the water as we approached, but the other remained obligingly on the bank, primitive and ancient, for photographs. Sunning unmoving and unblinking on the bank, the croc looked deceptively stolid and mechanical, belying its ability to move rapidly when hunting. I half-expected the croc to open its mouth like an animated figure from Disneyland just at the moment our boat passed. Seemingly an impenetrable creature of blind, instinctual actions, yet apparently intelligent enough to recognize a prey's routine and take advantage of it when hunting, as I had been warned on the Burdekin.

Rounding a bend, we came onto a large tree filled with roosting flying foxes. They hung from the branches like great black fruits and seemed out of place in the daylight as they "squacked" at each other, occasionally clambering about among the branches with their odd wing-hands. The night herons seemed to be roosting with them, in appearance strange bedfellows. We turned back where the vegetation began to thin, and I had a brief glimpse of the open, grassy plain where the river flows in great loops and meanders before entering the mangrove swamps at the edge of the sea.

I spent a day on one of these plains on the Mudginberri Corridor. During the dry season, the aquatic or semiaquatic life of Kakadu concentrates along the rivers or at the billabongs, expanding again across the plains during the general flooding of the Wet. These billabongs are pleasant places to spend a hot afternoon. White water lilies bloom in the clear, cool water, and delicately striped tiny fish that would grace a tropical aquarium swim among the slender grass stems. Beyond the billabongs stretch the backwater plains, heat-slurred in the midday sun.

We drove across the plains near Nankeen Billabong on twisting, rutted roads, bouncing on the hard seats of the old Land Cruiser. A frill-necked lizard trotted away from the road, comically dignified as it ran upright on its hind legs. Flocks of budgies and neon-colored parrots swooped at kamikaze speeds beside us. The plain was an absolutely flat, grassy expanse fringed to the south by a forest of eucalypts, pandanus, and paperbark, the Arnhem Land escarpment rising in tiers beyond. To the north the plain undulated into the heat waves, merging with the heat-pale sky. It was hot and silent beneath the intense sun; only the buzzing of the maddening flies broke the stillness. Off to the southeast the kites circled and dove for insects through the white smoke of a slowly burning bushfire. I squinted across the plain at the smoke twisting itself into willy-willies or feathering slowly upward. The forest fringe was hazed by smoke and humidity, and I could just discern the tall top of a palm protruding here and there. To the northeast, the green was broken by an orange blur at the edge of the forest, the rock outcrop of the Aborigines' "Sores Dreaming," off-limits to whites.

The vehicle started slowly across the hard-baked black soil of the plain, our bones and teeth jarring loose with each revolution. Little hummocks materialized on the plain, and the passengers retreated to the exterior of the vehicle, hanging precariously on to outer edges of the car, knees flexed to absorb the shocks hoping to settle into backbones, as the driver sped along. It was cooler and more exciting on the outside, the wind straining at my hair and shutting my eyes. I imagined myself intrepidly on safari, penetrating the secrets of an unknown continent. The grass grew thicker until patches of ground quaggy with moisture appeared, and the vehicle slowed. I jumped off and strode along, still shaken with the excitement of speed. We left the vehicle behind, the ground softer and softer toward the meeting of land and water, where we took a hand augur sample down through the thick, sticky black muck to the delicately pale gray-blue clay beneath, sweating heavily as we worked. Then back, wind and speed, across the plain to the shade of the big old paperbarks by the billabong. A billy boiling, I went exploring to the billabong, creeping slow and quiet with camera at the ready.

Two sides of the billabong were surrounded by low, emerald green trees, the water lying in a shallow black oval before them. Trees and water were filled with birds: brolgas, jabirus, magpie geese, ducks, ibis, a sea eagle. Brilliant white egrets perched in the bright green foliage like pearls amongst emeralds. My presence missed, one of the others came stealing quickly out from the lunch spot, warning of crocodiles. I nodded and continued circumspectly. The birds did what birds do, and I photographed them, returning unharmed to drink the billy tea with lunch.

As I ate, I watched a big drilling rig at work out on the plain, its metal frame shimmering in the heat waves as it pulled up cores of sediment. Our purpose in obtaining these cores was to reconstruct how the area had changed through time, based on the types of pollen and sediment contained in different levels of the core. Geologists work on a variety of temporal and spatial scales, from the process geomorphologist who may be concerned with the physics controlling the movement of a single grain in a sand dune during several minutes, to the structural geologist who may be inferring the movements of a continent over several hundred million years from the folds and faults preserved in a mountain chain. My work on the rivers of northern Australia focused primarily on the last 1,000 years, but the drilling on the coastal plains was directed at changes occurring during the last 10,000 years, the period during which global climate and sea level were stabilizing following the last major glaciation.

Through the heat of the day we dozed, examined the drill cores, talked casually of seas rising and falling over thousands of years — the arrogance of the geologist. Then we packed ourselves into the vehicle again and left the plain still torpid beneath the sun, somewhere in my mind the old idea of playing with pebbles on the beach before the whole vast, unknown ocean.

Despite the socializing in the field and in Jabiru, there were times when I got homesick. *Homesick:* small word for a large feeling that couldn't be fought with reason or activity. I felt it sometimes as a lack of something in my stomach and an empty weakness spreading up into my arms, like the feeling that comes just before fainting. Sometimes the loneliness was a physical urge, like panic, and I had to choke back a quick, fierce despair. A letter or phone call meant a lot. Did they still think of me? What were they doing? I'd think of what time it was back home — seven hours later but a day earlier — and imagine in minute detail the actions of their day.

Calling the States collect, a tenuous line reached out through a series of operators. Often the operators were chatty and friendly. Why was a Yank calling from an out-of-the-way place called Jabiru? They fit the old-fashioned stereotype of a country operator, and I imagined them listening in after the connection was made. Then, miraculously, the dearly loved voices of my parents at the other end, and I was taut with excitement and happiness, stumbling over my own words and interrupting. The euphoria lasted a while after I hung up, then smoldered out. Such a short, unsatisfying tie, without seeing or touching.

In early October, the air heavy with unfallen rain and held-back lightning, a postcard came. A happy postcard scene of the Arizona desert in spring bloom. I sat staring at the photo and knew what it would be like to walk into the scene, to have the sun's warmth on my head and shoulders. Pungent creosote smell overlaid with thousands of tiny wildflowers filling the gravelly spaces. Near sound of an occasional insect against the great silences of sweeping space. No place is as quiet with the easy absence of sound as the desert or as vibrant with color after spring rains. Sweep of land up to the mountains, so near and sudden in the clear air. The desert.

6
South to Uluru ~

Music has been in my heart all the time, and poetry in my thoughts. Alone on the open desert. . . . The world has seemed more beautiful to me than ever before. I have loved the red rocks, the twisted trees, the red sand blowing in the wind, the slow, sunny clouds crossing the sky, the shafts of moonlight on my bed at night. . . . I have been happy in my work, and I have exulted in my play. I have really lived.

Everett Ruess, as quoted by W. L. Rushton in
Everett Ruess: A Vagabond for Beauty

The words above were written by Everett Ruess about the deserts of the American Southwest, but they evoke the power of deserts everywhere. While working at the OSS I took two weeks off to travel south to Alice Springs and Uluru National Park to see the Red Center, the great arid outback of Australia that has fascinated people since the landing of the First Fleet. At last the climax journey lay clear before me, a fulfillment of the long-dreamed vision of utter desert at the heart of a continent.

My line of travel began at the Northern Territory capital of Darwin, the white Australians' hard-won toehold at the northern edge of the continent. From Darwin I journeyed inland along the sole paved highway linking the coast and the interior, and then retraced my route to the coast again. Viewed on a map, it is a pleasingly symmetrical route, connecting the geographic center to the northern coast at a point approximately midway between east and west. It is a line of travel pioneered by John McDouall Stuart coming up from the south and by the miners and telegraph construction gangs moving down from the north. Perhaps also by the Aborigines following the chants of the songlines that strung together and supported their whole known world.

The European explorers came to the center as to a blank space. Men like Stuart knew well the coastal outline of Australia, with its thin fringe of mapped and settled lands surrounding the blank interior. But they had little idea of what to expect from the interior, imagining everything from a sandy desert to a vast inland sea or lake. To the Aboriginal tribes of the interior, the region was anything but blank, being richly layered with meaning imparted to it by a history stretching back to the Dreamtime. Each feature of the landscape had its associated stories and taboos constituting the rules by which life was lived.

The first Aborigines to migrate into the area must also have faced a blank image on their mental maps, slowly filling in the details as they advanced. The white culture's written records of the history and geography of the center are thus only the latest addition to all the preceding conceptions of the region, from the scent tracks of small predators prowling the dunes by night, to the Dreamtime stories of the Aborigines. Each organism or community develops its own way of viewing the landscape, until a long-inhabited land comes to be steeped in meaning and association. This is like the progression followed by each individual discovering a landscape, a progression in which scenes of childhood or long residence are more subtly interpreted and fully known than the new lands.

I began my journey at Darwin. The city itself is fairly small, although the suburbs sprawling around it made it seem a major metropolis after Jabiru. I had some trouble both navigating and driving; red lights never last long enough to study a map.

The written records of Darwin begin with the stubborn British determination to settle the central northern region, a story told in Ernestine Hill's *The Territory,* Peter Spillett's *Forsaken Settlement,* and Barbara James's *No Man's Land.* Repeatedly, shiploads of thick-blooded temperate-zone British came out to colonize the tropical coast. Often they were fresh young sahibs with idealistic visions of civilizing the natives, claiming new territory for the Empire, and establishing a prosperous trade with the Dutch colonies. In the smooth flow of their dreams, they would eventually relax into a life of luxurious ease as tropical plantation owners.

Instead, they found themselves in an incomprehensible alien world. The natives would not be civilized, the land would not be claimed, and the trading partners stayed away. Fever and scurvy evaporated any energy and courage left after the heat and humidity had their way. Termites and mold destroyed supplies, and the despair of isolation and listlessness gave way to the delirium tremens of alcoholism. The would-be imperialists in distant Australia were puppets dancing to the changing whims of the

British navy and the Colonial Office. They needed five tries to establish a lasting settlement, which was itself nearly destroyed by cyclones more than once, as recently as 1974.

In the early nineteenth century, officials of the rapidly growing British Empire worried about losing the vast portions of Australia beyond their small southeastern settlements. Their primary rivals in trade and colonization were the French and the Dutch, who had both made exploratory forays into the region. British settlement on the Cobourg Peninsula of northern Australia was first suggested in 1823 by a British trader as a means of providing military security and reducing piracy in the area, as well as serving as a revictualing point for ships and strengthening Britain's claim to northern Australia.

In 1824 a shipload of convicts and their guards arrived at Port Essington, the port named by Phillip Parker King for his friend Admiral Sir William Essington, east across Van Diemen's Gulf from present-day Darwin. Unable to find fresh water in the harbor area, they sailed west to Melville Island, where they established Fort Dundas. They were to secure the north coast against possible French settlement and to trade with the Malay fishers, but nothing went right. Lost in a wholly unfamiliar world, they dropped in the heat from fever and scurvy. Their livestock died, the extremes of wet and dry ruined their crops, and the blacks stole their tools and speared the unwary. Five struggling, increasingly hopeless years later, in 1829, they were allowed by the colonial administration to abandon the settlement.

A similar attempt at Fort Wellington failed due to the long delays in receiving news. After a poor start in 1827 under Captain Henry Smyth, Fort Wellington grew into a settlement that had some chance of success under Captain Collet Barker. Barker worked hard to regain the confidence and trust of the Aborigines and took the welfare of the men in his command seriously. The settlers gave their hearts and their health to the constant uphill struggle against the climate and the isolation, but Smyth's negative reports of the state of affairs at the distant fort caused the colonial secretary to order its abandonment in 1829. Thus the isolated settlers were quite suddenly ordered to drop their work, not just to be relieved by others, but to see all their effort come to naught.

In 1838 the British government sent HMS *Beagle* to chart a safe route through the Torres Strait and to make a closer examination of the rivers and inlets discovered by King in 1818. Darwin Harbor was named by John Lort Stokes after former shipmate Charles Darwin, who made his famous world voyage in the *Beagle* in 1831–1836. The HMS *Alligator* arrived that same year with a new load of about forty-five would-be settlers, mainly Royal Marines and a few of their wives. Christened for the young Queen Victoria, the new settlement began hopefully but succumbed to many of the ills of its forebears. The new settlers withered in the stifling heat, seeing not a single ship for fourteen months at a time and quarreling with each other over how the settlement should be run. Poor diet and low morale favored illness; the hospital was the largest building in town. Even the doctor died of fever.

Leichhardt thought he had reached civilization when he stumbled in at the end of 1845. I suspect that the long-suffering settlers, unable to compare their situation with the horrors of Leichhardt's journey, would have disagreed with him. Two years later they were able to leave for their definition of civilization when a new garrison replaced the weary survivors of the first. Within a year, more than half the newcomers died of fever or were invalided home, and in 1849 the HMS *Macander* mercifully carried off the survivors, shelling the few huts that remained to prevent their falling into the hands of the blacks. The settlement was abandoned because it proved too expensive for the home government and did not fulfill its role of helping ships because it was too far off the main routes.

A fourth attempt at colonization (1864–1867), made at the ironically named Escape Cliffs, also failed.

Think of this: the date is 1867. The world is essentially modern in many respects. The Industrial Revolution is in full swing, and Charles Darwin has shattered human complacency in divine creation by publishing *On the Origin of Species*. In the United States the Civil War is over and the nation is looking westward, building railroads and steam-powered engines. This is the age of mechanical contrivances that reduce human labor, eat up the miles of space, and project messages farther and faster than a horse can run. And yet, on an edge of land far away from the bustle and progress of the great industrial cities with their sweatshops and streetlights, a group of white settlers cannot manage to eke out the barest existence from the land. Think of that if you would begin to understand the isolation and uniqueness of this place.

I tried to imagine what drove them. Australia: hope for a new life from an England that was too crowded — spread your elbows and you'd knock established privilege or the restraints of primogeniture. Better try another land, a new-old land where the "half-wild and half-child" natives could be bent to your will. Bent or broken, it mattered not. There was an empire to be built, extending the rightness of British life across the globe until the whole planet was British dominion and the sun never set on the Empire. It was fine to take your place with the builders of that empire, to do your bit for God, queen, and country, and make your own way in the world as well. So Australia it would be. God-forsaken jungles and swamps at the bottom of the earth, but British muscle, British sweat, and British blood would pull it up to the light of day. They would work for it to make it work for them, and when the spear-studded shadows were plowed into crops and pastures, and the neat ships sailed smartly on the milky blue sea, they could write a primer for the French and the Dutch on how it was done and walk them through the fields and ports in the pride of mastery and ownership.

But it was hot there, and heavy. The blood slowed down and stagnated in their veins, and a stiff shot of rum was hardly enough to help them walk down the street upright. Collars and buttons and vests weren't made for that climate. Better to be free and easy if a Christian man must sweat like a coolie to get through a day. God, it's hot and still. No wind, no ships. For all they knew the Apocalypse had come and taken the world, and this was hell. Do the damned know when they're in hell, or is there always the fear that this is not yet the worst?

Rain like the sky had ruptured and was draining to its death. Mud everywhere, water creeping slowly up the outside walls, and mildew spreading insidious through drawers and shelves. More rum, but the sky did not lighten, and still no ships. Then came the second thoughts — perhaps India, or the Cape. And the self-doubt: am I not strong enough for empire, or is empire a pipe dream, wafting up in the smoke of home hearths?

~ ~ ~

Following the arrival of the first livestock owners in what is today the Northern Territory, the region was placed under the control of the South Australian government, which claimed the land from Adelaide to the north coast. In 1869 the port of Palmerston (renamed Darwin in 1911) was named for the British prime minister. Grandiose hopes of a prosperous colony in the tropical north sprang resiliently to life again only two years after the latest failure. Surveyor-General G. W. Goyder of South Australia spent nine months laying out plantations in 130-hectare blocks and dividing the forests and billabongs into five counties and four towns. Goyder was appropriately nicknamed "Little Energy." The counties were Palmerston, Disraeli, Malmesbury, Rosebery, and Gladstone after the parliamentary peers of England, in an attempt to set the proper imperial tone. But the prosperous population was slow to materialize.

Throughout the late nineteenth and twentieth centuries, hopeful farmers in the Territory have experimented with coffee, rubber, coconuts, sisal, tobacco, maize, indigo, and rice, but each attempt has foundered on shortage of labor, distance from markets, or sheer mismanagement. There have been government projects to settle both small-scale mixed farms and large-scale plantations, but as in the case of the euphoniously named Humpty Doo, the crops were simply too expensive to grow. Instead of a planned, ordered city springing to life on demand, Darwin grew and shrank haphazardly with the chances of fortune.

In 1870 the government began building an overland telegraph line directly south across the continent from Palmerston to Adelaide. This line, linked to the undersea cable joining Palmerston with Java and Asia, revolutionized communication between the southern Australian population centers and the rest of the world. One hundred and sixty kilometers south of Palmerston the telegraph route crossed a highly mineralized zone, and in 1871 the surveyors found gold at Pine Creek. Most of the gold was in quartz, requiring capital and machinery to mine, and it was not until mid-1872 that an expedition from Adelaide, via Darwin by sea, began to work the area. Their success was cabled along the new line, causing a rash of speculation in the Adelaide market, and a steady stream of miners began to disembark at Palmerston.

They found a port without a jetty, and a town of mangrove sapling sheds. Advised to get a hat, Holloway's ointment, quinine, a tent fly, hammock, mosquito net, revolver (for the natives), and breech-loading gun (for the game), they were so many innocents facing the climate and the hostile Aborigines. The mines followed the telegraph line, never straying more than a few kilometers. Many proved to be rich, but the miners had outrun the pastoral frontier. The high cost of shipping and the impassable weeks of the wet season brought starvation and scurvy. Stamp mills were built and companies formed, but by 1875 the field was collapsing.

In an attempt to save the mines through cheap labor, a chartered ship to Singapore returned with indentured Chinese and Malays. Paid in rice, fish, and a low cash salary, they stayed on when their contracts expired and were soon resented by white Australians who accused them of monopolizing and ruining rich goldfields. In the 1880s legal restrictions were placed on their activities, but by 1888, 3,000 Chinese were working on the new Darwin–Pine Creek railway and by 1892 Chinese owned eight of the twelve crushing batteries in the Territory. They were probably significant in tipping the balance in favor of a permanent settlement in the region.

As pearl and trepang fishery prospered, a few farms began to appear, and slowly the town of Palmerston grew. A newspaper was founded in 1873 and a hospital in the early 1880s, when the population was 700 Europeans and 4,000–5,000 Chinese. In 1884 a jetty of termite-resistant jarrah wood from West Australia was built, to be eaten out in ten years. Then in 1897 fifty centemeters of rain fell in five hours. A population perhaps growing complacent was reminded of climatic reality when a cyclone destroyed most of the buildings in town, including the governor's residence and the government records. In *Green Mountains,* Bernard O'Reilly has described "the hammer blows of a raging cyclone," when the jungle roars like an angry sea and the air is full of flying leaves. In a city the air is filled with more dangerous things than leaves, and with the 1897 cyclone the coastal settlement of northern Australia again faltered.

But it hung on. People cleaned up the cyclone debris littered across the landscape and buried their dead, and I suspect that they found a new sense of community. They rebuilt in the unfailing human optimism that one disaster forestalls future disasters, and the world slowly found a path to their doorstep. In 1919 four young Australians pioneered an air route from England to Australia, stopping at Darwin, and the world grew dramatically closer. A regular airmail service was established in 1934, and by 1938 passengers were making the trip. Roads from the south steadily improved, and the population rose to 6,000. On February 19, 1942, disaster struck in a different form when ninety-two Japanese bombers destroyed the city and killed 243 people. Surviving civilians were rushed south, and for three years Darwin was a military frontier. Uranium discoveries to the south and east in the late 1940s and early 1950s rejuvenated the area, but on Christmas Eve 1974, Cyclone Tracy nearly wiped out the city again. Darwin is nothing if not resilient.

The city center of Darwin retains a colonial charm despite being surrounded by post-1974 American-style suburbs and indoor shopping malls. Considering Darwin's repeated destruction by cyclones and bombs, it is amazing that any historic buildings remain. The Old Vic, otherwise known as the Victoria Hotel (1894), is the centerpiece of these.

A two-story structure of stone and wood, it is surrounded by an open-air pedestrian shopping mall planted with palms and large-leaved shade trees. Patrons can have a counter lunch downstairs or a drink on the second floor balcony shaded by a profusion of magenta bougainvillea blossoms.

Two streets over is the Lyons Cottage, a stone building with a corrugated metal roof that in 1925 housed an executive of the British Australian Telegraph Company. Now it contains a museum of local history featuring the pearl luggers and trepang fishers. Looking at the old photographs and personal belongings, I began to understand what it was like to live in Darwin as recently as sixty years ago. Less than a single lifetime ago, Darwin was an exotic, tropical coast with closer affinities to Asia and Indonesia than to Australia. It was an isolated outpost where white people in white clothes lived on verandas shaded by brilliant pink bougainvillea vines, drank tea, and dealt with "brown and yellow" peoples. Today the city seems well integrated, its richness enhanced by the cultural blending of cuisines, clothing, art, and music.

The day was hot and humid as I walked along the Esplanade facing the harbor. The coast was flat to the point where it melted into the haze, and the water was a bright pale blue. Boats lay at anchor, beyond them a low, green island, and beyond that . . . Indonesia. The heavy, stifling atmosphere seemed to flatten the earth itself, and I felt close to the equator.

Indonesia has played an important part in the history of the Darwin region, as told in Ernestine Hill's *The Territory* and Hector Holthouse's *Ships in the Coral.* Not long after Cook explored the eastern shores of Australia, the Malay Bugis of Macassar drifted across the Arafura Sea, perhaps blown off course by a cyclone. The Malays called the new land Mareega, the Black Man's Land, and immediately set about altering it in the manner of new arrivals. From crevices in their ships and folds in their clothes, seeds slipped out, and tamarind trees appeared along the coast. Iron utensils and weapons were carelessly lost, or spirited away by the blacks, who were quickly enamored of this new hard-yet-malleable substance. The watchful blacks, haunting the deep shadows of the monsoon forest or advancing openly across the wave-washed sands, picked up shipbuilding technology and Mohammedan customs. Malayan words entered the Aboriginal vocabularies as the two groups talked together. The Malays also left their genes, seen in the broad shoulders and high cheekbones of the seacoast tribes.

The fleets of proas made from wood, grass, and bamboo came in each year with the northwest monsoon, sixty men to a ship, thirty to sixty ships spread out along the coast, the crew living on fish, rice, dugong, turtle, and coconuts. The proas anchored off the coast, and outrigger canoes paddled in to the shore to recruit blacks to dive for trepang, also known as bêche-de-mer or sea slug. The slugs were brought to shore to be processed: cut, gutted, boiled, dried, and smoked — oceanfuls of fantastically colored and ornamented creatures were reduced to shipfuls of dull-colored, leathery cargo.

The black laborers were paid in the novelties of a distant land. Sun-bright sarongs and beads; addictive sugar and tobacco; salted fish, rice, and arrack came to the tribes from the men in the ships. And the Malays salted their leathery trepang loads with the beauties of turtle and pearl shell, and pearls for the jewels of the Orient. There were misunderstandings, though, and the Malays were always well armed. From stolen iron the blacks forged deadly spears, and in return they got venereal disease, leprosy, yaws, and smallpox.

The Malays carried the dried trepang to China, where trepang soup was a delicacy supporting a trade worth millions. By the time Australia became aware of the commercial possibilities, the proas sailed under the protection of the Dutch, and customs agents rather than wholesale takeover were required to tap into the lucrative trade. In the early 1880s Alfred Searcy took up the post of customs agent, boarding and tolling the ships he could find, probably only a tenth of those actually fishing.

In the first decade of the nineteenth century James Aickin established the trepang fishery along the northeast coast of Australia. Trepang fishers gradually worked their way north along the shore, sending the trepang back to Sydney for transshipment to Canton. The lure of quick money attracted unscrupulous adventurers and rogues to the trade, and their raids on black camps to obtain laborers and women led to small-scale warfare. As matters grew steadily more vicious, trepang boats and camps on both the east and north coasts were likely to be ambushed suddenly and all hands killed. As late as World War I, the blacks were still exacting their vengeance with raids in obscure inlets.

Yet even as the Aborigines fought back, their culture was slowly dying as the population was decimated by disease or outright hostility. This was recognized by the whites who traveled and lived among them. Traveling inland from Sydney in January 1836, Charles Darwin attributed the rapid decline of the Aborigines to the introduction of alcohol, the decimation of wild game, and above all, the effect of diseases brought by the Europeans.

The condition of the Aborigines was particularly obvious to the Irishwoman Daisy Bates, who lived with the Aborigines of the arid outback for thirty-five years in the early twentieth century. Nicknamed Kabbarli (Grandmother) by the tribe she lived with, Bates learned their language, doctored their ills, and observed and wrote of their complex social and sexual taboos, their kinship groups, initiation rites, and occasional cannibalism. Bates lived apart in her own tent, keeping the formal Edwardian dress that was fashionable when she entered the outback in 1899. She never tried to alter Aboriginal culture, but she believed that she was observing a dying people and wrote that "the Australian native can withstand all the reverses of nature, fiendish droughts and sweeping floods, horrors of thirst and enforced starvation — but he cannot withstand civilization."

When it looked as though the Aborigines would soon vanish forever, the whites began to collect Aboriginal art. In the latter part of this century the Aborigines have experienced a cultural revitalization, creating new forms of art, and today the traditional and modern art styles can be seen together at the Northern Territory Museum of the Arts and Sciences. The Aboriginal gallery there displays the arts of a people close to the land: bark paintings, ceremonial costumes of feathers and bark, batik, cloth paintings interpreting the landscape through the actions of the Dreamtime, dilly bags woven from hair or bark, coiled baskets, and carved and painted totemic figures of wood.

The brilliant colors of the ceremonial feather ornaments caught my eye, and the gaunt, stylized features of the humanistic totemic figures were arresting. The most fascinating were the abstract designs of the bark paintings. The Aborigines work in colors that are especially pleasing and relaxing: burnt golds, oranges, reds, browns, white and black highlights. In *Arts of the Dreaming,* Jennifer Isaacs explains the cultural roles of Aboriginal art. All traditional Aboriginal art is symbolic, whether geometric and abstract, or representational. The most arresting paintings are those that use patterns of dots and lines to indicate events that occurred in a particular landscape. Often these patterns represent the tracks of creatures who created the landscape and its history, and the paintings embody the artists' spiritual identity and heritage.

The right to know and to paint certain events is earned by each individual, partly on the basis of ancestry. The Aborigines believe that a child is conceived by the entry of a spirit into the mother, often at the moment her husband performs a specific act, such as spearing a kangaroo. As soon as the woman recognizes her pregnancy, the tribal elders decide the most likely place and moment when the spirit-child entered the mother, and this determines the infant's totem. There is thus a bond between an individual and the tribal territory where his spirit dwelt before it became flesh, and one purpose of the celebrated walkabouts, or journeys into the bush, is to renew this bond.

An Aboriginal artist sings the proper songs while creating a design, so that the process becomes a religious act and a means of absorbing the power of the creation ancestors. These songlines are also a means of maintaining a mental map of the landscape, in which physical features are connected to creation events. The paintings preserve the social and ritual hierarchy rather than expressing an individual worldview, as do those of Western civilization. By keeping the paintings rigidly stylized and their interpretation relatively inaccessible, only the initiated, generally the older men, can understand them and use their power.

Late in the afternoon, I started south from Darwin on the highway named in honor of John McDouall Stuart. In the popular imagination, Stuart has never quite received the fame he deserves — the fame of Leichhardt or of Burke and Wills. Perhaps it is because he does not possess the glamour of having died while exploring, or perhaps because he failed twice before he succeeded. But he did succeed, crossing the Australian continent from south to north and north to south again, and he was the first to do so who lived to tell the tale.

The history of Australian exploration is that of a series of publicly sponsored expeditions, as traced by Marcia McEwan in *Great Australian Explorers.* The expeditions were initiated by the governments and prominent citizens of the competing colonies that became the six Australian states, and were generally intended to open up more land for settlement. Like the American dreams of a Northwest Passage or a southerly westward-flowing river (the Buenaventura) to equal the Columbia, Australian exploration is the history of the slow, unwilling death of a number of geographical fancies. Chief of these was a large inland sea in central Australia. This was the sea that would irrigate the surrounding bountiful pastoral lands. The myth of the blue sea and its green pastures was the daydream of a people wrestling with increasing aridity as they pushed inland from the coastal fringe. The myth was persistent, as myths often are, and many explorers suffered and died before the myth itself was laid to rest.

Edward Eyre was the first of the white men to explore the arid interior during his 1839–1841 treks from Adelaide west along the Great Australian Bight to King George Sound. He was followed by the parties of Charles Sturt; Stuart; Robert Burke and William Wills; Warburton; Giles; Sir Augustus Charles Gregory; John and Alexander Forrest; and Leichhardt. It is sobering to read their journals and study the original maps that they produced. Each epic of suffering produced a thin band of discovered topography nearly lost in the great white blank of the unknown, and the exercise makes you appreciate aerial and satellite photography.

The last formal expedition to uncover new territory in the interior was the Royal Society of South Australia's 1939 Simpson Desert Expedition. The expedition was financed by A. A. Simpson of Adelaide, after whom expedition leader C.T. Madigan named the 145,000-square-kilometer desert that all previous explorers had avoided. Madigan was a geologist, and the scientists composing the expedition team went out to collect and record as much as to map new territory. Fortunately the twentieth-century group traveled in relative comfort and never approached the terrible sufferings of their predecessors, although Baldwin Spencer would undoubtedly have maintained that they suffered in traveling on camels. The Madigan team communicated with the rest of the world by wireless, and the Australian Broadcasting Corporation arranged three broadcasts to the nation en route, thus bringing the great age of Australian exploration to a fittingly public close.

The physical and psychological agonies of the Australian explorers make an interesting counterpoint to the history of exploration in the western United States. Although the U.S. government sponsored expeditions like those of Lewis and Clark; Pike; Fremont; and Powell, these explorers always had other pathfinders on whom to rely. The earliest Spaniards crossing through the southwestern deserts of the United States relied on the knowledge and abilities of the resident Native Americans, and subsequent explorers of the American West either worked directly with the American Indians or with the white and half-breed trappers and mountain men who lived in the region. Although the western United States has some harsh environments, it has nothing to equal the vastly monotonous arid regions of Australia. It was the scale of the Australian deserts and the lack of cooperation between explorers and

Aborigines that resulted in the much greater suffering and death among the Australian explorers as compared to their American counterparts.

Like many of the great Australian explorers, John McDouall Stuart was a surveyor. He was born in Scotland in 1815 and emigrated to Adelaide in 1838, where he began working as a private surveyor and learning the lay of the land. In 1844 he volunteered to join the expedition of Charles Sturt to explore north into the interior of the continent. The expedition moved slowly onward for two years, looking for the fabled inland seas of Australia and seeking good pastureland for their flock of sheep. Instead, they found sand deserts and stony deserts, heat so intense that it destroyed their thermometers and killed one man, scurvy, thirst, and starvation. In 1846 they were at last forced to turn back to Adelaide. Stuart returned to surveying, spending much of his time alone in the bush. It is a measure of the man's character that when he discovered a profitable copper lode in the Flinders, he disinterestedly turned it over to his employers. Periodically he made forays into the interior, looking for new pastoral lands, and knowledge of his experience spread among official circles.

In 1859 the South Australian superintendent of telegraphs, Charles Todd, decided that an overland telegraph line to the far northern coast would ensure Adelaide's position among the colonial cities. When South Australian governor Sir Richard MacDonnell offered a reward of £2,000 to the first person to successfully cross the continent, the race was on. In Melbourne, the dashing Irish-born policeman Robert Burke was chosen by the Royal Society of Victoria to lead the most ambitious and expensive expedition in Australian history. A popular movie and Peter Oliver's novel *Burke and Wills* chronicle the expedition. Seventeen men, twenty-eight camels, twenty-eight horses, and an assortment of supplies set out from Melbourne in August 1860. Burke knew that Stuart had started north in March, and his anxiety to proceed quickly exacerbated his imperious manner, leading to unfortunate decisions that later cost lives. The news that Stuart, suffering from hostile blacks, exhaustion, and lack of provisions, had returned to Adelaide never reached Burke.

Midway through the expedition, Burke chose three companions, including his second-in-command, astronomer and surveyor William Wills, to make a dash for the Gulf of Carpentaria. They left in mid-December 1860 and reached the gulf in February, traveling over desert greened by a season of good rains. Then they turned south to retrace their footsteps 1,120 kilometers back to Coopers Creek, the last food depot on their route. As food began to run out and pack animals died, scurvy and fever set in. Morale strained to the breaking point, and the men quarreled over supplies. One man died of scurvy. The others reached the depot in mid-April, barely alive.

At the depot, they found a small cache of food and a note on a tree. A few months before, they had camped here with their entire party, young, healthy, high-spirited, and ambitious, the world and the fame of their accomplishments all before them. Now, broken in spirit and health, they read the note informing them that through a series of errors and misfortunes, many of the original party had died of scurvy, and the rest had assumed the leaders dead. The rearguard had departed nine-and-a-half hours before Burke and Wills arrived. Exhausted and still starving, Burke and Wills gave up. When friendly blacks tried to bring them food, the delirious explorers drove them away with weapons. Burke and Wills died at the end of June 1861; only one man of the original four barely survived with the help of the blacks until a search party rescued him three months later.

Meanwhile, Stuart, with two companions and a few packhorses, had reached Tennant Creek before being forced back by hostile blacks in April 1860. Scurvy and sun blindness tormented his party, but they reached the South Australian settlements by August 1860. Their tremendous success in having gone beyond the geographic center of Australia on the slim finances of an expedition privately backed by Stuart's employers inspired the public and the South Australian government. A government grant of £2,500, twelve men, and forty-nine horses, and Stuart was again on his way on January 1, 1861.

Two thousand, two hundred and fifty-three kilometers back to Attack Creek, another 240 kilometers on to Newcastle Waters. Each of those kilometers on foot or on horseback, each kilometer a decision on the spot, for there were no maps or native guides. So far and so hard, only 700 kilometers from present-day Darwin. But his men and horses were failing, and the supplies were just sufficient to make it back. Stuart knew that Burke and Wills were in the field, and he knew that to turn back would lose him the glory and the money, but his men were more important to him, so he turned back. He never lost a single man in all his years of exploring. Stuart never underestimated the rigors of the country he planned to traverse, and he came to know that country as did few other explorers: "Other deserts there are on the earth's surface," he wrote in his journal, "but they present not the steel-shod surface of this. The deathlike stillness of these solitudes is frightful and oppressive. We have not seen a living creature, either beast or bird, only the mirage, bright and continuous."

Back in Adelaide in September 1861, Stuart learned of the disappearance of Burke and Wills. When the search parties recovered the dead explorers' journals, Stuart knew that he had lost the race to reach the north coast by an overland route. But there was still no practical overland telegraph route, and in December 1861 he set off again with government support for his third attempt. Carefully and methodically moving his expedition from water supply to water supply, on July 24, 1862, he waded into the sea at Van Diemen's Gulf and washed his face in the salty water. I can only imagine his emotions at that moment, but there is a poignant line from a similar experience in the journals of Lewis and Clark: "Ocian [*sic*] in view! O! the joy."

The other members of the party carried Stuart into Adelaide on a stretcher in December 1862, almost blind, weak with scurvy, his exploring days over. Awarded £2,000, he returned to Britain and died in 1866, white-haired and broken in health at the age of fifty-one. I suspect that the look of Van Diemen's Gulf was in his mind's eye at the last.

The two-lane paved road now running north-south across Australia from Darwin to Adelaide is Stuart's monument. For a route with so short a written history, it is nevertheless rich in the memories of human experiences. Following the road south, I stopped briefly at Mataranka near the site of Jeannie Gunn's Elsey Homestead. Sometimes in a life everything comes together and you understand why you have long been preparing for what is. At the age of thirty-one, newly married Jeannie Gunn joined her husband, Aeneas, at the remote Elsey Homestead, leaving far behind the familiar world of Melbourne. They lived at Elsey for only a year before Aeneas died suddenly of fever, but that year was the flowering of Jeannie's life. Secure in the love of a man she loved, she reached out delightedly to the new people and new land of the Territory, and her delight sparkles across every page of her book *We of the Never-Never*.

A replica of the homestead used in filming the novel stands at Mataranka, containing a small museum on turn-of-the-century life in the Territory. I saw the movie while in Australia — a humorous, touching, well-crafted film, with a heavier touch of realism than the book. Standing at the old homestead site, I remembered some of the scenes from the book and tried to recreate in my imagination how it must have looked when

Jeannie Gunn came to it as a newlywed. A year of adventures and new experiences later, she buried her beloved husband there and left forever the Territory she had worked so hard to know and love. Now only a few graves remain in a grassy clearing in the forest, and if I had not read her book, I would have had no hint of the passionate lives lived out here.

How fortunate that Jeannie Gunn wrote of her experiences, but what of all the other lives that remain untold? Perhaps Australian writers not yet born will follow naturalist Donald Culross Peattie's example and "claim the poet's right to say he knows what they think and feel who are too headlong in life to make a song of it." Antoine de Saint-Exupéry wrote of the human skull as a treasure chest storing all the treasures of experience and emotion contained in the mind and memory. Each time an individual dies unrecorded, all of humanity loses the treasures of that chest.

Onward along the highway, I left the domain of caravan parks, left the domain of conveniences of any sort but for the occasional small town sprouted beside the road. I filled up my water bottles and had a wash in the public restrooms of these small towns, hoarding my water when I pulled off the road to camp at night. Lunches were eaten quickly, for when I opened the door for relief from the heat, the car was immediately invaded by flies. The trees thinned out and grew shorter as the land grew more broadly open, and I ran out of the range of Darwin's one radio station. I sang a good many of the songs I knew as I drove along through the monotonous landscape, but I began to doubt that I knew enough to get me to Ayers Rock and back. A single utility line of termite-discouraging metal poles ran beside the road. Large lizards crossed the track, and the soil grew more orange. I outran the mosquitoes, and the nights grew cool and pleasant, with little traffic on the road to disturb my sleep.

The Stuart Highway is two narrow, fairly bumpy, shoulderless lanes, but it is straight and level and does not require excessive concentration. Driving on that way, the movement itself became a purpose outside of any place toward which I was moving, and I had to force myself to stop occasionally. I stopped at the marker indicating Attack Creek, where Stuart's first expedition had to turn back. Getting out of the car, I promptly swallowed a fly, as Stuart undoubtedly did more than once.

The people who live in the outback stations each have their own ways of coping with the isolation of the desert spaces. I briefly met the families at two of these stations and saw the contrasts inherent in that life. "Frog" and Marcie run a station where the loose white sands of the channels glare like the Sahara, and midday can be stinking hot. Frog is a short, fat man, kind, but blunt and coarse. Marcie is tall and well-spoken, with a vaguely patrician air. Together they have built a new, temporary-looking homestead of a metal shed kitchen and house trailer surrounded by green trees and a lawn patrolled by geese. A satellite dish brings them news of the world, and their eight- and ten-year-old boys attend the School of the Air (broadcast by radio) and receive an organized trip to the south each year. The boys were polite and well behaved, but the older one is so ill at ease away from home that he vomits whenever he has to leave home and come in contact with other people.

Marcie talked of the station owners' worries and resentments toward the "Abs." The whites wear themselves out trying to make a go of it in a country where it is too dry, too wet, on fire, flooding in a cyclone — always something. Then they stand by in impotent anger while the government builds the Aborigines stations and community houses and facilities ("that's where all our tax dollars go"), which the Aborigines proceed to trash. The Aborigines announce that a site is sacred to them, and the hair of the white station owners curls in horror as a long-established white station has to "shift." It was rather like talking to someone under siege.

A couple of hundred kilometers farther on, Piet and Margaret have been running their station for twenty years. Piet built a house ideal for the climate: a single large, high-ceilinged room divided by three-quarter walls, with numerous large windows and screen doors, and shaded on all sides by a wide, screened veranda bordered by another open veranda. It is a home of gradual transitions built into, rather than on, its surroundings. And it was to me an ideal house, full of rustic wooden furniture and hundreds of good books. Piet came here from America and Margaret from Melbourne, and together they have made it a good place to live a life, raising children equally at ease in the saddle or curled up with a book.

I continued south, the wheels of the car revolving endlessly beneath me. I imagined the wheels unrolling a broad swath stretching to either side of me as far as I could see — the map of my mental consciousness. Before me lay terra incognita, haunted by the uncertain visions of my imagination, like the sea monsters lurking in the corners of the maps drawn by Europeans when they were just venturing out toward the new worlds. Behind me lay at least a slim strip of known images, the memory of terrain actually seen. As I later repassed the same terrain, returning north, I saw it in a slightly different light. Now my memory blends the two images into a composite map from which I draw individual scenes, like the multilayered overlays of Geographic Information Systems. These computer programs create a three-dimensional image of a terrain that can be called up with different characteristics highlighted. Even so does the human brain, the prototype computer, blend impressions of sounds and smells, different lights of day and weather, into a kaleidoscopic image of the complexity of the world.

The Aborigines keep a knowledge of their far-flung country through songlines. I imagine them, countless generations, chanting their paths along the vast, dry interior, from water hole to water hole. Singing a route across the landscape, singing for their supper. The songlines are a concentrated essence of the landscape, a mental map rendered down to narrow corridors through a land unforgiving of mistakes. All maps are such renderings — concentrations of the features deemed most important for travel and survival.

I once got lost in Australia because my informant and I focused on different features of the landscape. He drew me a "mud map," a sketch of the roads and gates etched across the station lands. I got lost trying to follow the roads from here — the station — to there — a canyon scores of kilometers away. He had misdrawn one turning on the map, and I was helpless. Could I have driven directly from the station to the canyon on a compass bearing, it would have been a simple matter, but I was confined to the tracks.

We lay out tracks in seemingly arbitrary ways. Often a historic purpose underpins a given route, but we continue to guide subsequent tracks along the original long after the purpose is gone. Game trail leads to wagon track, wagon track to graded dirt road, and then on to superhighway, so that we walk in the steps of our ancestors. These tracks, in turn, largely control our perception of landscape, for we seldom leave them. It is comforting to follow something linear, whether it be a river, a ridge crest, or a road. It gives a sense of purpose and accomplishment.

But if we have no knowledge of landscape beyond the track, we are lost when we lose or misread the track. I got lost on the Australian station because I had no compass, and the mud map included no topographic features by which to orient myself. As a geologist, I have been taught to orient myself by landforms or compass directions, and I now view the world within these confines of space and form. Yet it was not always that way.

When I remember the city I grew up in, my memories contain no reference to north. I dwelt in an isolated domain free of mathematical scale and magnetic direction, the underpinnings of maps. I had not yet learned to read maps, and my perceptions were not oriented in their terms. I had firm mental images of place, but the web extended unbroken only to those places within walking distance of home. If we had to drive to get there, a strand frail to breaking connected the outlier to the rest of my knowledge. The strand might be bolstered by landmarks like the steep hill and the tall apartments on the way to my father's office, but the route itself had only vague associations with street names.

Firmly anchored at the center of the web was our home. Close by and well connected were school, the corner candy store, the ice skating pond, the sluggish creek. The center of existence always occupies the center of our maps; it is our known starting point. The oldest surviving map of the whole earth is a Babylonian carved clay tablet from 1,000 B.C. On it, the world is a disk with Babylonia at the center. Centrist notions were still dying hard more than 2,500 years later, and Copernicus was long resented for unbalancing the geocentric universe.

Our maps are revealing for what they leave out, as well as what they include. We need ordered images of the world, and where the complexity outside our minds is overwhelming, we ignore it, substituting a dream of our own making. Study the art that was produced by the early explorers. Their maps inevitably concentrate on neatly laid out colonies that, at the moment of drawing, exist solely in the mind of the artist. These maps are their blueprints for the future, not a record of the landscape confronting them.

As a child I, too, used blueprints as a way of ordering my dreams and giving them tangible form. Tucked away in a drawer, I have a folder fat with laborious plan-view drawings of houses, libraries, museums, universities, shopping centers, whole communities — all the ideal worlds I planned someday to create. As an adult I continue to simplify, going about my city with a neatly ordered grid in my head. Sharp and clear are the streets I travel regularly between home and work, so that I follow them by rote, preoccupied with my thoughts. The streets are hard, geometric lines superimposed on the more subtle lineaments of the landscape of old river terraces and winding channels. If I think carefully, the two levels fuse in a composite map. Above my head is another dimension, where the restless geese fly each spring and fall. Long skeins of geese wind and unwind across the storm-gray skies, and I wonder about the maps they carry in their memories.

I have only recently come to the American city in which I now live, and each journey outward is like a plant sending out surface runners. All around me lies terra incognita, haunted by the uncertain visions of my imagination, like those sea monsters of the early maps. With each journey I take hold of a new strip of country and bind it into the system of the known. Blending impressions of sounds and smells, different lights of day and weather, I build a firm base held by the crisscrossing levels of memory and experience. This is sense of place, and the basis of mapmaking.

I often think about maps, because so much of what I do involves measurement. To explain features or processes, you must first describe them. In science the description must be precise and reproducible to be accepted, and this requires measurement. How does slope angle correlate with landslide size? Are the pools along a gravelly stream channel equally spaced? Do these dunes all have the same alignment with respect to the prevailing wind? Maps are a tool of measurement and description. At the broadest level, topographic maps already in existence highlight features of interest. Notice the low, irregular mounds aligned parallel over this broad plain — relict dunes. At progressively finer levels of detail, maps are drawn to delineate a feature. This is a means of sorting data that have not yet been perceived as a pattern, in order to search for the patterns as clues to understanding. You cannot understand what you cannot see; you must first perceive pattern, order, predictability. Here the visual nature of maps is crucial. What appears an impenetrable thicket as a cluster of numbers, suddenly resolves itself into a flight of marine terraces when the numbers are plotted by location. It becomes important to see maps not merely as planar objects, but as representations of three-dimensional geometries. You learn to look beyond the map for clues to the nature of what it represents.

And this closes the circle of understanding, for maps represent both an external reality and the mapmaker's perception of that reality. For the Aborigines following their songlines, time and distance are inseparable. They reckon distance between two water holes as the number of days' walk to travel between. Their drawn maps are water holes connected by lines of travel, and their language reflects their preoccupations. As explained by Pat Lowe and Jimmy Pike in *Jilji,* the nomadic Walmajarri of the central desert have more than a dozen words for each cardinal point of the compass, differentiating far south and near south, for example.

I eventually located myself on that deserted Australian station by relying on the perception of landscape with which I am most comfortable. I pulled out my topographic maps, which did not include tracks but which showed the range before me. Studying the range on the map and the range in front of me, I matched the notches and spires until I found myself. Then, secure in the knowledge of topography, I continued on to my destination.

There are no speed limits and certainly no police on those stretches of the Stuart Highway, and in a fairly short time I extended my mental map to Alice Springs, 1,500 kilometers from Darwin and just above the Tropic of Capricorn. Through the Tanami Desert, where the water-saving stratagems of the plants recalled the Sonoran desert; past Central Mt. Sturt, geographic center of the continent; beyond the tropic, and into the low, rocky hills culminating in the rampart of the MacDonnell Range seemingly stretched across the girth of the continent.

The town of Alice Springs lies at the base of the range, where the dust-dry bed of the Todd River cuts a gap through the towering rock. I stopped only briefly in the town for petrol before seeking a camping place beyond. The night was just cool enough to make snuggling into my sleeping bag comfortable, and I thought back over the day's long drive. I was beginning to truly appreciate Stuart's feat in crossing the continent from south to north and back on foot. I thought of the vast, unpopulated spaces that I had traveled through, but in my mind's eye they refused to transform themselves into populous cities of the future; it seems I am not an empire builder.

The heat of the day had vanished with the setting of the sun, and the cool night air was smooth as silk. Lying on my back on the stony desert floor, I saw the stars clearly for the first time in months. Each point of light came from one of a multitude of sharply defined sources massed together without blending, and the song of the crickets rang out crisp and staccato in the still air. My skin felt cleanly smooth and supple, no longer the clammy, suffocating envelope of the monsoonal regions. I could sense the uncluttered space around me in the darkness, and the ease and grace of space.

I woke to a cloudy sky the next morning and continued on to Ayers Rock, south past Alice another 200 kilometers, then west at Erldunda past a camel farm, relic of the pre-automobile days. Spencer traveled by camel on the 1894 Horn Expedition and reserved some of his choicest descriptions for "these uncouth, malodorous beasts" that chew "their filthy cud, which they have a habit of spluttering about if you go near them, watching you all the time with evident contempt and dislike." "For filthiness, viciousness and crass stupidity it would be impossible to beat [a camel]."

The rust red land rolled grandly on in broad, low buttes and mesas where the desert-pale plants could hardly gain a roothold. Low, stabilized dunes collected by winds now stilled appeared beside the road, and the colors of the landscape leapt into life under the returning sunlight. Ayers Rock gradually stood out from the horizon, followed by the low bulbs of the Olgas to the west.

The Olgas and Ayers Rock are opposite limbs of an anticline, two abrupt masses of rock twenty-two kilometers apart in a flat sand sea stretching to the horizons. Both are of red-orange arkosic sandstone and conglomerate weathering into pock-marked knobs and humps. As is frequently the case, the Aboriginal name for the Olgas is a more poetic reflection of their appearance. The Aborigines call these rounded knobs rising from the plain Katatjuta, or Many Heads. The prosaic European name was given to them by the explorer Ernest Giles in 1873 to honor the queen of Spain.

From a distance the many heads present a united front, but a closer approach reveals the broad, green-brushed swales that divide them. A few stunted trees grow in these swales, but mostly the landscape supports only shrubs like spinifex growing in compact little clumps like immobile echidnas, most noticeable when you brush painfully against them.

I drove to the Olgas first and climbed up to Katatjuta Lookout. Walking along the windswept top of Katatjuta, I held on to my hat and exulted in the clean, bright desert. For 360 degrees I looked down on the vast, red, sandy land spreading to the horizons, with only the occasional punctuation of a low mountain range. People below me in Windy Valley were small, white specks against the red rocks, and across the plain the alien-looking mass of Ayers Rock, seeming to melt beneath the desert sun, could have been dropped from outer space.

Ayers Rock, the Olgas, and the surrounding desert make up Uluru National Park, dedicated in 1958. Development in the park has largely been confined to the Yulara Tourist Resort, a 50-hectare compound containing the national park visitor center, accommodations, shops, and restaurants. After setting up camp and exploring the resort, I drove out late in the afternoon to Sunset Strip, a vantage point for Ayers Rock and the Olgas. The Rock reflects the moods and hours of the day, its opaque, granular surface miraculously transforming the ambience of the surrounding light and air into a vast mass of color. At midday the Rock stands pale and bleached beneath the direct rays of the sun. As shadows pool on the ground and the sun sets, the slanting rays fire the Rock from orange to red. At the last, the Rock glows a subdued maroon as powder blue twilight settles over the desert, and the Olgas stand black against the fiery western sky. Each day before sunrise the cycle begins anew with the Rock pale brown in the early morning light and the Olgas glowing maroon against a sky purple-blue with clouds or serene with the promise of clarity and heat.

As the color of the Rock changes with time, so the texture changes with distance. What is a single, solid lump of rock from afar resolves into striated humps at a few kilometers. Then the long parallel grooves running down its sides become visible, conjuring up a Dreamtime image of a giant running his fingernails over the surface. Orange-and-gray mottles appear at closer quarters, and the rock surface is suddenly full of motion, with flutes and grooves swirling across and tunneling through it.

It is a landscape in which to believe in magic. As Spencer wrote, "The Arunta [member of an inland tribe] lives in an age of magic. Everything that is of importance to him in life, whether it counts for pleasure or discomfort, for good or for evil, is a matter of magic." Traveling across the inland early in this century, Englishman E. L. Grant Watson wrote of "the subtle yet penetrating psychic aura of the Australian tribesmen": "I entered the bush with a rationalistic, scientific bias. I thought magic to be a kind of infantile make-believe. . . . [and] I witnessed daily the power of magic. . . . I came to believe in it."

As I began to climb the Rock, my footsteps rang hollowly on the surface flaking off in plate-sized pieces like rusty iron. I toed my way up the steep lower slopes, the friction of the rough surface providing secure footholds. Then the grade decreased and I followed a white path undulating across a badlands petrified in stone, suspended in air 400 meters above the red desert. Extremely windy at the top, rain hanging in the distance, and the top itself a world apart. Even under dark clouds, the Rock glowed with a rich orange color, and emerald green pools filled the occasional small hollows in its surface. The flat red desert sands with their sparse olive green vegetation stretched away in every direction to the rims of the world, where tiny, distant mountain ranges cropped up. A few other high points stood alone in the midst of the flatness, dark silhouettes against the coming rain. I descended again, reaching the base of the rock just as the rain came. As I sat in the car waiting out the storm, the look of the rain hanging from the clouds over the sulky blue distance was familiar.

Baldwin Spencer camped at the base of Ayers Rock during his travels with the Horn Expedition:

> It was truly a wild scene. Our fires lighted up the rocks that hemmed in the chasm in which we were camped and shone on the bodies of the natives. As we rolled our rugs around us on the hard ground and watched the stars shining down through the cleft in the great Rock, we realised that we had been carried far back into the early history of mankind and that we had enjoyed an experience such as now falls to the lot of few white men. We had actually seen, in their primitive state, entirely uncontaminated by contact with civilisation, men and women still living in the Stone Age.

When the Rock again glowed orange in the sunlight stealing down through a storm-dark sky, I set off on a tour of circumnavigation. Ecologists have designated four basic habitat types in the park, and I glimpsed each of them as I followed the winding base of the Rock. Above me was the Rock itself, pitted by water and wind swept along in the flow of time. Furtive creatures sheltered in the caves and crevices of the Rock — bats and reptiles, small marsupials and birds. Down the slope from them the whittlings of the Rock formed debris piles that caught the dust and sand forever blowing by and soaked up the water of the brief rains. Acacias sprout from these tenuous footholds, as do fig trees with vines, and less conspicuous shrubs and grasses. Where there are plants, animals come to feed on them, and the debris piles echo to the thumping bounds of the euros, or hill kangaroos.

Out on the plains beyond the Rock the occasional rains come hard and fast, and the tight-gripped desert soil never opens fast enough to soak up the sudden abundance of water. So there is drought, and then a flood, and then drought again, and the bloodwood and mulga each follow their own strategy of waiting out the dry times. The blood red dunes, for all their look of harsh aridity, carry the richest flora. Desert oaks and mulga shadow ground-hugging flowers, and spinifex bristles beneath grevilleas and myrtles. The sands are delicately tracked by a thousand small feet

The base of Ayers Rock, showing some of the unique erosional features
attributed to the activities of dreamtime ancestors by the Aborigines; people at
the lower middle left for scale.

creeping or skipping through the night and by the prints and trails of their
hunters. A multitude of life, if you but know how to look for it.

The runoff from the recent rains had concentrated at the base of the
Rock, and low-growing shrubs were flowering in spring colors of yellow
and white, pink, blue, and purple. Desert varnish streaked the sides of the
Rock black, and cavernous weathering pitted them with alcoves. A few
Aboriginal paintings were visible, although most of the sacred sites
around the base of the Rock are closed to visitors. Many of these are
women's sites, which men are forbidden to enter.

The recognition of Aboriginal women's sacred sites represents an
encouraging reversal of a century of misinterpretation of Aboriginal
culture, as explained by Diane Bell in *Daughters of the Dreaming.* In
traditional Aboriginal society, men and women had separate physical
tasks and ritual responsibilities that involved upholding the law and
performing initiations and the Dreamtime rituals that cared for the land.
Both sexes had knowledge, power, and respect, but the balance was upset
by the imposition of white cultural values. The Victorian anthropologists

and officials who came in contact with the Aborigines assumed that Aboriginal women were subservient and that Aboriginal men could be considered adequate tribal representatives. Thus, in their dealings with the Aborigines, white male officials consulted only tribal males. The process was further complicated by the structure of Aboriginal society, which permitted Aboriginal women to talk only to white females.

Aboriginal women's positions were also undermined by the replacement of gathering, in which women provided a large percentage of the group's food, with rations given to male "heads of family" by white officials. Movement from traditional land, where women were looked to as judges and arbiters due to their knowledge of traditions, to settlements, where women's land-derived religious power was gone, further weakened the women. The Aboriginal women's traditional role as nurturer has been overshadowed by the advent of white schools, hospitals, and doctors.

The important role played by women in Aboriginal society has only recently been recognized as female anthropologists have begun field research. Traditional Aboriginal life provides a large supportive social network for the individual, and men and women often live separately in groups of their own sex, making it difficult for outside observers of either sex to adequately understand the role of both sexes. Aboriginal society emphasizes the group rather than the individual. An individual's prestige derives from an ability to maintain the rituals and traditions of community knowledge rather than from personal creativity, and people are defined by their relation to the land rather than by personality traits or actions. An individual's association with various places is determined by birth, ancestry, and relations and by his or her knowledge of oral history as preserved in songs. When an individual dies, his or her songs about an area become taboo, but someone else may re-dream the songs and change some of the names and thus become associated with that country. The recognition by whites of Aboriginal women's sacred sites is thus also a recognition of the importance of women in the traditional structure of Aboriginal society.

Ayers Rock as a whole is sacred to the Pitjantjatara tribe (who call themselves the Anangu), which leases the land to the park service and participates in management decisions. The Pitjantjatara people have stories to explain all of the features of the Rock, features that were created by various ancestral figures during the Tjukurpa, or Dreamtime. The Rock itself was made during the play of two young boys at the time of the creation and then used and remade through the actions of other Tjukurpa creatures. For example, there were the snakes. The Kuniya (carpet snakes) and Liru (poisonous snake species) traveled over the land from different directions. They met at the Rock and fought, marking the landscape in their struggles, and the Kuniya are still inside the rock today. The Mala (hare wallaby) people passed by, too. They arrived from the north and scampered across the bumps and ridges of the Rock until Kurpanngu (a devil dingo) arrived stealthily from the west and pursued the Mala southward. Today these sites at Uluru are points on a number of intersecting Tjukurpa journeys whose tracks link the Pitjantjataras of the area to others living hundreds of kilometers away.

In my solitary hike around the Rock, I came to understand its choice as a sacred site. The Rock dominates the landscape from a distance, a lone island in the sand sea. At close range the sheer mass of its bulk inspires awe. With the sensuously rounded, nearly vertical walls climbing beside me in a pulsating orange toward the cool blue sky, I felt the power of the Rock. It was only a small step to recognize life in that power: whether you come to the landscape from the perspective of twentieth-century science or tenth-century mysticism, the Rock records the events of history, and you must interpret your own existence in the context of those events.

I began the return journey to Alice late in the afternoon, camping beside the road. The next morning came in cold and clear, with a lyrical bird calling over and over again as the morning stars faded. After stopping briefly for petrol in Alice, I turned west to Spencer's Larapinta Land and H. H. Finlayson's Luritja Country — the MacDonnell Range named for South Australian governor Sir Richard MacDonnell. The range is a structural geologist's paradise of folded and faulted sandstone, quartzite, breccia, and granite, with strata dipping and plunging in every direction. Like Uluru, the reddish orange rocks dominate the landscape, glowing fiercely at sunset.

Simpson's Gap, Standley Chasm, Glen Helen Gorge, Ormiston Gorge: the MacDonnells are cut by a series of deep, narrow, sheer-walled water gaps, like so many knife gashes. As you approach the range from the surrounding valley, there is often little hint of these sudden cuts. Trails wind through scrub of wattles, mulga, and corkwoods. Near the dry, sandy river courses, bright-leaved ghost gums stand tall, spreading their massive white branches above the twisted, mottled red trunks of the river red gums lining the channel. Then the rivers abruptly squeeze into the rock, and the trails follow them from the open brightness into silent, shadowed ways where footfalls echo slightly. Here rugged rock walls rise straight from cool-shaded beds nurturing red gums and MacDonnell Range cycads. Small rock wallabies leap agilely about the cliffs high above. At high noon the sunlight careens down the long walls to the innermost depths of the canyon, until the air itself vibrates with the fiery red pulsating out between sun and rock.

Coming out of the rock-girt canyons, drowsy with heat and sunlight late in the day, I found the air heavy with the scent of flowers blooming at the base of the slopes. It had obviously rained recently, and everything was blooming in the yellow exuberance of the desert after a deluge. Ground, shrubs, and trees looked as if they had received a rain of pollen dust.

The region was first explored by Englishman Ernest Giles in the course of three expeditions searching for a route to the western coast during the years 1872–1876. Giles was financed by the German botanist Baron von Mueller, curator of the Melbourne Botanic Gardens, and many of the place-names Giles bestowed on central Australia reflect a strong Teutonic influence. Retracing Giles's tracks fifty years later, H. H. Finlayson wrote: "To read Giles's simple account of those terrible rides into the unknown on dying horses, with an unrelieved diet of dried horse for weeks at a time, with the waters behind dried out and those ahead still to find, is to marvel at the character and strength of the motive which could hold a man constant in such a course."

Giles's connections with Victoria prompted the South Australian government to equip explorers of its own, rather like the Burke-Wills versus Stuart contest. Colonel Peter Edgerton Warburton, South Australian commissioner of police, headed northwest from Alice Springs in April 1873 and reached the coast eight months later. William Gosse of the South Australian Surveyor-General's Department chose a more southerly route, and although he did not reach the coast, he explored the Olgas and discovered and named Ayers Rock.

I camped at Trephina Gorge in the western MacDonnells and walked off a slight restless loneliness toward evening as the birds were singing their vespers. The eastern wall of the gorge glowed in the light of the sinking sun, the trunks of the ghost gums growing in the gorge's crags forming a fine network of white tracings against the rock.

I settled in for the usual solitary evening back at camp, lost in a book peered at in the dim interior light of the car. Solitude had become habitual, and a social caller an unwelcome interruption. But there was another solitary traveler at the car door, a slender, wistful young man inviting me for tea, tea in the Queensland sense — early evening meal — not a "cuppa." In my solitude I had fallen into careless habits, like peanut butter and jelly sandwiches for supper. He cooked a splendid meal of tinned beef, boiled potatoes, brussels sprouts, and bread, with tea as beverage. The trunk of his car was methodically arranged, with quantities of food and camping gear carefully sorted. It was an old sedan, sagging a little, paint fading after many miles.

We sat in lawn chairs, and I watched the evening wind ruffle his fine hair. He perched in his chair like a bird, thin limbs sheltered from the cool air in turtleneck and corduroys, and as I savored the food, he talked with the eagerness of one who has found few kindred spirits. He had been a telephone company technician for ten years and was a native son of Brisbane, Queensland, on a three-month holiday tour of Queensland and the Territory. His talk amazed me, not in the facts of his life, but in the thoughts behind them. From nowhere appeared a conversationalist at ease with topics ranging from existentialist philosophy to Australian and American national characteristics.

With a fluent eloquence, he lay before me thoughts matured slowly and carefully, and I heard in them a resonance of my own thoughts. He discussed Donald Horne's 1964 book *The Lucky Country,* in which Horne writes of the Aussie mistrust of ideas and achievers and the Aussie emphasis on mateship and sport, whereas Americans emphasize creativity, individual expression, and achievement. My new friend speculated that Australians lack a national identity. Americans sense the forward movement, power of the future, great deeds under presidents who lead the world, manifest destiny. The English have their past, a solid historical tradition supporting their existence. But the Australians struggle in a void, strive for pleasure, mistrust ideas.

The sun set, and the night was cool and windy. He talked on and on, quietly, earnestly. His great ambition was to write a philosophical novel or play, and he gave me Sartre's *The Age of Reason,* which I later read and found too negative and tired by the heaviness of life. I questioned the stimulation of his job, and he spoke of a need to work with his hands. I, too, felt the need, satisfied in hobbies of woodworking and quilting. We exchanged addresses, and I finally left. But I was troubled by him, and I lay awake long that night. He was too hungry — half-starved. Someone so lonely can stifle.

The night was just pleasantly cool, and all the birds began singing lustily while the last stars were still visible. After breakfast I went back to Alice and made a day of it. Darwin and Alice Springs are the only cities in the Territory, places like Jabiru, Katherine, and Tennant Creek being towns, and the others just making settlement status. Although slightly infamous for its dives and down-and-out Aborigines living along the dry course of the Todd River, Alice is one of the major tourist rendezvous of the Center and has a couple of pleasant streets of shops and cafes, an art gallery, and a museum devoted to the overland telegraph.

The general bustle and color of the streets were alluring, and I could see why a swagman, a ringer (cowboy), or any bushie would be attracted to the town and go on a binge after a long sojourn in the outback. Alice was a "bonza town" of about 20,000 people, mainly government employees and tourists. The residential sections were very modern, with suburban lawns surrounding brick or stucco ranch-style houses built temperate-style on the ground. Where the sandy course of the gum-shaded Todd River winds through Heavitree Gap, the residents hold the annual Henley-on-Todd Regatta, famous as a boat race run on a dry river.

My first stop was the museum at the old Overland Telegraph station north of town. It was situated beside a spring named Alice, after the wife of Sir Charles Todd, for whom the Todd River was named. In 1855 Charles Todd, a Londoner who had been a student of astronomy at Cambridge, came to Australia and took up the post of government astronomer and superintendent of telegraphs for the colony of South Australia. Todd's deeds in Australia are vividly recounted by historian Ernestine Hill in her panoramic account *The Territory*. Todd opened the first South Australian telegraph line in 1856, providing the prototype for the telegraph lines that were soon to link the major Australian towns and change the nature of development in them.

In the 1860s Australia was still isolated from the rest of the world, and news entering by ship was two months old when it arrived. The first port of call was often Adelaide, South Australia, from which news was telegraphed to Melbourne and Sydney, providing South Australia with a rich revenue from transit charges. With the development of undersea cables, a proposal to lay a cable from India to Singapore to Java to Brisbane in Queensland threatened to destroy this revenue, and in 1859 Todd proposed a transcontinental telegraph line from Adelaide to Darwin that could link up with Java via undersea cables. But the continent had not yet been crossed from north to south, and the stage was set for the explorations of Stuart and of Burke and Wills.

Following Stuart's successful crossing of the continent in 1862, the way was open for construction of the telegraph line. Jurisdiction over what is now the Northern Territory was transferred in 1863 by royal decree from New South Wales to South Australia, which retained control of the Territory until 1911, when it passed to the Commonwealth. The telegraph line was completed in 1872 after eighteen months of feverish work. Todd divided the work into three sections, subcontracted the north and south sections, and superintended the more difficult central section himself. Twelve repeating stations about 300 kilometers apart were planned, and 3,000 kilometers of iron wire and 36,000 insulator poles were ordered. According to Ernestine Hill, two questions were asked of prospective laborers on the line: "Are you sound in mind and limb?" and "Can you live on bandicoot and goanna?" Hill noted that "wages were 25 shillings a week and 'found'. If you were lost you ate what you found till you were found, if you were found."

Bully beef, the famous Australian tinned beef, was invented to keep 500 hungry men alive, and for almost two years it was bully beef for breakfast, dinner, and tea. The first into the interior found their way by prismatic compass and a tracing of Stuart's map, and they lived on flour, tea, jerked beef, and an occasional crow. Behind them came the construction gangs of 200 men, 800 horses, 200 bullocks, stores, express wagons, and drays. Caravans of 100 camels led by Arab and Afghan drivers carried poles and gear. It must have been a pageant and a spectacle equal to the greatest Hollywood extravaganzas. Imagine men of a score of nationalities, each clothed in their own costumes and cursing in their own idioms, pursuing the destiny of a continent through what the Aborigines termed a "singing string," the telegraph line.

They struggled mightily, and I suspect that they celebrated mightily when they succeeded. Wagons stuck in sand or floated away in flash floods. The party on the northern section was ruined by a Wet that bogged wagons, drowned horses, and washed telegraph poles out of their holes. I can picture a telegraph party that had endured through the long dry heat of winter only to be stranded on a hilltop island by the rising waters of summer. In the spring, fever struck camps equipped with a medicine chest of Holloway's pills, boracic, eye lotion, and castor oil. In other areas wells could not reach water, and pack animals died of thirst. The

Aborigines were terrified by the Singing String and killed workers when they found them alone.

Early in 1872 Ralph Milner, the first drover to successfully make the journey from south to north, reached the workers with 4,000 sheep, having lost 3,000 sheep and some of their drovers along the way. By autumn (March) the skies cleared after the storms of the Wet, and Todd battled on. On June 26, 1872, the first message was relayed with the help of a horseback messenger to bridge the remaining 500-kilometer gap, and on August 23 the line linking Australia to the world was completed. Shiploads of bearded workers arrived in Adelaide to draw two years' worth of pay and celebrate the biggest "knockdown night" in Australian history. Todd became Sir Charles.

Until 1930 the Overland Telegraph was Australia's lifeline to the news of the world, and the guiding track across the outback. Miners, cattlemen, and explorers followed it. Travelers perishing of hunger and thirst shot the insulators and severed the line to alert rescuers to their location. Alice Springs, Tennant Creek, Katherine, and Daly Waters grew up along the line, but it was a continual struggle. Perhaps, like Robert Frost's wall, there is something that doesn't like a straight line in the landscape.

Termites ate the telegraph poles, and Aborigines stole the glass insulators to make spearheads to kill the telegraphists in their lonely repeating stations. The wire rusted and snapped. Imagine all the bad things that could happen to a thin, wire line stretched vulnerably along the breadth of a continent. Cyclones blew the line down, and lightning struck it. Cockatoos nipped through the wire, and floods engulfed the poles. Through it all, the linesmen rode up to 200 kilometers on horseback to repair the damage, and the messages kept coming.

The museum north of Alice is a monument to all of these men, a reconstruction of the original buildings of one of the main stations and a way of life now gone. I find the human sense of duty and purpose unfathomable when I think of the telegraphists ensconced in these small fortresses across the vast outback so that a merchant in Adelaide could know the latest on the market in London.

I walked around the central shopping area of Alice and had a steak-and-egg sandwich, a Territory specialty, although beef is costlier and of lesser quality now that Australia exports it to Japan and the United States. At the Araluen Art Center I found a collection of Aboriginal landscape paintings done in the representational style of Europe. Albert

Namatjira pioneered this approach among Aborigines, painting landscapes of central Australia featuring a ghost gum backed by desert ranges. Today his works command large sums.

Up the next day at first light and heading north, I felt again the vastness of the uninhabited distances — plenty of elbow room. I stopped at Ryan's Well, an abandoned homestead now merely the shell of a stone house. There was a vague sadness about the place, where so much hard work and hope invested in its building had ended in this way. On past Stuart's camp at Daly Waters, today a settlement of three houses and a comfortable-looking pub with a red roof and shady veranda, to Katherine.

Of primary interest to me in Katherine was the Katherine Gorge National Park, where an eight-kilometer trail wound through a scrubby forest of woollybark and sand palm to outcrops of spheroidally weathered granite on the gorge rim. Below the rim lay the 500-meter-deep gorge of jointed orange rock, the broad river at its base green and still. My doctoral adviser, Victor Baker, came here in 1983 to study flood deposits along the Katherine River, and he was instrumental in encouraging me to take up similar studies on other Australian rivers three years later. So in a sense, this last river I visited in Australia was also the starting point for my work.

There were several purposes in initiating what has turned into a decade-long study of floods on northern Australian rivers. The first was to extend the record of large, infrequent floods over a longer time scale than that covered by the relatively short gauge records of river discharge. A second was to determine the distribution of floods through time in order to relate this distribution to fluctuations in climate. A third purpose, which has come to dominate my work, was to understand the role of floods in shaping channel morphology.

It seems intuitively obvious to most people that floods play an important role in controlling channel shape. Floods are dramatic and abrupt, and in their wake there are obvious changes in channel appearance. What are not so obvious are the subtle, gradual channel changes that may occur over a period of years or centuries between large floods.

In 1960 American geomorphologists M. Gordon Wolman and John Miller published a classic paper in which they compared the effects of large floods and smaller, more frequent flows. Using U.S. Geological Survey records of river discharge and sediment transport, Wolman and Miller concluded that the fairly small floods that recur every year or two are responsible for transporting the most sediment and thus largely controlling channel morphology on many of the rivers they studied. Wolman and Miller included caveats in their interpretation: their results applied primarily to low-gradient rivers with alluvial channels in humid-temperate climatic regions. As too often happens, however, their caveats were sometimes forgotten by subsequent investigators, and the role of extreme floods in shaping channel morphology was often downplayed. It took more than a decade before other geomorphologists began to document the important role of floods in channels that had either high boundary resistance or extreme hydrologic variability.

Channels formed in bedrock or amid large boulders may be said to have a high boundary resistance because the water flowing over them must exert relatively high levels of shear stress before the channel bed and walls begin to deform and change shape. In these conditions, only large floods may generate the shear stress necessary to effectively shape the channel. Similarly, in arid or seasonal tropical regions, rivers may alternate between extremes of very low or no flow, and large floods. Again, under these conditions large floods may transport the greatest amount of sediment, as well as creating channel features that are not completely reworked by subsequent low flows before the next large flood occurs. Large floods may thus be the dominant control on channel morphology in some settings, but it was necessary to develop a series of individual case studies in order to document the importance of these floods. This has been one of the primary contributions of the northern Australian flood studies.

Back at the town of Katherine, a single row of buildings lined the road like worn photographs of frontier towns in the western United States. Everything seemed to droop under the intense heat and glare of midday, and the flies clung maddeningly. The long distances were bleached to a monotonous gray-green color, and I felt devoid of energy and will in the heavy air. I made a quick stop for groceries, the heat and the hours of driving weighing heavily on me. I took a big hunk of watermelon to the small city park, where groups of Aborigines squatted beneath the trees like darker shadows.

Swaddled in damp, clinging clothes, I ate the sticky-sweet melon at a shady picnic table. Three young Aboriginal girls came over, playing around the table and talking to me. I smiled at them absentmindedly and finished the melon, my thoughts elsewhere, until a small boy toddled up and climbed onto the table. Naked and pale chocolate, he was chubby like a cherub. He waddled over to where I was sitting, frowning at me as he came, and picked up the rind. There was a moment of hushed silence from the girls before they asked in quick excitement if they could have it. It had all happened too quickly, and my reason had not caught up to embarrassment. It was only a rind, but they fell on it with gusto. I couldn't watch and got up, driving quickly on into the heat-wavering plains, feeling sheepish, pampered, bewildered, angry, but mostly embarrassed. It was disturbing to watch children make a meal on my scraps.

Continuing on, I found myself once again surrounded by abandoned World War II airstrips, relics of the panic following the bombing of Darwin. The landscape closed in, distances limited by haze, forest, and flatness. At the Adelaide River Inn I had chips and a buff burger in revenge on the water buffaloes that had disturbed my camp on the East Alligator River. However, the beeflike meat was so tough and stringy that it nearly destroyed my jaws. After lunch I drove into Darwin, passing through the Americanized suburbs built after Cyclone Tracy in 1974. I stopped at the large, modern indoor shopping mall of Casuarina Shopping Centre, where I walked about gaping like a bush hick. What would the old imperialists struggling to maintain a sense of white superiority in the tropic heat have thought of this?

At the Lameroo Hotel beside the Greyhound Terminal, seven dollars got me a linenless bed in a four-person room, with the bathroom down the hall. The room contained an old dresser and mirror, a closet, and four metal bunks. Two of the walls were adjustable louvers, and a slowly rotating ceiling fan kept the room just bearably stifling. I took a much needed shower, but most of my clothes were dirty, and everything smelled vaguely of mildew.

Late in the afternoon one of my roommates turned up, a Londoner in Australia on a six-month work visa. She had a clerical job in a government office and told interesting stories of life in Darwin. Drinking provides a refuge from the unpleasant climate, and her office had two refrigerators, one for beer and one for wine, with drinking commencing each day around 3 P.M. I had noticed that the faces of the people in Darwin presented a blend of European, Aboriginal, Asian, Indonesian, and various mixed castes, and Liz told me that Darwin was the only Australian city with a Chinese mayor. She spoke of people in from the bush whom she had met in pubs: they came in intending to stay one night and left three days later when their drunk had worn off. For the time being, she found life in Darwin more interesting than that in London and appreciated the easygoing friendliness of the people. She seemed to be an international wanderer, having worked in New York for three months, traveled the East Coast between Boston and Florida, and arrived in Darwin via Bangkok, Burma, Thailand, and Bali.

Her friend Trish dropped in and spoke of her work as cook and deckhand on fishing trawlers. It was a hard life of night shifts and salt water, fish smells and seaweed. Five to six people had to work out a community equilibrium for periods of up to eight months, their only direct contact being with supply barges. Trish, a very attractive blonde, was the only woman on the boat, but "if you tell the blokes a couple a' times that you won't stand no nonsense, they leave you alone."

We had a good, cheap supper in the hotel cafeteria. Roast meat, boiled vegetables, and baked dessert, food that had fed the English and their colonies for hundreds of years. After supper we walked down to the pub of the Old Vic Hotel. It was dusk, the streets quiet, only a drunk staggering along here and there. The life of the city had drained out along the roads to the east, to suburbs like Casuarina, and the Old Vic was one of the few night spots in the old downtown. As we walked along the pedestrian mall fronting the hotel, we heard the drums in the pub beating a pulse for the night.

Passing below a balcony hidden by vegetation, we climbed dark stairs and were suddenly in the heated light and noise of the pub. We found a scarred wooden table out on the balcony, a little away from the blaring jukebox. Steamy night. As I drank cold Foster's, the sweat rolled down inside my shirt, sliding my arm off the table. I looked through a screen of magenta bougainvillea blossoms and bright green coconut palm fringe, and beyond was the deep blue-black velvet sky of a tropical night. A live band much too loud succeeded the jukebox, and it was not really a cheery spot. Beyond our table were too many alone and lonely men, and everyone was trying too hard to have a good time. My companions talked of an upcoming experiment in tomato picking and marvelled at a notice in the hotel for nondrinking traveling companions. How can you travel without drinking? What else is there to do? Ten o'clock, three glasses of beer, and I no longer noticed the lonely men or the hot heaviness of the night. Sleep was needed.

We walked back to the hotel, happily noisy and disjointed in the deserted streets. Even the drunks of dusk had gone to sleep. Inside the hotel the walls closed in until I found it hard to breathe. The air was thrice used, worn out. I lay on the bed, feeling the damp, unclean bedding the length of my body. On my back with my eyes closed, I alternately rose and sank through water as a wavy sensation began at my head, flowed smooth and swift to my feet, and sloshed back to my head again. The greasy old ceiling fan whirred and creaked in the heavily resistant air. Exhausted, I slept little. The bed gave off a heat of its own, and the stifling air weighed down on me. Slowly the air faded from black to gray until I woke early to a slightly cooler morning. A quiet ride back to Jabiru, heavy-headed with sweated sleep, and then a warm welcome and a stack of mail.

Part III
And So, Contrary to Reality, an End ~

I was still the same, knowing myself yet being someone other.

T. S. Eliot, "Little Gidding"

In reality my Australian experience has no definite end. I may be physically in or out of Australia, but the effects of my sojourns there are more fluid and pervasive, for I am no longer limited to an American viewpoint and can see my own country from the context of another culture. In my mental geography of the world, the rather gray, undistinguished map of the southern continent has been replaced by the vibrantly colored images of detail. Australia has expanded to a whole complex of experiences and memories that will continue to condition my life in ways I have not yet perceived.

The most obvious effect of my experiences in Australia is that they have to some extent determined the direction of my subsequent work. I went to Australia with the intention of developing a chronology of floods on a few northern Australian rivers in order to relate that chronology to climatic fluctuations. Through the work of Australian climatologists and hydrologists, I knew that periods of less frequent floods corresponded to periods of decreased or shifted cyclone activity around northern Australia in association with El Niño–Southern Oscillation conditions. Similarly, periods of enhanced flooding corresponded to the opposite climatic conditions. These correlations had been demonstrated for the period of approximately 100 years covered by systematic, or instrumental, climatic and hydrologic records. I hoped to extend the possibility of this relation over 1,000 years by demonstrating that periods of enhanced or decreased flooding had also occurred at time scales longer than a century.

When I combined the flood records from the Burdekin, Herbert, and East Alligator Rivers with the records developed for other northern

Australian rivers, the pattern they formed was a little hazy. Over a time span of 1,200 years, I could discern a period of increased flooding during the last century and periods of no floods from 900 to 1,100 and from 450 to 650 years ago. However, the pattern was not overwhelmingly convincing, because the recent increase could be caused by the greater preservation and resolution of the younger sediments, and there were simply too few data points to be sure that the 900–1,100 and 450–650 "gaps" really indicated a regional absence of floods rather than an absence of floods on just a few rivers. So I was left with what must be the most common "conclusion" in science: here are my hypotheses, but I need more data to verify them.

Since my initial trip to Australia in 1986 I have returned repeatedly in order to get the additional data, and I have begun to do similar work in other regions of the world. Once you become known for a particular type of work among your professional colleagues, it is often easier to continue that work than to branch out into other areas, because you have a record of success on which to argue for further research funding. Now that I am known for my work on paleofloods, there are invitations to do that work elsewhere, and my choice of a dissertation topic has influenced my career in ways that I did not foresee.

I was already both desperate with homesickness and taut with excitement when I boarded the airplane for Australia. I had traveled fairly extensively in Europe, but never so far from home, family, and friends for so long. Why was I sending myself into exile? Luckily, from the moment I landed in Australia, the novelty and fascination of my surroundings eclipsed fear and unhappiness, and although I had occasional twinges of homesickness throughout the year, I never approached the violent unhappiness of the first few hours of the journey to Australia.

The contrast of Australia helped me to define the United States and its citizens. I saw my first Americans in Cairns, after I had been in Australia for two months. With their high standard of living, the Australians dress well, and there are no particular facial or bodily characteristics that separate them from the average American, but I immediately recognized the four people walking toward me on the Cairns street that day as compatriots. Their speech confirmed it when they got closer, and I laughed to myself. Encountering Americans again three-and-a-half months later was a culture shock. I was flying to Canberra from Darwin via Alice Springs, and a group of American tourists got on the plane at Alice. They stuck out like sore thumbs, and all of the unpleasant stereotypes about traveling Americans proved true in this case: they were loud, boisterously friendly, and yet clannish in their obliviousness of the surroundings. They were not behaving offensively toward any individual, but they were noticeably exclusive in their concentration on having a good time among themselves.

Understandably, the Australians have some ambivalence about us. During World War II the United States stepped into Britain's fostering role with regard to Australia. Its influence began with military and economic supply during the war, when Australia was facing the threat of Japanese invasion, and it continued after the war through large infusions, whether active or passive, of science, technology, and popular culture. Imports of the latter have been steadily accelerating since the war, to the point where some Australian intellectuals are justifiably alarmed that Australia is losing its identity and becoming an American clone. Ford and GM cars, McDonald's, Burger King, and Kentucky Fried Chicken, shopping malls and suburbs, movies and television shows, rock music and blue jeans: at every level of Australian life I saw influences of Americanism, which Australian literature and history demonstrate to be a recent phenomenon. Pine Gap, a U.S. military installation for which the Australian people have never been given any explanation or details, is now a focal point for the Australian disarmament movement, and I wonder whether Australians will eventually come to feel for Americans the same love-hate relationship they have with the British.

Love-hate is not an inappropriately strong term to describe Australian attitudes toward Britain. Judging by their literature, the Australians have always had an inferiority complex with regard to Britain. They were proud to be part of the mighty British Empire that carried civilization to the dark corners of the world. Britain set the standards in politics, science, industry, and culture, to the point that native-born Australians saw their land through British eyes and found it odd and inhospitable.

Naturally, when Australian-born intellectuals began to develop their own tradition, they rebelled fiercely against this often sneering dominance by all things British. This rebellion is perhaps best expressed by Xavier Herbert, a mid-twentieth-century Australian novelist who unmercifully castigated the latter-day, would-be cultural imperialists who came to Australia from Britain. But the disenchantment has not yet thoroughly permeated society. Australia still has a British governor general who has the power to depose an elected Australian prime minister, and the January Australia Day festival that I attended in Canberra was officially opened by present governor general Sir Ninian Stephen. In certain disciplines it is still an unwritten requirement that your doctorate be from a British university if you want to join an Australian university faculty, and in my field many professors are not Australian-born.

The first major disillusionment with Britain came during World War I. Australia suffered heavy losses during the war, and every little country town that I visited prominently displayed its army memorial. The Australian soldiers had little regard for discipline, but they amassed a splendid battle record and came to have a low regard for the fighting ability of the British. The Australians and other colonials like New Zealanders and Canadians were often sacrificed before British troops were sent in (as at Gallipoli), and the Australian attitude toward Britain and the Empire changed from admiration to distrust. For the first time, Australia began to view itself as an independent nation apart from the British Empire.

Australia's dependence on Britain or America, and the resulting doubt in its own worth, has been strongly expressed in attitudes toward the land. The relationship between people and the land is a major theme of Australian literature, as social position and wealth are of English literature. As Australian historian Geoffrey Blainey expressed it in his book *A Land Half Won:* "The physical mastering of Australia was swift and often dramatic, but the emotional conquest was slow. . . . Most Australians were still strangers in a new land. The land was only half won."

In reading Eleanor Dark's novels *The Timeless Land* and *Storm of Time* about the early years of the Australian colony, I realized how much greater a psychological readjustment was required of the first English settlers in Australia than of the first English to settle the eastern coast of North America. Whereas there were some similarities between Britain and the New World, in Australia the first settlers faced wholly different flora and fauna, different stars, reversed seasons, and the memory of a seemingly interminable journey between themselves and home. Among many of the earliest, involuntary convict-settlers, there was a protracted struggle to find comfortable images of the land, and the feeling of exile highlighted the importance of heritage, with its sense of continuity in legends and history. English and Irish legends did not transplant particularly well to Australia, but it would have been unthinkable for the early colonists to adopt the legends of the blacks, whom they considered inferior. The new settlers had to learn to look at this different world through new eyes — almost to learn again how to live — a lesson not yet completed.

The process of learning how to look at a new landscape is fascinatingly preserved in the progression of Australian landscape paintings from pseudo-European landscapes painted by both foreign- and Australian-born artists to truly Australian landscapes that manage at last to capture the unique qualities of light, space, and natural vegetation of the continent. These paintings demonstrate the old truism that you see only what you look for. So long as artists approached the Australian landscape with European trees and mountains and light in their eyes, they re-created Europe on their canvases. Only when they learned to look at Australia unprejudiced by the forms of another world did they catch its essence, bringing the very scent of dry gum leaves to their art.

Where America has been regarded as a New World and a land of opportunity, fresh beginnings, and optimism, Australia is often described in very different terms. Australian writers always describe the bush as a thing totally apart and unique from any other land. This distinction usually takes the form of such descriptions as silent, timeless, sleeping, subtle, and ancient. Australians like Miles Franklin could view the land as full of unfulfilled potential, and thus hopeful, but until recently a more common reaction seemed to be that of English writer D. H. Lawrence, who in his novel *Kangaroo* described the land sometimes as dark and brooding, sometimes as light and airy, but always as aloof and apart from humanity, with a sense of menace and oppression.

The dichotomy is represented by two of Australia's most popular nineteenth-century poets: writing of the life led by the itinerant wanderers of the bush in "Clancy of the Overflow," A. B. (Banjo) Paterson described "the vision splendid of the sunlit plains extended." Henry Lawson's characters struggled bitterly with lives harshened by a physical environment of heat, flies, dust, glaring sun, drought, and isolation. Lawson focused on people, but the land was always present as a background for misery and ultimate futility.

Hostility toward the land, and a consequent nostalgia for the tamed, cool green of England, rose mainly from the experiences of families like that of Lawson's parents, who were small selectors (settlers) struggling to earn a living on agriculturally marginal land. Most of Australia is arid. The secret to living successfully in an arid landscape, of learning which activities the land can sustainably support and which it can be forced to do for only a short time before it and its tenants are exhausted, is a lesson still being learned today in both the United States and Australia. Much of the bitterness toward and alienation from the Australian landscape may be due to the difficulty and implacability of this lesson.

The absence or abundance of water is the crucial control on Australian pastoralism. Much of Australia's soil is lower in fertility than that of other arid regions, and the refusal to recognize this has caused repeated disasters. Australia had a dust bowl in the 1930s equal to that of the Great Plains of the United States, and as in the United States, the deadly erosion of topsoil continues today. In 1983 the city of Melbourne was crippled by an immense dust storm. The farming failures of Henry Lawson's time were repeated after World War II, when returning servicemen were encouraged to become self-sufficient farmers on small irrigated plots. Sometimes the soil simply blew away. In the mallee country of the Murray-Darling Basin, the hot sun sucked up the water and left salts encrusting the soil and killing the crops. Today stretches of the region remain a wasteland of glittering white cankers.

On the other side of the coin came hundreds of thousands of sheep and cattle, far too many for the range to support. Compacting the soil, the animals John Muir called "hoofed locusts" destroyed the food sources of the native herbivores and opened the weakened range to the inroads of introduced species like prickly pear. The Australian land is vulnerable to abuse by callous, ignorant people. In her 1967 account of a visit to Australia, Elspeth Huxley quoted a portion of James McAuley's poem "The True Discovery of Australia," in which he described the Australians passively sitting on their verandas taking tea and watching floods and cyclones completing the work of the pioneers by "shifting all the soil into the ocean."

The sense of alienation from the Australian landscape may also be due to a weaker literary tradition in Australia, as compared to that of the United States, of natural history and environmental philosophy. I have grown up reading John Muir, John Burroughs, Aldo Leopold, Sigurd Olsen, Edwin Way Teale, Henry Thurston, Joseph Wood Krutch, Rachel Carson, and, more recently, Edward Abbey, Annie Dillard, Ann Zwinger, and Barry Lopez. These are only the leaders of a veritable school of writing, and collectively they have extended my consciousness of the American wilderness far beyond the areas that I have actually visited. I found less evidence of a similar tradition in Australian writing, either through my own readings or through conversations with others. Although there is a large market for natural history works like guidebooks,

Australia does not seem to share the U.S. tradition of environmental philosophy and wilderness advocacy.

There are, of course, some books dealing with these subjects, such as E. J. Banfield's 1908 *Confessions of a Beachcomber,* a rambling collection of anecdotes and observations from the author's life on Dunk Island off the Queensland coast, or Francis Ratcliffe's *Flying Fox and Drifting Sand,* about the research of a government scientist in humid Queensland and arid South Australia in the 1920s and 1930s. Two recent books are Eric Rolls's *A Million Wild Acres* and Graham Pizzey's *A Separate Creation.* The former is an account of the natural and land-use history of a portion of southeast Australia; the latter is a collection of excerpts from the accounts of early Australian explorers and naturalists describing the continent's unique fauna, illustrating the great changes that have been wrought on seemingly pristine landscapes since European colonization.

Probably a third factor in the Australians' attitude toward their natural environment is the pattern of settlement in Australia. Australia is a highly urbanized country, with less than 15 percent of the people living in rural areas. This is in direct contrast to the popular image of Australia as a nation inhabited by people scattered across the outback in lonely stations. Most Australians, being relatively unfamiliar with the bush, have not learned to fully appreciate it. They do not seem to have the powerful sense of identification with the land itself that characterizes citizens of the United States. Even many Australians who know the bush emphasize its bizarre qualities, in terms of its differences from the more "familiar" Northern Hemisphere biota.

Rather than recognizing that the world has a range of unique natural communities and accepting their natural world on its own terms, many Australians view their land as a variant of the prevailing norm. This has fostered a sense of isolation and defensiveness, as though they must prove that separate really is equal (which, indeed, they have had to prove in the face of prevailing British arrogance). This has hurt the Australians, both in terms of developing a positive, healthy natural identity and in terms of appreciating and caring for their natural environment.

A similar view is expressed by Xavier Herbert in his massive novel *Poor Fellow My Country,* in which he portrays white Australians as a dispossessed race alienated from their country. Because they have no love for or understanding of their country in terms of the land itself, they have been dominated by other nations, primarily the British. Herbert offers the solution of assimilating Aboriginal beliefs and attitudes in order to develop a sense of identity and unity with the land. This, he believes, might provide a continuity of the sort that Stonehenge or the Icelandic sagas give to European culture.

The rise of environmentalism since World War II has increased the awareness of, and appreciation for, the bush by native Australians. The Australian environmental movement is not yet as organized or as politically active as its counterpart in the United States, but it has already expanded beyond its own continent by taking on Antarctica as a special cause. Perhaps in future the land will be wholly won, and both people and land will be winners.

There will always be individuals who are powerfully drawn to the Australian outback. Consider the German Leichhardt, nearly killing himself more than once in his insatiable quest for discovery and returning yet again to finally lose his life. Or Irish Daisy Bates, for whom the "virus of research" grew into a "labor of love" absorbing forty years of life. As recounted by Elizabeth Salter in *Daisy Bates,* Bates became famous and wrote a European best-seller about her work, despite having to fight pedigreed academics for respect as a researcher. On retiring to civilization she spent the remainder of her life torn between the worlds of the blacks and the whites.

There were thousands of men and women who chose the pastoral life of the outback over the crowded struggle of the cities and stuck by their choice through miseries they faced alone. There were men like the classically educated Lutheran pastor C. Strehlow of Germany, who buried themselves in the bush in service to their fellow men. As described by T.G.H. Strehlow in *Journey to Horseshoe Bend,* Strehlow spent twenty-eight years at the Hermannsburg Mission in the western MacDonnells before dying en route to medical help in October 1922. He was a firm, fair man who protected the Aborigines against unscrupulous whites and taught both races by example. He could have fought his battle against inner darkness anywhere, but I suspect that the Australian bush itself played some role in keeping him there once he arrived.

And there are the people of our own time who continue to follow the allure of challenge and adventure into the still-unknown interior. Women like Robyn Davidson, traveling by camel from Alice Springs to the west coast and recording her changing attitudes in *Tracks.* Men like the OSS technician Johnny Mac, whose extensive library of Australiana traced the growth of his dream to live and work in an outback region like Jabiru.

And finally people like myself, passing travelers caught unexpectedly in the diaphanous web of romance spun from the southern land, who believe that the golden ages are not all past.

Selected Bibliography

Archer, Michael, Suzanne Hand, and Henk Godthelp, 1986, Uncovering Australia's Dreamtime. Chipping Norton, New South Wales: Surrey Beatty and Sons.

Baird, David, 1970, The Incredible Gulf. Adelaide, South Australia: Rigby.

Banfield, E. J., 1908, The Confessions of a Beachcomber. South Yarra, Victoria: Currey O'Neil.

Bates, Daisy, 1938, The Passing of the Aborigines. London: John Murray.

Beebe, William, 1921, Edge of the Jungle. New York: Henry Holt.

———, 1949, High Jungle. New York: Duell, Sloan, and Pearce.

Bell, Diane, 1983, Daughters of the Dreaming. Melbourne, Victoria: McPhee Gribble.

Blainey, Geoffrey, 1982, A Land Half Won. Melbourne, Victoria: Sun Books.

———, 1978, The Rush That Never Ended. Carlton, Victoria: Melbourne University Press.

———, 1975, Triumph of the Nomads. Melbourne, Victoria: Sun Books.

———, 1982, The Tyranny of Distance. Melbourne, Victoria: Sun Books.

Blong, Russell, and Richard Gillespie, 1978, "Fluvially Transported Charcoal Gives Erroneous C-14 Ages for Recent Deposits." Nature 271:739–741.

Carson, Rachel, 1964, Silent Spring. Greenwich, Connecticut: Fawcett Publications.

Chaloupka, George, 1985, "Chronological Sequence of Arnhem Land Plateau Rock Art," in Archaeological Research in Kakadu National Park, Rhys Jones, ed. Australian National Parks and Wildlife Service, Special Publication 13, 269–280.

Chamberlin, Thomas C., 1897, "The Method of Multiple Working Hypotheses." Journal of Geology 5:837–848.

Clarke, D. E., and A.G.L. Paine, 1970, Explanatory Notes on the Charters Towers Geological Sheet. Bureau of Mineral Resources, Geology and Geophysics, 1:250,000 Geological Series.

Conrad, Joseph, 1990, Heart of Darkness and Other Tales. New York: Oxford University Press.

Cook, Captain James, 1984, Voyages of Discovery. Gloucester, England: Alan Sutton.

Crowley, F. K. (editor), 1986, A New History of Australia. Melbourne, Victoria: William Heinemann.

Dark, Eleanor, 1966, Storm of Time. London: Collins.

———,1988, The Timeless Land. Sydney, New South Wales: Collins.

Darwin, Charles, 1964, On the Origin of Species. Cambridge, Massachusetts: Harvard University Press.

———, 1962, The Voyage of the Beagle. New York: Doubleday.

Davidson, Robyn, 1980, Tracks. New York: Pantheon Books.

Davies, Gordon L., 1969, The Earth in Decay: A History of British Geomorphology 1578–1878. New York: Elsevier.

Davis, William Morris, 1954, Geographical Essays. New York: Dover.

Edwards, Hugh, 1989, Crocodile Attack. New York: Harper and Row.

Finlayson, H. H., 1936, The Red Centre: Man and Beast in the Heart of Australia. Sydney, New South Wales: Angus and Robertson.

Flood, Josephine, 1983, Archaeology of the Dreamtime. Sydney, New South Wales: Collins.

Frith, Clifford, and Dawn Frith, 1985, Australian Tropical Birds. Townsville, Queensland: Tropical Australian Graphics.

Gould, Stephen Jay, 1977, Ever Since Darwin: Reflections in Natural History. New York: W. W. Norton.

———, 1980, The Panda's Thumb: More Reflections in Natural History. New York: W. W. Norton.

Grant Watson, E. L., 1946, But to What Purpose: The Autobiography of a Contemporary. London: The Cresset Press.

Gunn, Mrs. Aeneas, 1982, We of the Never-Never. Sydney, New South Wales: Angus and Robertson.

Herbert, Xavier, 1989, Capricornia. North Ryde, New South Wales: Angus and Robertson.

———, 1975, Poor Fellow My Country. Sydney, New South Wales: Collins.

Hill, Ernestine, 1940, The Great Australian Loneliness. Sydney, New South Wales: Angus and Robertson.

———, 1977, The Territory. Sydney, New South Wales: Angus and Robertson.

Holthouse, Hector, 1986, Ships in the Coral. Sydney, New South Wales: Angus and Robertson.

Horne, Donald, 1964, The Lucky Country: Australia in the Sixties. Ringwood, Victoria: Penguin Books.

Hudson, W. H., 1916, Green Mansions: A Romance of the Tropical Forest. New York: Alfred A. Knopf.

Hutton, James, 1795, Theory of the Earth, With Proofs and Illustrations, 2 vols. Edinburgh, Scotland.

Huxley, Elspeth, 1967, Their Shining Eldorado: A Journey Through Australia. New York: William Morrow.

Idriess, Ion, 1932, Flynn of the Inland. North Ryde, New South Wales: Angus and Robertson.

Isaacs, Jennifer, 1984, Arts of the Dreaming: Australia's Living Heritage. Sydney, New South Wales: Lansdowne.

James, Barbara, 1989, No Man's Land: Women of the Northern Territory. Sydney, New South Wales: Collins.

Lawrence, D. H., 1955, Kangaroo. London: Heinemann.

Leichhardt, L., 1847, Journal of an Overland Expedition in Australia From Moreton Bay to Port Essington, a Distance of Upwards of 3,000 Miles, During the Years 1844–1845. London: T. & W. Boone.

Lowe, Pat, and Jimmy Pike, 1990, Jilji: Life in the Great Sandy Desert. Broome, Western Australia: Magabala Books.

Lumholtz, Carl, 1889, Among Cannibals. London: John Murray.

Madigan, C. T., 1946, Crossing the Dead Heart. Melbourne, Victoria: Georgian House.

Martin, Paul S., and H. E. Wright, 1967, Pleistocene Extinctions. New Haven, Connecticut: Yale University Press.

McEwan, Marcia, 1979, Great Australian Explorers. Sydney, New South Wales: Bay Books.

Meier, Leo, and Figgis, Penny, 1985, Rainforests of Australia. McMahons Point, New South Wales: Weldons.

Neidjie, Bill, Stephen Davis, and Allan Fox, 1985, Kakadu Man. Brisbane, Queensland: Mybrood.

Oliver, Peter, 1985, Burke and Wills. Dingley, Victoria: Budget Books.

O'Reilly, Bernard, 1941, Green Mountains. Brisbane, Queensland: W. R. Smith and Paterson.

Ovington, Derrick, 1986, Kakadu: A World Heritage of Unsurpassed Beauty. Canberra, Australian Capital Territory: Australian Government Publishing Service.

Pizzey, Graham, 1981, A Separate Creation. South Yarra, Victoria: Currey O'Neil Ross.

Pownall, Eve, 1986, Australian Pioneer Women. South Yarra, Victoria: Lloyd O'Neil.

Ratcliffe, Francis, 1970, Flying Fox and Drifting Sand. Sydney, New South Wales: Angus and Robertson.

Reader's Digest, 1984, Reader's Digest Book of the Great Barrier Reef. Sydney, New South Wales: Reader's Digest.

Rolls, Eric, 1981, A Million Wild Acres. Ringwood, Victoria: Penguin Books.

Russell-Smith, Jeremy, 1985, "Studies in the Jungle: People, Fire, and Monsoon Forest," in Archaeological Research in Kakadu National Park, Rhys Jones, ed. Australian National Parks and Wildlife Service, Special Publication 13, 241–268.

Salter, Elizabeth, 1971, Daisy Bates. New York: Coward, McCann, and Geoghegan.

Spencer, Sir Baldwin, 1928, Wanderings in Wild Australia. 2 volumes. London: Macmillan.

Spillett, Peter G., 1972, Forsaken Settlement. Dee Why West, New South Wales: Lansdowne Press.

Strehlow, T.G.H., 1969, Journey to Horseshoe Bend. Adelaide, South Australia: Rigby.

Stuart, John McDouall, 1975, Explorations in Australia: The Journals of John McDouall Stuart. William Hardman, ed. Adelaide: Libraries Board of South Australia.

Wallace, Alfred Russel, 1869, The Malay Archipelago. London: Macmillan.

Warburton, P. E., 1875, Journey Across the Western Interior of Australia. London: Sampson Low, Marston, Low, and Searle.

White, Patrick, 1957, Voss. New York: Viking.

Wolman, M. Gordon, and John Miller, 1960, "Magnitude and Frequency of Forces in Geomorphic Processes." Journal of Geology 68:54–74.

Wright, Judith, 1971, Collected Poems 1942–1970. Sydney, New South Wales: Angus and Robertson.

Index